Questioning Technology

"*Questioning Technology* is a superb piece of work...I see it as quite simply one of the best books in the field of philosophy of technology, as well as one which I think will be of most interest to students."
Andrew Light, SUNY Binghampton

"Andrew Feenberg's *Questioning Technology* is a cutting edge book which provocatively argues for subjecting technology to democratic debate and reconstruction. One of the most important books on technology in the present era."
Douglas Kellner, UCLA

In this extraordinary introduction to the study of the philosophy of technology, Andrew Feenberg argues that technological design is central to the social and political structure of modern societies. Environmentalism, information technology, and medical advances testify to technology's crucial importance.

In his lucid and engaging style, Feenberg shows that technology is the medium of daily life. Every major technical change reverberates at countless levels: economic, political, religious, and cultural. If we continue to see the social and technical domains as being separate, then we are essentially denying an integral part of our existence, and our place in a democratic society.

Questioning Technology convinces us that it is vital that we learn more about technology the better to live with it and to manage it.

Andrew Feenberg is Professor of Philosophy at San Diego State University. He is the author of *Alternative Modernity*, *Critical Theory of Technology*, *Lukács, Marx and the Sources of Critical Theory*, and co-editor of *Technology and the Politics of Knowledge*.

Questioning Technology

ANDREW FEENBERG

London and New York

First published 1999
by Routledge
11 New Fetter Lane, London EC4P 4EE

306.46
F2958
1999

Simultaneously published in the USA and Canada
by Routledge
29 West 35th Street, New York, NY 10001
Reprinted 2000, 2001, 2003
Routledge is an imprint of the Taylor & Francis Group

© 1999 Andrew Feenberg

Typeset in Adobe Garamond by
Juliette Robbins for Danielseed Design
Printed and bound in Great Britain by
TJ International Ltd, Padstow, Cornwall

British Library Cataloguing in Publication Data
A catalogue record for this book is available
from the British Library

Library of Congress Cataloguing in Publication Data
Feenberg, Andrew.
Questioning Technology / Andrew Feenberg.
p. cm.
Includes bibliographical references and index.
1. Technology–Social aspects. 2. Technology–Political aspects.
3. Technology–Philosophy.
HM221.F3843   1999
306.4'6–DC21   98–37421
CIP

ISBN 0–415–19754–6 (hbk)
ISBN 0–415–19755–4 (pbk)

Contents

List of Charts

Preface

For two centuries now, great democratic movements have swept the globe, equalizing classes, races, genders, peoples. As these movements expand the definition of humanity, they also extend the boundaries of the political to embrace more and more of social life. At first, law was taken from God and king and brought under human control. Then, Marx and the labor movement placed the economy on the political agenda. In this century, political management of the economy has become routine, and education and medicine have been added to the list of contestable issues. As a new century begins, democracy appears poised for a further advance. With the environmental movement in the lead, technology is now about to enter the expanding democratic circle.

This marks a fateful change in our understanding of technology, in its position on the conceptual maps of theory and critique. Formerly, the democratic movement gave its fullest confidence to the natural processes of technological development, and it was only conservative cultural critics who lamented the price of progress. The Ruskins and the Heideggers deplored the dehumanizing advance of the machine while democrats and socialists cheered on the engineers, heroic conquerors of nature. However, all agreed that technology was an autonomous force separate from society, a kind of second nature impinging on social life from the alien realm of reason in which science too finds its source. For good or ill, technology's *essence*–rational control, efficiency–ruled modern life.

But this conception of technology is incompatible with the extension of democracy to the technical sphere. Technology is the medium of daily life in modern societies. Every major technical change reverberates at many levels, economic, political, religious, cultural. Insofar as we continue to see the technical and the social as separate domains, important aspects of these dimensions of our existence will remain beyond our reach as a democratic society. The fate of democracy is therefore bound up with our understanding of technology. The purpose of this book is to think that vital connection.

The same kind of ignorance that bound men to the gold standard for centuries maintains the illusion that technology is an alien force intruding on our social life from a coldly rational beyond. The forces of the market were believed to transcend the will of peoples and nations. The economy was treated as a quasi-natural system with laws as rigid as the movements of the planets. The social nature of exchange had to be discovered against tremendous ideological resistance. Today it seems absurd that modern societies renounced control of their own economic life to a second nature they had themselves created. Yet where technology is concerned we remain in willful submission to a second nature just as contingent on human action as the economy. Liberation from technological fetishism will follow the course of liberation from economic fetishism. The same story will someday be told about machines that we tell today about markets.

Just insofar as democracy challenges the autonomy of technology, the "essentialist" philosophy of technology around which there used to be such general consensus, is challenged as well. The time has therefore come for an anti-essentialist philosophy of technology. We have had enough of generalizations about technological imperatives, instrumental rationality, efficiency, enframing, and similar abstract categories. I offer here a concrete alternative to the approach of such influential representatives of essentialism as Ellul, Borgmann, Heidegger, and, for reasons I will explain in chapter one, Habermas as well.

Essentialism holds that technology reduces everything to functions and raw materials. Goal oriented technological practices replace practices which embody a human meaning. Efficiency sweeps away all other norms and determines an autonomous process of technological development. From this standpoint any attempt to infuse the technical with meaning appears as external interference in a rational field with its own logic and laws. Yet rational though it may be, technology engulfs its creators, threatening both spiritual and material survival.

The methodological dualism of technique and meaning has political implications. On the one side, technology undermines traditional meanings or communicative action, while on the other side we are called to protect the integrity of a meaningful world. Because the essence of technology is unaffected by changes in particular technologies, technological reform is irrelevant to the philosophical issues, desirable though it may be, on practical grounds. Universal technologization must be resisted by drawing boundaries around the technical sphere. But do these oppositions make sense at the end of the 20th century?

This approach leaves me skeptical, not because it affirms the existence of social pathologies linked to technology, but because it forecloses in principle any serious action to address them. But huge changes are occurring in fields such as medicine and computers under the influence of political protest and public involvement in design. The environmental movement has been deeply and quite concretely involved in the question of technology for the last twenty years. The technological world we will inhabit in the years to come will be a product of public activity to a great extent. How can one know in advance that all this debate and contestation will have no effect, positive or negative, on the fundamental problems identified by the critics of technology today?

I would argue that their approach is a function of our professional culture as humanist scholars and our relationship to the cultures of the technical disciplines, and has nothing to do with the realities of our time. This cultural relationship is peculiarly ambiguous. Technical disciplines are constituted around devices conceived as *essentially* functional, and therefore as *essentially* oriented toward efficiency. In the pursuit of efficiency, technical disciplines systematically abstract from social aspects of their own activities. Presumably, those aspects are the concern of humanistic disciplines. Essentialism accepts this division of labor. Like the technical disciplines, it views technologies as devices oriented toward efficiency. The only difference is that essentialism deplores the social consequences of technology the technical disciplines ignore.

This, I think, points to the basic weakness of essentialism. It has produced a powerful critique of the obsession with efficiency that is indeed prevalent in our society and reflected in the design of many devices and systems, but it has not shown that that attitude reveals the essence of real technology as it has existed historically, as it exists today, and as it may exist in the future. If essentialism is unaware of its own limitations, this is because it confounds attitude with object, the modern obsession with efficiency with technology as such.

No doubt real dangers do lurk in modern technology. And I can agree that it must have some general features that allow us to distinguish it and on the basis of which we can *sometimes* decide on its appropriate and inappropriate range of application. Although I see the logic of drawing boundaries narrowly in such cases, I cannot agree that this is the whole story. The "essence" of actual technology, as we encounter it in all its complexity, is not simply an orientation toward efficiency. Its many roles in our lives cannot be captured so simply. This is the burden of constructivist sociology of technology, which affirms the social and historical specificity of technological systems, the relativity of technical design and use to the culture and strategies of a variety of technical actors. Constructivism, in short, has introduced difference into the question of technology.

Yet constructivism so disaggregates the question of technology that it is sometimes difficult to see its relevance to the legitimate concerns of essentialism. I believe there is a single fundamental distinction among technical actors that enables us to link social to philosophical issues. This is the distinction between the dominant and the subordinate subject positions with respect to technological systems. There are, as essentialists argue, technological masters who relate through rational planning to a world reduced to raw materials. But ordinary people do not resemble the efficiency oriented system planners who pepper the pages of technology critique. Rather, they encounter technology as a dimension of their lifeworld. For the most part they merely carry out the plans of others or inhabit technologically constructed spaces and environments. As subordinate actors, they strive to appropriate the technologies with which they are involved and adapt them to the meanings that illuminate their lives. Their relation to technology is thus far more complex than that of dominant actors (which they too may be on occasion.)

Empirically inclined students of technology often complain that philosophy of technology defends its positions with very abstract generalities illustrated at best with simple examples such as Heidegger's famous hammer. This may be why so many philosophers have overlooked the significance of the distinction between these two types of actors. To illustrate my thesis, I therefore propose to consider a more complex but also more typical example of a technical object, the house.

The house, you may ask? The house is not a device but an extremely rich and meaningful life environment. Yet it has gradually become an elaborate concatenation of devices. Forget the old manse. A house today is the center of electrical, communications, heating, plumbing, and of course mechanized building technologies. To its builder, it is *essentially* these things. The fact that we who occupy the house romanticize it, hide many of its devices or shroud them in traditional facades, and dwell inside it rather than handling it like a tool obscures its basically technical character. It has in fact become the "machine for living" foreseen by Le Corbusier in the 1920s already.

But the house also undeniably belongs to our lifeworld and is not merely an efficient device for achieving goals. Of course it does achieve goals, for example sheltering us from the weather, but it obviously does far more than this and belongs to the realm of meaning as much as anything we can name. We have "domesticated" the technicized house and made it ours in all sorts of ways that have little or nothing to do with efficiency. The essence of technology, whatever that is, ought to encompass this complexity in principle. It ought to have categories under which we can recognize aspects of the house that are not reducible to a means-ends relationship.

Essentialists reply that this example falls apart analytically into the two halves of their dualistic view. The house considered as a concatenation of devices is at least conceptually different from the house as a human environment. The one belongs to the realm of technology, the other to the lifeworld of meaning. Thus there is an analytic distinction between the operation of the electric circuit as a technology and the experienced warmth and light of the space we inhabit, made possible by electricity no doubt but taking on a meaning in terms of traditional archetypes such as the hearth.

This distinction has a certain validity. Without it there would be no technical disciplines. But what starts out as an analytic distinction ends up as an ontological difference, as though technology could really be separated from society as two types of things—or in more sophisticated formulations, two "practices"—interacting on their boundaries. Essentialist dualism cuts across the lifeworld of technology, in which both these dimensions are immediately present, and disconnects the technical as such from the experience of it. But from an experiential standpoint these two dimensions—device and meaning, technical and lifeworld practice—are inextricably intertwined: the user is perfectly aware of the electrical source of the warmth that signifies security and welcome as he or she returns home in the evening. Both aspects of the experience qualify each other.

Of course users' "subjective associations" with technology seem irrelevant to home builders pursuing a profit or the technical disciplines on which they rely, which work exclusively with relations of cause and effect. Thus if one bases philosophy of technology on the self-understanding of the dominant technological actors, one might conclude that meaning is extrinsic to the technical as such. Yet this would be a mistake. Even if meaning plays no role in technical disciplines at any given point in time, *it is relevant to the history of technology*. Lifeworld meanings experienced by subordinate actors are eventually embodied in technological designs; at any given stage in its development, a device will express a range of these meanings gathered not from "technical rationality" but from past practices of its users. Technology as a total phenomenon thus must include an experiential dimension since experience with devices influences the evolution of their design. This is a conclusion generously documented in constructivist sociology and social history of technology.

This non-essentialist approach has political implications. Awareness of the meanings embedded in technology is more immediately available to ordinary users than to managers and technical personnel. The manager may see the new machine as more efficient, but the worker condemned to using it notices that it also removes skill and initiative from the shop floor. The polluter is less likely to see the relevance of environmental ethics to technology than the victim of pollution. And so on. Thus what essentialism conceives as an ontological split between technology and meaning, I conceive as a terrain of struggle between different types of actors differently engaged with technology and meaning.[1]

Concern for workers' skills and the environment could of course be dismissed as merely contextual, as not belonging to technology per se. But to understand its full complexity, we need to take seriously Don Ihde's remark that "technology is only what it is in some use-context" (Ihde, 1990: 128). The contexts of technology include such things as its relation to vocations, to responsibility, initiative, and authority, to ethics and aesthetics, in sum, to the realm of meaning. In the concluding chapter of this book I develop a socio-historical theory of technology to account for the role of context. I argue that the invariant elements of the constitution of the technical subject and object are modified by socially specific contextualizing variables in the course of the realization of concrete technical actors, devices, and systems. Thus technologies are not merely efficient devices or efficiency oriented practices, but include their contexts as these are embodied in design and social insertion.

I believe my approach can incorporate much of essentialism's critical

---

[1] The background of this argument is to be found in Lukács's theory of the reifying and dereifying forms of consciousness associated with different class positions. He writes, for example, "The quantitative differences in exploitation which appear to the capitalist in the form of quantitative determinants of the objects of his calculation, must appear to the worker as the decisive, qualitative categories of his whole physical, mental and moral existence" (Lukács, 1971: 166). I have generalized this approach beyond production to technology as a whole.

contribution while also opening up reflection on the reform of technology. I do not see how one can come up with a similarly positive program from the essentialist standpoint. Rather, the best one can do is to suggest that boundaries be drawn more tightly around the sphere given over to technological power. But that approach offers no criteria for improving life within that sphere.

This is not a fruitful stance, as activists in technical fields have discovered. Here is the paradox of essentialism: critical though it is, it ends up agreeing implicitly with technocrats that the actual struggles in which people attempt to influence technology can accomplish nothing of fundamental importance. But since technology embraces more and more of social life, these struggles promise to become more frequent and more significant. Can we rest content with a philosophy of technology that is unable to comprehend them? Real change will come not when we turn away from technology toward meaning, but when we recognize the nature of our subordinate position in the technical systems that enroll us, and begin to intervene in the design process in the defense of the conditions of a meaningful life and a livable environment. This book is dedicated to that project.

The issues raised here are of concern to people of all political persuasions, but I believe they have a special significance for the left. Marxism claimed most fundamentally that the technological mediation of work would create a new kind of lower class with an unprecedented potential for self-determination. Revolution was supposed to follow from this transformation. Marxism has been eclipsed by identity-based movements as a result of the failure this prediction. These new social movements generally signify themselves according to the actors involved, as women's movements, movements for gay rights, of environmentalists, professionals, workers. Unfortunately, no unifying articulation has emerged through which these various movements can join together to offer a politically convincing alternative. The promising notion that radical democracy could serve this purpose has so far had little impact. It is so abstract it determines no substantive policies, and in fact does little more than certify the left credentials of the very divisions it hopes to overcome (Laclau and Mouffe, 1985). But perhaps it can begin to take on content through the question of technology.

Obscured in the identitarian classification of the new social movements is the potentially unifying articulation supplied by technology, which is often the stakes in their struggles. For example, when women demanded changes in childbirth procedures, when AIDS patients demanded access to experimental treatment, they challenged technical medicine to incorporate a wider range of human needs in its structure. Environmentalists demanding changes in production technology to preserve nature and human health should be able to recognize themselves in such struggles. Similarly, when workers protest the intensification of labor made possible by the computer and demand different ways of realizing its benefits, they are attempting to change technology and the preconceptions realized in its design. The computer users in France and the US who introduced human communication on networks originally designed for the distribution of data accomplished a liberating technical innovation.

In all such democratic interventions, experts end up collaborating with a lay public in transforming technology. The process is intermittent and conflictual today, but it is reasonable to suppose that social control of technology will eventually spread and be institutionalized in more durable and effective forms. What are the implications of this prospect for democracy? That is the political question of technology. Marx's answer was socialism, the administration of production by the assembled producers. And indeed, this question still takes us back to Marx, to the idea that technological mediation opens new possibilities for intervention from below. But the limitation of technology to production in Marx's day has long since been transcended. Only through a generalization of the political question of technology to cover the whole surface of society does it again become relevant to our time. In this form it may someday provide a theme around which the left can articulate a utopian vision of a redeemed modernity.

Questioning Technology is the third in a series of books I have written on these problems. *Critical Theory of Technology* (1991) focused on contradictions in the Marxist approach and made the connection between labor process theory and the Frankfurt School's critique of the domination of nature. The argument of that book is based on the contrast between capitalist and "subversive" forms of rationalization. In the context of a more developed analysis of technical politics, I now call the latter "democratic rationalization" although in certain fields, such as artistic production, "subversion" may still be the more appropriate term. *Alternative Modernity* (1995) introduced a constructivist formulation of the basic argument which it applied to the critique of technocracy and postmodernism. That book analyzed case histories in medicine and computerization, and extended the approach to a consideration of problems of national culture with special reference to Japan. *Questioning Technology* now completes the cycle with an account of the radical political roots of non-essentialism, and a direct challenge to major thinkers in the philosophy of technology.

This is a propitious moment for such a project. According to Francis Sejersted we are entering a new phase of normative reflection on technology informed by a long development "from technological determinism to social constructivism, and then on to a political theory of technology" (Sejersted, 1995: 16). The reaction against determinism brought the contingency of technological development into focus, which in turn has opened the way to a reassertion of the political. This exactly situates the argument of this book. I will begin with the problem of determinism and the political reaction against it in the new left and the environmental movement, proceed to draw out the implications of that reaction for social theory, and then turn to basic problems in the renewal of philosophy of technology.

The writing of this book has placed me in debt to a great many people. Francis Sejersted invited me several times to the TMV center for research on technology and culture at the University of Oslo where several chapters were written and first presented. I owe to Augustin Berque an invitation to spend a month at the Ecole des Hautes Etudes en Sciences Sociales in Paris. Versions of several other chapters were written for that occasion. Much of the work on this book was done under a grant from the EVIST program of the National Science Foundation. I want to thank Rachelle Hollander of the NSF staff for encouraging me to apply. Dean Paul Strand of San Diego State University and my Department Chair, Tom Weston, lent sympathetic ears to requests for special equipment.

Much of chapter 7 was thought through in online dialogue with Thomas Krogh and David Ingram. Lorenzo Simpson also contributed to a fruitful exchange of views. I am grateful to many others who gave me a forum in which to present the ideas in this book, including Phil Agre, Andrew Light, Scott Noam Cook, Paul Durbin, Jerry Doppelt, Richard Smith, Martin Jay, Hans Sluga, Ryosuke Ohashi, Birgit Jaeger, Alain Gras, and Dan Williamson. Thanks are also due to Walter Murch for his help with the cover, Juliette Robbins for the book design, and Anne-Marie Feenberg for her many contributions to the writing of this book.

Several chapters of this book are based on published articles: "Heidegger, Habermas, and the Essence of Technology," Special Studies Series of the Center for Science and Technology Policy and Ethics, Texas A&M University, 1997; "Marcuse or Habermas: Two Critiques of Technology," *Inquiry* 39, 1996; "The Commoner-Ehrlich Debate: Environmentalism and the Politics of Survival," in D. Macauley, ed., *Minding Nature: The Philosophers of Ecology*, Guilford Publications, 1996; "Remembering the May Events," *Theory and Society*, July 1978; "Subversive Rationalization: Technology, Power and Democracy," *Inquiry* 35, 1992.

Andrew Feenberg
La Jolla, August, 1998

1. Technology, Philosophy, Politics

DETERMINISM AND SUBSTANTIVISM

In this introductory chapter, I will sketch the main themes of this book in the context of a brief account of the growth of interest in technology in the humanistic disciplines. This process has not been an easy one and its full implications are still unclear.[1]

If the human significance of technology is largely unmapped territory, this is mainly due to the idealism of Western higher culture. Only recently have scholars outside the technical fields become interested in their problems and achievements. In earlier times the humanities rejected discourse on technology as unworthy. That tradition goes back to the ancient Greeks who lived in aristocratic societies in which the highest forms of activity were social, political, and theoretical rather than technical.

Humanist scholars first took technology seriously in the modern period, especially with the publication of Diderot's *Encyclopédie*. However, as Langdon Winner explains, modern political theory subsumed technical activity under the economy and did not raise the same kinds of issues about rights and responsibilities in relation to it that are considered relevant to the state. Common sense instrumentalism treated technology as a neutral means, requiring no particular philosophical explanation or justification. So once again it was pushed aside; as an aspect of private life, it was considered irrelevant to the basic normative questions that concerned the thinkers of the great tradition in political theory such as Hobbes, Rousseau, and Locke (Winner, 1995).

There is, however, another fateful path by which technology enters the larger conversation of modernity: the historicizing trend in the emerging biological and social sciences of the late 18th and 19th centuries. This trend was firmly rooted in the idea of progress, which found its surest guarantee in the promise of technology. By the end of the 19th century, under the influence of Marx and Darwin, progressivism had

---

[1] For another more detailed account of these problems, see Mitcham (1994).

become technological determinism. Following the then common interpretation of these materialist masters, technical progress was believed to ground humanity's advance toward freedom and happiness.

Note the link between humanism and determinism. Of course progressive thinkers were well aware of the social divisions that prevented humanity as such from acting as the concrete subject of its own history. However, they regarded competing social groups and nations as proxies for the human race and so ignored this detail. Their universalistic treatment of cultural differences was similarly expeditious. They assumed that the ends which technology serves are permanent features of our biological constitution. Technology was thought to be neutral since it did not alter these natural ends but merely shortened the path to them. This neutralization of technology removed it still further from political controversy. If technology merely fulfills nature's mandate, then the value it realizes must be generic in scope. In fact this is the story that is so often told: technology's advance is the advance of the human species. The editorial "we" intervenes often in this story: "we" as human beings went to the moon.

The great success of modern technology in the early years of this century seemed to confirm this view. But that success also meant that technological decisions affected more and more of social life and had obvious political impacts. From this one can draw diametrically opposed conclusions: either politics becomes another branch of technology, or technology is recognized as political. The first alternative leads straight to technocracy: public debate will be replaced by technical expertise; research rather than the uninformed opinion of the voters will identify the most efficient course of action. The idea of replacing traditional normative paradigms of politics with technical ones dates back to Saint-Simon, but it achieved its greatest popularity in the 1950s and 1960s. The "end of ideology" was much discussed then as it is today for different reasons.

In opposition to this technocratic trend, there is a grand tradition of romantic protest against mechanization going back a century and more. These "substantive" theories of technology attribute a more than instrumental, a substantive, content to technical mediation. They argue that technology is not neutral but embodies specific values. Its spread is therefore not innocent. The tools we use shape our way of life in modern societies where technique has become all pervasive. In this situation, means and ends cannot be separated. How we do things determines who and what we are. Technological development transforms what it is to be human.

Heidegger is the most prominent advocate of this position, which he formulated in ontological terms. In Heidegger's view, we encounter our world in action as a concrete whole, revealed and ordered in a definite manner that belongs to our epoch. Technology is such a mode of "revealing," a way in which what is appears. As the mode of revealing of our time, technology is no mere instrumentality. It forms a culture of universal control. Nothing escapes it, not even its human makers. They, like the things they appropriate technically, are reduced to raw materials through the technological revealing. Everything loses its integrity as a part of a coherent world and is leveled down to an object of pure will (Heidegger, 1977a).

According to substantivism, modernity is also an epistemological event that discloses the hidden secret of the essence of technology. And what was hidden? Rationality itself, the pure drive for efficiency, for increasing control and calculability. This process unfolds autonomously once technology is released from the restraints that surround it in premodern societies.

Something like this view was implied in Max Weber's dystopian conception of an "iron cage" of rationalization. In his account modernity is characterized by a unique form of technical thought and action which threatens non-technical values as it extends ever deeper into social life. However, Weber did not specifically connect this process to technology. Jacques Ellul, another major substantive theorist, makes that link explicit, arguing that the "technical phenomenon" has become the defining characteristic of all modern societies regardless of political ideology. "Technique," he asserts, "has become autonomous" (Ellul, 1964: 6). In Marshall McLuhan's melodramatic phrase: technology has reduced us to the "sex organs of the machine world" (McLuhan, 1964: 46). Ellul is as pessimistic as Heidegger and calls for an improbable spiritual transformation in response to the domination of technology.

Substantive critique has affinities with determinism. For both, technological advance has an automatic and unilinear character. What makes substantivism so very gloomy, where determinism started out as a cheerful doctrine of progress, is the additional assumption that technology is inherently biased toward domination. Far from correcting its flaws, further advance can only make things worse. I call this view essentialist. Essentialism holds that there is one and only one "essence" of technology and it is responsible for the chief problems of modern civilization. I will offer both a critique of essentialism, which continues to set the terms of most philosophy of technology, and an alternative to it, in the concluding chapters of this book.

LEFT DYSTOPIANISM

Surprisingly, substantivism became a new popular culture of technology in the 1960s and 1970s, showing up not only in political discourse but in films and other media. In the United States, the dystopian viewpoint replaced traditional liberalism and conservatism to such an extent that current politics is still largely determined by vulgarized versions of the substantivist categories and sensibility (Feenberg, 1995: chap. 3).[2]

It is not easy to explain the dramatic shift in attitudes toward technology that occurred in the 1960s. By the end of the decade early enthusiasm for nuclear energy and the space program gave way to technophobic reaction. But it was not so much technology itself as the rising technocracy that provoked public hostility.

By "technocracy" I mean a wide-ranging administrative system that is *legitimated* by reference to scientific expertise rather than tradition, law, or the will of the people. To what extent technocratic administration is actually scientific is another matter. In some cases new knowledge and technology really does support a higher level of rationalization, but often a hocus-pocus of pseudo-scientific jargon and dubious quantifications is all that links the technocratic style to rational inquiry. In terms of social impact, the distinction is not so important: reliance on technocratic arguments evokes similar reactions from the administered whether the computer is really "down" or the employee behind the counter too lazy to consult it. The up-to-date excuse for inaction tells a tale all its own. What makes a society more or less "technocratic" is largely its rhetoric rather than its practice. But the fact that the term is ideological does not mean it is without consequences. On the contrary.

That those consequences were political was due to the intellectual arrogance of the Kennedy and Johnson administrations. The Vietnam War was conceived by the US government and sold to the public as a technical problem American ingenuity could quickly solve. Today one is astonished to read behaviorist discussions of strategy from the 1960s: villages were bombed to "condition" their inhabitants to reject the communists—some advisers wondered whether cutting off ears might not be more effective. Support for the counter-cultural critique of technocracy grew tremendously during the War and gradually spread to encompass

---

[2] By "dystopia" is meant the sort of negative utopia described in Huxley's *Brave New World* and Orwell's *1984*. See Aldridge (1984, 1978).

the whole liberal agenda. In a benign vein, the "War on Poverty" proposed to achieve a smoothly functioning social system through enhanced administrative control. Similarly, the creation of the "multiversity" involved integrating a hitherto somewhat marginal and tradition-bound institution to the industrial system. These rationalizing ambitions too appeared as a dystopian threat to many young people and became part of the inspiration for the new left. (Today the same dystopian fears are mobilized in a far more confused form by the right.)

These popular movements transformed the dystopian themes they shared with the critics of modernity. The cultural elitism of discouraged humanists gave way to populist demands incompatible with substantivism. This shift redefined the question of technology as political, and showed that it could be addressed from the left. The left in this period called for democratic control over the direction and definition of progress, and reformulated socialist ideology on these terms. These socialist positions were more or less tied to traditional Marxism, and so may appear outdated today. But, as we will see, they also anticipated a new micropolitics of technology which engages the issue of progress in concrete struggles of a new type in domains such as computers, medicine, and the environment.

Part I of this book therefore includes two chapters on particularly revealing events and debates of the late 1960s and early 1970s. I have chosen subjects which seemed important to me at the time and which shape the philosophy of technology presented in this book. I do not claim that these examples are typical, but I do believe that close attention to them opens a window on the revolution in thinking about technology that continues to this day.

The French May Events was the culminating new left movement. In the spring of 1968, a national student protest began in Paris. It was soon seconded by a general strike which led in turn to the collapse of most of the institutions of the French state. Some 10 million strikers in every sector of the economy brought France to a crashing halt for over a month, threatening the capitalist system. Despite its working-class ideology, the May Events articulated its demands in a distinctively anti-technocratic language. Soviet-style socialism was denounced in the same breath as advanced capitalism: two peas in the technocratic pod. The students and their working-class allies demanded self-management as an alternative. This demand was a response to dystopian anxieties linked to the growth of the technocratic state under de Gaulle. Chapter 2 explores this movement through examples drawn from documents of the period.

In chapter 3, I address a second domain in which technology emerged early as a political issue: the environment. I analyze in some detail the debate between Paul Ehrlich and Barry Commoner that divided environmentalists in the early 1970s. This was one of the first serious attempts to introduce the question of technology into the environmental movement.[3] Commoner rejected antigrowth environmentalism in favor of democratic control of industrial development. The lasting significance of this debate lies in the sharp focus it brought to bear on the conservative political implications of determinism in the environmental arena and the need for a new philosophy of technology emphasizing contingency and social shaping.

The movements of the 1960s created a context and an audience for the break with technocratic determinism that had already begun in the theoretical domain in the works of Mumford and a few other skeptical observers of the postwar scene. Soon they were joined by a host of critics responding to the changed political climate. It was in this context that an American school of philosophy of technology emerged which incorporated elements of substantivism in a democratic framework. Several members of this school, Langdon Winner, Albert Borgmann, Don Ihde, will be referred to frequently in this book, which itself belongs within this tradition (Achterhuis, et al., 1997).

Marcuse and Foucault stand out in this period as the most powerful critics of the role of scientistic ideologies and technological determinism in the formation of modern hegemonies (Marcuse, 1964; Foucault, 1977). They rejected the idea that there is a single path of progress based on technical rationality, and opened a space for philosophical reflection on social control of technological development. At the same time, they argued, apparently inconsistently, that modern forms of domination are essentially technical. I describe their position as a "left dystopian" critique of technology.

These thinkers were strongly influenced by substantivism. Marcuse was a student of Heidegger and clearly learned a good deal from him. His discussion of technology in *One-Dimensional Man* is explicitly phenomenological (Marcuse, 1964: 153–154). Foucault too claimed to be a sort of Heideggerian. Although the connection is less direct than for Marcuse, the case can be made for significant similarities between

---

[3] In addition to Commoner, another influential source of new thinking was Schumacher's notion of "appropriate technology."

Heidegger's critique of technology and Foucault's writings on power, especially in the period of *Discipline and Punish* (Dreyfus, 1992).

In any case, both Marcuse and Foucault agree that technologies are not just means subservient to independently chosen ends but that they form a way of life, an environment. Whether it be an assembly line or a panoptic prison, technologies are forms of power. But Marcuse and Foucault differ with substantivism in introducing a more socially specific notion of domination. Although it sometimes seems so, they do not really claim that technology is autonomous. Rather, they relate technical domination to social organization and argue that technology has no singular essence but is socially contingent and could therefore be reconstructed to play different roles in different social systems.

The left dystopians reject essentialism and argue for the possibility of radical change in the nature of modernity. This position has a certain similarity to the common-sense view that technology is a neutral means available to serve any end. The difference is that here the choices are not at the level of particular means but at the level of whole means-ends systems. I call the availability of technology for alternative developments with different social consequences, its "ambivalence." At stake in the ambivalence of technology is not merely the limited range of *uses* supported by any given technical design, but the full range of *effects* of whole technological systems. Not all of these effects belong to any given technology through all the stages of its development, and not all are "uses" in the usual sense. Some are contextual requirements of the employment of a technology. Others are side-effects. All are relevant to technical choices. Given the range and consequence of the effects for which technologies are responsible, it is not surprising that these choices are often political.

The Frankfurt School expressed a similar view in claiming that technology is materialized ideology. The ideological bias of technology can be understood in different ways, several of which are discussed in later chapters. Habermas, for example, treats technology as a general form of action that responds to the generic human interest in control. As such, it transcends particular political interests and is politically neutral in itself. Value controversy, and hence politics, belongs to the communicative sphere on which social life depends. Technology only acquires a political bias when it invades the communicative sphere. This is the "technization of the lifeworld." It is reversible through reasserting the role of communication.

For Marcuse, technology is ideological where it imposes a system of domination, and forces extrinsic ends on human and natural materials in contradiction with their own intrinsic growth potential. What human beings and nature are and might become is subordinated to the interests of the system. This view has some similarity to substantivist critique, although Marcuse holds out the possibility of a radically transformed technology in the future that would be more respectful of its objects, that indeed would recognize nature as another subject (Marcuse, 1972: 65). The debate between Habermas and Marcuse is the subject of chapter 7.

Foucault's critique of the social construction of rationality does duty for the Frankfurt School's concept of technology as ideology. He explores the "subjugated knowledges" that arise in opposition to a dominating rationality. The view from below reveals aspects of reality hidden from the hegemonic standpoint of science and technique (Foucault, 1980: 81–82). As in Marcuse, so in Foucault technocratic rationalization meets its limit in the resistance of its human objects. But there is also a significant difference between them: while Marcuse demanded an "Absolute Refusal" of one-dimensional society as a whole, Foucault called for new forms of local struggle without any overall strategy. Something like this view is reflected in the action theory of Michel de Certeau, discussed in chapter 5 in connection with Bruno Latour's theory of actor networks.

Regardless of these differences within the critical tradition, the notion of technology as ideology has definite political implications. If one can loosen up the public vision of technology, introduce contingency into it, technical elites will have to be more responsive to a democratically informed public will.[4] These theories thus have a demystificatory aspect which is sometimes viewed as anti-technological. But they also reject the traditional humanistic contempt for technology one still finds in Heidegger and Ellul. In left dystopianism, politics and technology finally meet in the demand for democratic intervention into technical affairs. This is a significant turning point that promises to enlarge the range of the democratic public sphere to encompass issues formerly conceived as "purely" technical. In Part II I attempt to develop and apply this new democratic conception of technology in the light of what social constructivism has taught us in the intervening years.

---

[4] For a critique of this assumption, see Pippin (1995).

Chart 1: The Varieties of Theory

Technology is:	Autonomous	Humanly Controlled
Neutral (complete separation of means and ends)	Determinism (e.g. traditional Marxism)	Instrumentalism (liberal faith in progress)
Value-laden (means form a way of life that includes ends)	Substantivism (means and ends linked in systems)	Critical Theory (choice of alternative means-ends systems)

Simplifying tremendously, the theoretical variety that has unfolded over the long history reviewed above can be represented in a table with two axes. The theories differ with respect to the role of human action in the technical sphere, and the neutrality of technical means. Common sense assumes both the possibility of human control and the neutrality of technology. Deterministic theories, such as traditional Marxism, minimize our power to control technical development, but consider technical means to be neutral insofar as they merely fulfill natural needs. Substantivism shares determinist skepticism regarding human agency but denies the neutrality thesis. Ellul, for example, considers ends to be so implicated in the technical means employed to realize them that it makes no sense to distinguish means from ends. Critical theories, such as Marcuse and Foucault's left dystopianism, affirm human agency while rejecting the neutrality of technology. Means and ends are linked in systems subject to our ultimate control. This is the position defended here, although I work it out rather differently from Marcuse and Foucault.

SOCIAL CONSTRUCTIVISM

The new left and the left dystopian theories of the 1960s and 1970s changed the boundaries of plausibility in thinking about science and technology. Where formerly challenges to the dominant positivism and determinism were easily dismissed as romantic irrationalism, they now gained a certain credibility.

With the decline of the left interest in dystopian critique declined as well, but the mainstream of technology studies retained its skepticism regarding the hegemonic claims of science and technology. The influence of Kuhn and Feyerabend grew among social scientists in the 1980s and it became intellectually respectable to study the history and sociology of science and technology on terms similar to other cultural domains. Early heroic expressions of a critical politics of technology were left behind and technology was approached as a normal social phenomenon without political afterthoughts. The stage was set for the current view of technology as a dimension of society rather than as an external force acting on it from an epistemological or metaphysical beyond. This shift in attitude eventually led to the rise of constructivism.[5] This new approach reaffirmed two central notions of the dystopian critique, the link between means and ends and contingent development.

I will return to constructivism in more detail in chapter 4. For now, let me offer a rough sketch of this complex approach. Constructivism breaks with the standard view according to which society conditions the pace of progress but not the nature of technology itself. Constructivists argue that many paths lead out from the first forms of a new technology. Some are well-trodden while others are quickly deserted. The "principle of symmetry" holds that there are always viable technical alternatives that might have been developed in place of the successful one. The difference lies not so much in the superior efficiency of the successful designs, as in a variety of local circumstances that differentiate otherwise comparable artifacts. Like other institutions, artifacts succeed where they find support in the social environment (Pinch and Bijker, 1987).

Constructivism focuses on the social alliances that lie behind technical choices. Each configuration of components corresponds not only to a technical logic, but also to the social logic of its selection. A wide variety of social groups count as actors in technical development.

---

[5] I use the term "constructivism" loosely here to refer to the range of theories and authors to be found in two influential collections published by MIT Press, Bijker, Hughes, and Pinch (1987), and Bijker and Law (1992).

Businessmen, technicians, customers, politicians, bureaucrats are all involved to one degree or another. They meet in the design process where they wield their influence by proffering or withholding resources, assigning purposes to new devices, fitting them into prevailing technical arrangements to their own benefit, imposing new uses on existing technical means, and so on. The interests and worldview of the actors are expressed in the technologies they participate in designing.

The process of "closure" ultimately adapts a product to a socially recognized demand and thereby fixes its definition. Closure produces a "black box," an artifact that is no longer called into question but is taken for granted. Before closure is achieved, it is obvious that social interests are at stake in the design process. But once the black box is closed, its social origins are quickly forgotten. Looking back from that later standpoint, the artifact appears purely technical, even inevitable. This is the source of the deterministic illusion.

Constructivists believe that technology is social in much the same way as are institutions. It is neither neutral nor autonomous as many technologists and humanistic critics of technology have maintained. But if this is so, then technology must surely have political implications. In particular, specific technical choices rather than progress as such would be involved in the deskilling of work, the debasement of mass culture, and the bureaucratization of society. Constructivism could contribute to the study of the replacement of traditional forms of power, based on myths, rituals, and coercion, with technologies of control and communication. It could lend support to Foucault and Marcuse's political critique of technology.

But so far most constructivist research has confined itself to the study of the strategic problems of building and winning acceptance for particular devices and systems. Studies tend to be narrowly focused on the specific local groups involved in particular cases and lack any sense of the political context. Social resistance is rarely discussed, with the result that research is often skewed toward a few official actors whose interventions are easy to document. The frequent rejection of macro-sociological concepts such as class and culture further armors the research against politics by making it almost impossible to introduce the broad society-wide factors that shape technology behind the backs of the actors.

Thus, although constructivist sociology has placed particular technologies on the agenda in new ways, the basic questions of modernity posed by an earlier generation of theorists are rarely addressed today in

terms of the general problematic of technology.[6] Where the old determinism overestimated the independent impact of the artifactual on the
social world, the new approach has so disaggregated the question of
technology as to deprive it of philosophical significance. It has become
matter for specialized research. And for this very reason, most scholars in
the humanities and in philosophy in particular now feel safe in ignoring
technology altogether, except of course when they turn the key in the
ignition.

Constructivism's narrow empiricism goes along with a purely academic conception of the history of technology studies. Kuhn's break with
positivism is often cited as a founding act. But Donna Haraway argues
that the emergence of new approaches owes as much to the environmental and feminist movements, and, I would add, the contributions of
thinkers such as Marcuse and Foucault (Darnovsky, 1991: 75-76). It is
ironic that the currently dominant social theory of technology seems to
have no grasp of the political conditions of its own credibility.

To be sure, there is some justification for rejecting traditional concepts of politics. Contemporary technology studies would not be much
advanced by rehashing outdated models in which engineers offer
options while goals are neatly set by parliaments and sovereign consumers. Technological development actually involves another kind of
politics, or rather, several other kinds of politics in which the actors cross
all these boundaries between roles. And just because the rise of constructivism is so closely, if unconsciously, linked to increased resistance to the
dominant technical institutions of our society, it can contribute to a necessary reconceptualization of the politics of technology. In chapter 5, I
will show how actor networks can be interpreted as the basis for a revised
political constructivism that incorporates micropolitical resistances in its
understanding of technology. And in chapter 6, I apply this approach to
debates within political theory over the nature of democracy in an age of
technology.

THE POSTMODERN DILEMMA

As the memory of the 1960s faded, social philosophy took an entirely
different path from social science and simply abstracted from technology's broader social and cultural impact. Technology as such canceled
out as its normative implications were identified with the social and

---

[6] Wiebe Bijker has recently taken up the challenge of drawing out the implications of
constructivism for democracy. See Bijker (1998).

political institutions to which it was supposed to be merely instrumental. Thus Rawls and Nozick acquired tremendous influence in the 1970s and 1980s despite the absence of any reference to technology in their work. After an early interest in technology, Habermas and most of his followers abandoned discussion of it to focus on other problems. Most of the work on Heidegger that deigns to notice the central importance of technology for his critique of metaphysics is exegetical. As a result, there have been few original contributions to philosophy of technology in recent years.

In abstaining from the philosophical debate over technology, philosophy left it to other disciplines, such as "postmodern" literary theory and cultural studies.[7] These approaches are associated with multiculturalism, which defends the very differences the substantivist tradition believes to be threatened by progress. According to that tradition, as technology affects more and more of social life, less and less will remain free of its influence to constitute a cultural difference. Yet to the extent that technology is discussed philosophically today, the currently fashionable position claims exactly the contrary, namely, that difference is not only desirable, but ineffaceable.

But multiculturalism cannot be taken for granted so long as theories of convergence in a singular model of modernity are not persuasively refuted. The demonstration, in the course of endlessly repeated case histories, that modern scientific-technical rationality is not the transcultural universal it was thought to be may advance the argument, but does not settle the question. Nor is the persistence of cultural particularity in this or that domain especially significant. Perhaps the Japanese and the Americans will disagree on the relative merits of sushi and hamburgers for generations to come, but if that is all that remains of cultural difference it has ceased to matter. The problem is to show how differences might be *fundamental* and not merely minor accidents certain to be effaced or marginalized in the future.

Epistemological relativism seems to be the predominant way of showing this in the postmodern framework. The new picture emerging from social studies of science and technology does give us excellent reasons for believing that what we call rationality is more similar to than different from other cultural phenomena, and like them relative to social conditions. The anti-technocratic significance of such arguments is

---

[7] See, for example, Penley and Ross (1991).

obvious but of little practical value. Practical questions of technology are not decided on epistemological grounds. Whatever the ultimate status of scientific-technical knowledge, it is what we *use for truth* in making policy. We need far more specific arguments against technocracy that can play at that level.

Furthermore, it is implausible to dismiss rationality as merely a Western myth and to flatten all the distinctions which so obviously differentiate modern from premodern societies. There is something special captured in notions such as modernization, rationalization, and reification. Without such concepts, derived ultimately from Marx and Weber, we can make no sense of the historical process of the last few hundred years.[8] Yet these are "totalizing" concepts that seem to lead back to a deterministic view we are supposed to have transcended from our new culturalist perspective. Is there no way out of this dilemma? Must we choose between universal rationality and culturally or politically particularized values? That is the principal philosophical question of technology I hope to address in the final chapters of this book through a critique of the account of technical action in Habermas, Heidegger, and, as an instance of contemporary philosophy of technology, Albert Borgmann.

ESSENCE AND HISTORY: ON HEIDEGGER AND HABERMAS

Recognition of technical phenomena in Habermas's early philosophy and in Heidegger's later thought seemed like the start of a welcome revolution in social theory. At last philosophy would grapple with the real world! However, neither fulfilled the initial promise of their breakthrough. Both developed essentialist theories that fail to discriminate significantly different realizations of technical principles. As a result, technology rigidifies into destiny in their thought and the prospects for reform are narrowed to adjustments on the boundaries of the technical sphere. They hope that something—albeit a rather different something—can be preserved from the homogenizing effects of technical systems, but they give us little reason to share their hope. In the third part of the book, I will attempt to preserve these thinkers' advance toward the critical integration of technical themes to philosophy without losing the conceptual space for imagining a radical reconstruction of modernity.

It may appear strange to discuss Habermas and Heidegger in the same breath, and especially to compare their views on technology since

---

[8] It is of course easy to renew the vocabulary in which these things are discussed, but that is a far cry from actually breaking with the tradition.

Habermas has written practically nothing on the subject in the last 25 years. But Habermas's preoccupation with technocracy provides a link between his present concerns and his earlier views on technology. I believe there is enough similarity between his critique of systems rationality and Heidegger's theory of the *Gestell* to justify a comparison.

That comparison reveals several interesting complementarities, but also a common problem. Both Habermas and Heidegger rely on the Weberian hypothesis that premodern and modern societies are distinguished by the degree to which previously unified domains such as technology and art have been differentiated from each other. And both argue, for different reasons, that differentiation has made scientific-technical progress possible while reifying the object of technical action and degrading it to a lower plane of being than the subject which acts on it. Each emphasizes a different aspect of this process, Heidegger the object, Habermas the subject. As I will try to show in chapter 9, these complementary emphases provide the basis for a powerful theory of technology. Yet they each develop their contribution in an essentially unhistorical way which is no longer credible.

In Heidegger and Habermas, modernity is governed by a very abstract concept of technical action. I call this view "essentialist" because it interprets a historically specific phenomenon in terms of a transhistorical conceptual construction. The weakness of this approach shows up most strikingly in problems with historical periodization. The construction of the distinction between the premodern and the modern in terms of essentialized characteristics of technical action is unconvincing. Are we really more "rational" or uniquely oriented toward control by comparison with earlier social formations? And if indeed this is what distinguishes us as modern, what can be done to reform our society short of regression to a more primitive condition? There are thus both theoretical and practical reasons to doubt such blanket distinctions between eras and types of society.

The difficulty is inherent in the essentialist project: how to fix the historical flux in a singular essence? Two strategies are available: either deny all continuity and treat modern technology as unique — Heidegger's solution; or distinguish earlier from later stages in the history of technical action in terms of the degree to which it has purified itself of the admixture of other forms of action—Habermas's solution.

Heidegger represents modern technology as radically different from the one other model of technical action he recognizes, premodern craft. He emphasizes the reduction of the object of modern technology to a decontextualized, fungible matter cut off from its own history. This reduction is value charged, or more precisely in Heideggerian terms, it brings "value" into being by canceling the intrinsic potentialities of the object, which craft respected, and delivering it over to alien ends. The modern process of differentiation constitutes a sharp ontological break for Heidegger, a new dispensation, not a continuous social change. Modern technology is no merely contingent historical phenomenon but a stage in the history of being. Perhaps because of this ontologizing approach, Heidegger allows no room for a different technological future. Modern technology remains fixed in its eternal essence whatever happens in history. Not technology itself but "technological thinking" will be transcended in a further stage in the history of being that we can only await passively. This essentializing tendency cancels the historical dimension of his theory.

For Habermas, on the contrary, modernity does not reveal being but human activity in a new and purer light. In premodern societies the various types of action are inextricably mixed together, with no clear distinction between the technical, the aesthetic, and the ethical. In modern societies these action types are differentiated practically and theoretically. At first Habermas identified technical action with technology, but in his later work he focuses on economic and political forms of success-oriented action which he treats much as he had earlier treated technology. In either case, because he continues to interpret technical action through the generic concept of instrumentality, he grants it a kind of neutrality in the limited sphere where its application is appropriate. Its political implications appear where it interferes with human communication in essential lifeworld domains such as the family or education. He ends up arguing that in modern societies the "coordination media," money and power, extend ever more deeply into these domains to their detriment. His goal is the restoration of a healthy process of social communication capable of providing direction to market and administration and especially of limiting their influence.

Habermas's notion of history is less idiosyncratic than Heidegger's, but for him the culturally variable nature of technical action systems is not a question of rationality; he treats it as a minor sociological issue of the sort from which he routinely abstracts. His alternative thus offers an avowedly non-historical conception of technical rationality which effaces any fundamental difference between culturally distinct achievements in what he calls the "cognitive-instrumental" sphere. All the important differences now come down to the degree of development on an apparently absolute scale, and the location of the boundaries between spheres.[9]

The basic problem is essentialism. Heidegger and Habermas claim that there is a level at which instrumental action in modern societies can be considered as a pure expression of a certain type of rationality. However, as such, it is merely an abstraction. Real action always has a socially and historically specific context and content. What do they actually mean by the enframing of being or the objectivating, success oriented relation to nature? Can abstract definitions such as these serve the foundational purpose to which they are destined in these theories?

In chapter 7 I confront Habermas's theory around these questions. I show that while the general framework of his media theory is useful, he fails to work out its relevance to technology, which has social consequences similar to money and power. I argue, as Habermas himself once did, that the design and configuration of technology does more than merely accomplish our ends; it also organizes society and subordinates its members to a technocratic order. Only by including technology in the media theory can we arrive at an adequate account of what Habermas calls the "technization" of the "lifeworld."

In chapters 8 and 9, I amplify this approach with a theory of the essence of technology as a social phenomenon quite different from Heidegger's. Where philosophy of technology has long sought to explain its object in terms of asocial categories such as the Frankfurt School's "instrumental rationality," or the Heideggerian "enframing," I propose an account in which social dimensions of technological systems belong to the essence of technology as well. This essence includes such features as the impact of these systems on workers' skills and the environment, their aesthetic and ethical aspects, and their role in the distribution of power. This "instrumentalization theory" attempts to embrace the wide variety of ways in which technology engages with its objects, its subjects, and its environment. A social account of the essence of technology enlarges democratic concerns to encompass the technical dimension of our lives. It offers an alternative to both the ongoing celebration of technocracy triumphant and the gloomy Heideggerian prediction of techno-cultural disaster.

---

[9] For a provocative attempt to develop a philosophy of technology under the influence of Habermas, see Krogh (1998).

Part I.

THE POLITICIZING OF TECHNOLOGY

The chapters in this section offer case histories in the politicizing of technology in the late 1960s and early 1970s. At this turning point in the public understanding of technology, two major social movements challenged traditional approaches, the student movement and the environmental movement. In a first chapter I will discuss the high point of the student movement in Paris in 1968. Anti-technocratic themes played a central role as the French students claimed the right to define progress in their own terms. This is precisely what the environmental movement soon demanded as well, and much more concretely than any previous critique of technology. A second chapter presents the emergence of the technological alternative in environmentalism through the example of the early debate between Paul Ehrlich and Barry Commoner. The still current issue dividing them is whether modern technology can evolve in environmentally sound directions, or whether we must return to more primitive conditions to save the planet. With these movements, the theoretical question of technological determinism became a practical question of the limits of political action in modern societies.

Part I.

THE POLITICIZING OF TECHNOLOGY

2. Technocracy and Rebellion: The May Events of 1968

INTRODUCTION: AN HISTORIC INTERSECTION

Nineteen sixty eight was the climactic year of New Left protest all over the Western world, and especially in France where in May of that year ten million workers transformed a student protest into a revolutionary movement by joining it in the streets. In the short space of a month France was overthrown and restored, but not without suffering a shock which resounds to this day. Like many an unsuccessful revolution before it, the May Events had an enormous impact on the culture of the society that defeated it in the streets. Although the Events occurred in France, they reveal many of the underlying causes of student protest throughout the advanced capitalist world, including the United States.

The May Events lay at the intersection of three histories: not only did the New Left of the 1960s peak in France in 1968, but France gave the first signal of the political instability that overtook much of Southern Europe in the 1970s. In 1968 no one imagined that the Events would be relayed by an electoral movement such as Eurocommunism. Then the talk was of the "senility" and "sclerosis" of the official opposition parties. In fact the May Events overthrew not the Gaullist state, but the narrow ideological horizons of the old left it challenged in challenging capitalism in new ways. The Events transformed the popular image of socialism in France, contributing to the collapse of moribund Stalinist and social democratic traditions, and prepared Mitterand's eventual victory in the early 1980s.

However, that victory failed to yield radical social change. The Socialist and Communist Parties flirted with the ideas circulating in the extra-parliamentary Left since 1968, but in the end implemented a banal program of nationalizations followed by a hasty retreat into fiscal conservatism. Disappointed, the new social movements, such as the environmental and feminist movements, finally came out from under the shadow of the established Left parties.[1] Meanwhile, French intellectuals

---

[1] For a measured account of the long-run impact of the Events, see Weber (1988). For histories of the Events themselves, see Singer (1970), and Hamon and Rotman (1987).

were also liberated from the moral burden of communism that had weighed on them since World War II. New theoretical movements associated with Foucault, Deleuze, Baudrillard finished the break with the old left begun in 1968.

In this chapter I will reconsider the May Events in the light of four central themes, illustrating the analysis with documents from the period. The themes on which I will focus are: the logic of the student revolt; the relations between workers and students; the ideological crisis of the middle strata; and the new libertarian image of socialism.

The struggle against technocracy played a central role in each of these domains. As giant corporations and state agencies swallowed up more and more of society, as technology threatened to invade hitherto protected domains such as education and medicine, progress through blind technological advance was finally challenged. One student leaflet called "The Amnesty of Blinded Eyes" put it like this: "Let's categorically refuse the ideology of PROFIT AND PROGRESS or other pseudo-forces of the same type. Progress will be what we want it to be" ("L'Amnistie des Yeux Crevés").[2] In challenging both the French government and its official opposition around this theme, the May Events invented a new politics.

TECHNOCRACY AND STUDENT REVOLT

"Why do they fight? Because they refuse to become the watchdogs of the bourgeoisie" ("Roche Démission").

In modern societies, the hierarchy of wealth and power is supposed to reflect gradations in the population's ability. No longer does mere wealth or birth justify privilege. Now education and competence have this function. This is the essential argument of postindustrial technocracy. Of course, technocracy is more an ideology than a reality. While it is true that technological advance has transformed modern bureaucracy, technocratic administration in both state socialist and advanced capitalist societies rationalizes the exercise of power by political and economic elites; in neither does it replace them.

But if technocratic ideology is not altogether true, it is plausible enough and believed enough to change the image of the university,

---

[2] This and other documents of the May Events cited in this chapter are available on microfilm at the library of San Diego State University. All translations are mine. Schnapp and Vidal-Naquet (1971) contains an excellent bibliography on the background to the May Events.

that breeding ground of technical competence. In the late 1960s, student resistance was directed at first against the growing pressure to achieve a technocratic integration of the university and society.[3] In France a profoundly traditional university viewed the rise of technocracy with dismay and resisted adaptation to a world it rejected. In America the movement arose simultaneously with the creation of the modern "multiversity," in the service of business and government as never before.

Mass education certainly made for a less agreeable and prestigious college experience. However, the movements of the 1960s were not merely reactions to the declining quality of student life. Still more important was the students' relation to society in general and their perception of the university as a social institution. During the May Events "L'Amnistie des Yeux Crevés" became something of a manifesto of the movement. It began: "There is no student problem. The student is an outdated idea." This leaflet, like many others, claimed that student revolt was not about the situation in the universities. One could observe this same refusal to concentrate on student issues in the American, Chinese, Italian, Mexican, indeed most of the other major student movements of the 1960s (*Daedalus*: Winter, 1968). Although changes in the university often formed the background to these revolts, students quickly graduated from demands for university reform to protest in the name of universal goals such as peace and freedom.

Most student movements of the 1960s were defined by solidarity with the oppressed in whose name they made these universal demands. In the United States the student movement struggled on behalf of blacks and Vietnamese; it is comprehensible only in terms of the bonds of solidarity, imaginary or real, that linked it to these oppressed groups. The French student movement was similarly based on solidarity with workers. The universalism of these movements was particularly surprising in the West, where student revolt supplied a practical refutation of the supposed "end of ideology."

The new university was called a "knowledge factory," a factory in which knowledge and the knowledgeable are produced (Kerr, 1963). It supplies the technocratic hierarchy with its members, and it is also the place in which the new scientific knowledge used by this hierarchy is first discovered. The struggle, a leaflet asserts,

---

[3] The theme of technocracy was a central one for commentators on May 1968. Touraine (1968) is the most famous discussion of it. The analysis presented here is independent of Touraine's.

is motivated in particular by the fact that the University has become a more and more essential terrain: the intensification of the repressive reality of the University, its increasing role in the process of social reproduction, its active participation in maintaining the established order (cf. the social sciences in particular), the role of science and research in economic development, all require the institution of a right to permanent contestation of the University, its goals, its ideology, the content of its "products" ("Camarades," *Action*, no. 1, 7 Mai 1968: 4).

Furthermore, the university resembles a technocracy in that it too is divided into the trained and the untrained, the knowledgeable and the ignorant. There is thus a metaphoric equivalence between society, which professes to be based on knowledge, and the university, which actually is so based. Judging by the many leaflets and articles they wrote during and after the Events, French students saw the university as an idealized model of the social world in which differences in knowledge justified different functions and privileges. One leaflet comments: "For us the faculty and the student body are only grotesque miniaturizations of social classes, projected onto the university milieu, and this is why we reject the right of the faculty to exist as such" ("Université de Contestation").

Although most French students were poor in 1968, they were predestined to take their place in the hierarchies of business and government after graduation. They could not define themselves in terms of poverty and exploitation, and were in fact seen by workers as incipient oppressors. The only significant resemblance between workers and students was their lack of qualifications. In any other society, this particular equation between them would be irrelevant, but in a society dominated by technocratic ideology, in which all forms of subordination are justified in terms of levels of expertise, students could be said to suffer in its purest and most abstract form the same domination as workers. The emergence of unemployment among university graduates made the analogy all the more plausible. Thus the students confronted the tasks to which they were destined, both as teachers and executives, and rejected them. They hoped to change the system before it became their job to run it:

Today the students are becoming conscious of what is being made of them: the executives of the existing economic system, paid to make it function better. Their fight concerns all the workers because it is everyone's fight: they [the students] refuse to become professors serving a teaching system which selects the sons of the bourgeoisie and eliminates the others; sociologists designing slogans for the government's electoral campaigns, psychologists charged with organizing "work teams" in the interests of the boss; executives applying to the workers a system which subjugates them as well ("Pourquoi Nous Nous Battons," *Action*, no. 1, 7 Mai 1968: 4).

And just as the perception of domination could be universalized along the lines laid out in technocratic ideology, so could the demand for more freedom and initiative. Carrying the analogy between the university and society one step further, students discovered the general arbitrariness of the established structures of power in the society at large. This helps to explain why students sought not so much the destruction of the hierarchy of learning in the university, as its destruction in the larger society they had soon to enter. Dissatisfaction with the university was displaced from the learning process and its administration along the pathways set up by technocratic ideology, toward the government and the economic system. A leaflet of the March 22 Movement states:

> The college and high school students, the young unemployed, the professors and the workers did not fight side by side on the barricades last Saturday to save a university in the exclusive service of the bourgeoisie. This is a whole generation of future executives who refuse to be the planners of the needs of the bourgeoisie and the agents of the exploitation and repression of the workers.
> ("Continuons la Lutte dans la Rue")

The language of these leaflets has a deceptively outmoded air. It conjures a long history of French intellectuals placing themselves in the service of the working class through the good offices of the Communist Party. But as we will see the French students of 1968 had nothing in common with classical intellectuals motivated by philanthropic concern for the welfare of their social inferiors. In fact, one graffiti on the walls of Paris read: "Do not serve the people. They will serve themselves." New causes were disguised in the old language of the movement. Thus despite the borrowings from Marxism, the French Communist Party was suspicious of the students and condemned the movement as profoundly alien to its traditions, as indeed it was.

Is there not an implicit anti-intellectualism in the students' rejection of their own role? The charge has often been made. Yet it would be more accurate to say that the revolt within the university was a struggle against the use of arguments from technical necessity and intellectual authority to justify a system of domination. Thus it was not intellect the students rejected, but technocracy when they wrote that they did "not want to be ruled passively any longer by 'scientific laws,' by the laws of the economy or by technical 'imperatives'."

The "Amnesty of Blinded Eyes" continues:

> Let's categorically refuse the ideology of PROFIT AND PROGRESS or other pseudo-forces of the same type. Progress will be what we want it to be. Let's refuse the trap of luxury and necessity—the stereotyped needs imposed separately on all, to make each worker labor in the name of the "natural laws" of the economy. . .

> WORKERS of every kind, don't let's be duped. Do not confuse the TECHNICAL division of labor and the HIERARCHY of authority and power. The first is necessary, the second is superfluous and should be replaced by an equal exchange of our work and services within a liberated society ("L'Amnistie des Yeux Crevés").

In sum, the students found themselves at the leading edge of a contradiction that cuts across all modern societies, the contradiction between the enormous knowledge and wealth of these societies and the creativity they demand of their members, and the mediocre use to which this knowledge, wealth and creativity is put. And they believed they had a solution to the problem in a transformation of the place of knowledge—and their own future role—in the social structure. They wrote, "We refuse to be scholars, cut off from social reality. We refuse to be used for the profit of the ruling class. We want to suppress the separation of execution, reflection and organization. We want to construct a classless society" ("Votre Lutte est la Nôtre").

THE WORKER-STUDENT ALLIANCE

"Freedom is the crime which contains all crimes.
It is our ultimate weapon" (Graffiti from the walls of Paris, 1968).

In a society which pretends to be based on knowledge, revolt in the university can be seen as a refutation of all the claims of the social hierarchy. It shows that there is something profoundly wrong in the citadel of knowledge itself. Insofar as the university is understood ideologically on the model of the society, student revolt can appear to students to be the model for social revolution.

But for revolution actually to occur, the model-reality relations experienced in the university must be reversed. Students could universalize their movement because the university appeared to them as a metaphor to the society. But for others outside the university to understand the significance of the student movement, they had to perceive its similarity to their own struggles. This was the purpose of much student propaganda which described the student movement on the model of a classic revolutionary struggle in order to make it an example for the whole society. Then the circle of ideology and reality could be closed, and the model being taken reciprocally as metaphor and reality, it could become the symbol of generalized social struggle.[4]

The labor movement provided the dominant metaphor in terms of which the French students described their own struggle. This choice flowed both from a realistic sense of the limitations of an isolated student revolt, and from the prestige of traditional Left ideology. Thus leaflets like the following one were widely distributed in the first days of the movement to justify its violence to workers and to provoke them to violence as well.

WORKERS,
— You too are forced to struggle against the offensives
of the government to defend your gains.
— You too have encountered the CRS and the Mobile Guards,
come to break your resistance.
— You too have been slandered by the Boss's press and
by the government Radio.
You know that violence is in the nature of the existing social order.
You know that it strikes down those who dare to challenge it:
the batons of the CRS answered our demands, just as the rifle
butts of the Mobile Guards answered the workers of Caen,
Redon and Mans
("D'Où Vient la Violence").

Soon student leaflets began to draw the parallel between student and labor demands: "Between your problems and ours there are certain

---

[4] For a more elaborate discussion of the relations between workers and students, see the analysis of Vidal in P. Dubois et al. (1971).

similarities: jobs and opportunities, standards and work pace, union rights, self-management" ("Camarades Ouvriers").

The factory occupations which quickly followed showed the reciprocity of the model-reality relation: they were coded simultaneously in terms of the student occupation of the Sorbonne, begun on May 13, and similar factory occupations in 1936, which latter could themselves be described as the model for the students' actions. One leaflet that was widely distributed to workers was entitled "Your Struggle is Ours!" In it the students said, "Your struggle and our struggle converge. We must destroy everything which isolates each of us from the other (habit, the newspapers, etc.) We must make the connection between the occupied factories and the campuses" ("Votre Lutte est la Nôtre").

How successful was this strategy? The French student revolt provoked a general strike by millions of workers. The strikers seized hundreds of factories all over the country, paralyzing commerce and transportation for over a month. The government was largely helpless as well, and only the police and professional army actively supported the tottering state.

Yet it is difficult to gauge labor support for the actual goals of the student movement. The students had little influence on the major working-class organizations such as the Communist Party and the Communist-led union federation, the Confédération Générale des Travailleurs (CGT). Continuing for the most part to confine the union struggle to wages and working conditions and the political struggle to elections, the Party completely misunderstood what was new about the movement: its demand for workers' self-management and for the transformation of daily life and culture. As a result, the communists found the new student opposition contesting their own leadership of the working class from the left.

The communists counterattacked by charging the students with *"gauchisme"*—ultra-leftism, to which the students responded by accusing the Party of another equally serious deviation, "opportunism." The stale insults had flown back and forth for years, but unlike earlier struggles between French communists and the old anarchist, Trotskyist and Maoist sects, this time the students broke out of their traditional isolation. Never before had such a profound social crisis been orchestrated against the will of such a strong communist party.

In a leaflet entitled "Toward a Mass Leftism," a Trotskyist group commented: "The role fulfilled by the *'gauchistes'* was, within certain limits, that which an authentically revolutionary leadership would have played: foreseeing the course of the movement (and this is not a question of dates), organizing it, directing it" ("Vers une Gauchisme de Masse").

That such results could have been achieved, shows that the communists had disastrously underestimated the political consciousness of the workers they were attempting to lead.

The second largest union federation, the Confédération Française Démocratique du Travail (CFDT), was drawn into the movement, adopted the symbols and goals proposed by the students, at least verbally, and pushed for a strategy of structural reforms far to the left of anything considered by the communists. In a major leaflet distributed by the CFDT on May 18, this organization addressed workers with an interpretation of the movement close to that of the students.

> The intolerable constraints and structures against which the students rose exist similarly, and in a still more intolerable way, in the factories, construction sites, and offices . . .
> The government yielded to the students. To freedom in the university must correspond freedom in the factories. Democratic structures based on self-management must be substituted for industrial and administrative monarchy. The Moment Has Come To Act ("La CFDT s'Addresse aux Travailleurs").

In spite of this verbal support, student activists decided to appeal over the heads of the unions directly to the workers. To a certain extent they were successful, although they could not overcome in a few weeks the effects of years of mutual ignorance. In any case the students were encouraged to try by the massive strike which began independent of the parties and unions; by the rejection of a settlement the unions negotiated with the government and corporations; by the brief radicalization of the Communist Party at the end of May when under pressure from the grass roots it demanded de Gaulle's resignation; and by the appearance of revolutionary workers at the Sorbonne, on the barricades, in factory and union meetings.

In fact two groups of workers were deeply influenced by the student strategy, and it was their opposition to ending the strike and their participation in the street fighting that makes it possible to speak of a real worker-student alliance during May. The first of these two groups was the technicians, particularly those organized by the CFDT, which over the years had become their chief representative. The idea of self-management had more immediate appeal to these workers than to any others. They were highly trained and felt competent to run the factories in which they were employed. The CFDT had responded to this sentiment long before the May Events by demanding a share in management.[5]

Young workers were drawn to the students for other reasons. They proved to be tremendously combative and impatient for revolution. Many of them joined the students on the barricades and fought the police. They served on worker-student coordinating committees and influenced student thinking about workers while being influenced in their turn by the students. In some cases they were inspired by the Events to join one or another of the Maoist and Trotskyist *"group-uscules"* which flourished at the time.

These young workers argued for violent and immediate revolution, sometimes with contempt or condescension toward their seniors and the Party for having failed to do the job in the past. Many older workers, they seemed to feel, had resigned themselves but they had no intention of following in their fathers' footsteps; they were not going to "swallow" defeats and humiliations without making their try for freedom whatever older, wiser heads from the unions might advise.

Parallel phenomena occurred in the following two years among young workers in Italy, particularly those of Southern origin. They were even less integrated into established union and party organizations than their French counterparts, a factor which seems directly related to their intense combativity. Often first-generation immigrants to the cities, with no proletarian roots at all, they unhesitatingly attacked structures and practices which seemed "natural" to the older or more urbanized workers. In Italy this included the entire organization of manual labor: systems of piecework, the assembly line, the wage hierarchy, pay supplements for dangerous work, etc.

A few years later rather similar struggles occurred in the United States, the most famous of which was the Lordstown strike of 1971-1972. There too young workers dissatisfied less with the rewards than the servitudes of industrial labor made a new kind of strike indicative of profound changes in the expectations of workers in advanced capitalist societies (Aronowitz, 1973: chap. 2).

The New Left was thus not exclusively a student affair. Industrial workers, who were believed to be content with receiving periodic wage increases, also came forward in this period with demands for power and control over the labor process. In France such struggles dovetailed with

---

[5] The classic discussion in the French literature of the attitudes of technicians is Serge Mallet (1963). Later Mallet (1971) argued that the May Events confirmed his approach.

the students' attack on the organization of labor from above, supported by many employees in the professions and the bureaucracies.[6]

IN THE SERVICE OF THE PEOPLE

"Obedience begins with conscience and conscience with disobedience" (Graffiti from the walls of Paris, 1968).

The struggles of May briefly dislocated one of the structural bases of capitalist democracy: the allegiance of the middle strata to the established parties and institutions. Opposition exploded among teachers, journalists, employees in the "culture industry," social service workers and civil servants, and even among some middle and lower level business executives. So much for the image of a politically and socially conformist middle class, put forward in the classic analyses of "white collar" labor of C. Wright Mills and William Whyte. The students soon found their own revolt embedded in the much broader movements of the occupational groups to which the university licenses the entry.

The May Events produced a flowering of theories to explain this phenomenon.[7] This is not the place to review these discussions. The study of the role of the employed middle strata in the May Events cannot entirely resolve the theoretical problems, but it can teach us how they understood themselves and acted in support of a developing revolutionary movement. This perspective shows the artificiality of attempts to squeeze the middle strata into the procrustean bed of traditional class theory.

During the May Events there were brave attempts to convince the middle strata that they were ordinary workers. Roger Garaudy, among others, argued that engineers, technicians, office employees and executives have been "proletarianized" "because the mechanization of administrative tasks and managerial functions increasingly eliminates the frontier between the employee as a manipulator of computers, to give an example, and the laborer working under conditions of automation"

---

[6] The importance of the aspiration for power in the May Events is supported by statistical evidence in an article by Seeman (1972), 399.

[7] For new working-class interpretations, see Touraine (1968) or Glucksmann (1968). For a defense of the traditional view of the middle strata as part of the petty bourgeoisie, see the Maoist response to Glucksmann, Centre Universitaire d'Etude et de Formation Marxiste-Leniniste (1968). The Communist Party was divided by this debate, with the traditional option predominating during the period of the Events. Cf. Claude Prévost (1968). Roger Garaudy (1968) presented an alternative view.

(Garaudy, 1968: 9). This account simply ignored the fact that these same "proletarianized" employees manned the technocracy that controlled the society. More traditional Marxists misinterpreted this phenomenon too by consigning the middle strata to the petty bourgeoisie, as though there was a significant similarity between running a corner grocery store and a branch of the state or corporate bureaucracy.

In practice, the middle strata in revolt did not see themselves as members of either the ruling or the working classes and, in contrast with the latter, their demands were primarily social and political. Their protest focused on the absurdity of "consumer society;" they denounced the bureaucratic organization of their work and demanded the right to participate in the determination of its goals. The most advanced struggles of the middle strata were distinguished in another way from those of workers. The workers' movement spoke in the name of the "people;" the middle strata expressed their desire to switch their allegiance from the state and capital to the "people." This language tended to imply that they were indeed in the middle of the social hierarchy, neither rulers nor ruled. Their intermediary position reflects the ambiguous role of "knowledge workers" in a technocratic society, caught between traditional elites and the mass of the population. Some examples may make this clear.

1. *Education.* During the May Events high schools and universities in solidarity with the movement declared their "autonomy." As one leaflet explained it, "The autonomy of public education is a political act of secession from a government which has definitively failed in its task of defending the real interests of the community in the educational sphere" (*Le Mouvement*, no. 3, June 3, 1968).

But what did "autonomy" mean? Did the university in revolt hope to isolate itself from society? In a lengthy leaflet a group of leftist faculty explained why it could not do so:

> The principal victims of the present functioning of the . . . educational system are, by definition, outside the system because they have been eliminated from it; consequently, the groups whose voice has not been heard in university discussions, discussions between beneficiaries of the system, are the very ones who would have the most direct interest in a real transformation of the system . . .
>
> Every attempt to call into question academic institutions which does not bear fundamentally on the function they serve in eliminating the lower classes, and consequently, on the socially con-

servative function of the school system, is necessarily fictive . . .

In declaring the University 'open to the workers,' even if it is only a question here of a symbolic and illusory gesture, the students have at least shown that they were open to a problem which cannot be resolved except by acting on the mechanisms which forbid certain classes access to higher education (Schnapp and Vidal-Naquet, 1968: 695).[8]

It was out of reflection on problems such as these that the students concretized their demand for "autonomy" with proposals for "permanent education for all." Autonomy was thus not an end in itself; it was precisely through autonomy that the university was to switch its class allegiance and reduce the social distance that separated it from the society at large. The demand for *more* autonomy from the state implied *less* autonomy with respect to the population which was invited to participate in the reform of the university.

2. *Communications*. The communications industry was also thrown into turmoil during May. The nationalized sector was struck by employees demanding "a radio and television in the service of all and not of a party" (*Téléciné*, no. 143, July 1968). This was the counterpart of student-faculty demands for a democratization of education. "Autonomy" was also the slogan under which the personnel of the Radio-Télévision sought liberation from the stifling supervision of the Gaullist state. In essence, they demanded the right to tell the truth. But in the context of the Events, that demand had a fairly clear political significance: it meant supporting the movement by mirroring its own activities back to it. Thus here too autonomy from the state implied a closer relation to the people.

3. *Civil Service*. Many government ministries were closed during May by their own employees, on strike in solidarity with the movement. The pattern of protest was similar in every case: a combination of demands for more democratic working conditions and an end to policies the civil servants judged to be opposed to the interests of the people.

Even the usually staid Ministry of Finances was involved. The model of the student movement was reenacted there, complete with occupations, general assemblies and reform commissions. A descriptive leaflet tells the story:

---

[8] Among the signatories were P. Bourdieu, R. Castel, J. Cuisinier, A. Culioli, J. Derrida, L. Goldmann, J. Le Goff, E. Leroy-Ladurie, L. Marin, J. B. Pontalis and P. Ricoeur.

While the students rose in all the universities of France and ten million strikers united against the iniquities of the economic system, the prodigious popular movement of May 68 touched the civil servants of the principal ministries, where the traditional structures of administration have been profoundly shaken.

The general assembly of the personnel of the central administration of economy and finances, meeting the 21st of May, decided to continue the strike. At the Ministry of Finances, as in the majority of associated services and at the National Institute of Statistics, the civil servants stopped work and occupied their offices.

On May 21 a demonstration in the Rue de Rivoli drew 500 civil servants from Finances demanding an administration in the service of the people and a "radical change of economic and social policy." ("Grève au Ministère des Finances: On Debré-Ye")

Similar events occurred in the Ministry of Urban Affairs and Housing, which issued a leaflet containing the following significant paragraph.

Civil servants in the service of the community, we have become, paradoxically and for many of us against our will, the symbol of red tape. An erroneous conception of the role of the Administration, together with the absence of consultation in the making and implementing of decisions, have as a consequence that, instead of being the driving force of Urban Affairs and Housing, we are the brakes that all concerned would like to see disappear ("Grève Sur Place au Ministère de l'Equipement (20 Mai - 8 Juin)," *Cahiers de Mai*, no. 2, July 1968).

In cases like these the professionalist ideology of "public service" glides imperceptibly into the Maoist rhetoric of "service to the people." Civil servants, like students and communications workers, attempted to include the previously excluded, and to switch their allegiance from the state to the population as though they themselves represented a middle term.

4. *Business Executives.* No doubt most business executives were hostile to the movement, however, a significant minority supported it. As one commentator noted:

In the Loire-Atlantique executives were in solidarity with the workers in impressive numbers, something which had never before been seen. But support for wage demands was not the essential point: it was the theme of management methods which cemented the union. Executives are frustrated by the excessive centralization of public enterprises: they remain in their offices signing papers, but they have no power of decision ("Toute une Ville Découvre le Pouvoir Populaire," *Cahiers de Mai*, no. 1, May 15, 1968: 6).

On May 20th 1500 executives met at the Sorbonne and declared their sympathy with the movement. Several hundred of them seized the Paris headquarters of the principal union of executives and engineers and called for a general strike. In a leaflet issued on May 24, they demanded "The elaboration of concrete solutions for the democratization of management and the general economic decision-making process. The goal of fulfillment of the personality in work as well as in leisure must be substituted for the usual goals of profitability and expansion" ("Manifesto").

5. *Technical Experts.* The Events even reached a government funded think-tank. The researchers there earned good livings making surveys and studies for various ministries, usually concerning public works projects. Yet even before May they suffered from a distinct malaise. They were aware that their work, on becoming the "property" of the purchasing ministry, served to justify pre-established policies or was ignored where it conflicted with them. Often the researchers felt these policies were not in the best interests of the very populations they had been called on to study. This is an alienating situation and during May, "It suddenly seemed intolerable that the researcher should have in the final analysis no control over the product of his work" ("Les Bureaux de Recherches," *Action*, June 24, 1968).

Yet there could be no question of claiming control for the sake of personal satisfaction. No sooner had the researchers gone on strike than they attempted to join up with the people whose interests they wished to serve. Their union declared, "The workers of the National Union of Social Sciences affirm their will to see their work placed in the service of the workers and not in the service of management and the capitalist state apparatus" ("Les Bureaux de Recherches," *Action*, June 24, 1968). Concretely, they provided financial aid to poorer strikers and, in one case made a free study of employment in the Paris suburbs at the request of the local unions.

These examples illustrate a common pattern. In May 1968 the French middle strata did not so much feel useless or guilty about their privileges as misused by those in command of the society. Their radical stand is best understood as an appeal to the population to redirect their work into more humane and productive channels. In 1971, when the French Communist Party revised its attitude toward the middle strata, its theoreticians described their new political potentialities.

> Before these transformations emerged, the support for working-class struggles by the middle strata and especially by intellectuals appeared as a rallying to the proletarian cause. Today there is no longer any question of individuals rallying to the cause, but of an entente to be established between social strata having common interests and which can build a democratic future together (*Le Capitalisme Monopoliste d'Etat*, 1971: I, 240).

This statement of the case reflects the experience of the May Events and helps to explain the subsequent rise of the electoral alliance of the Communist Party, primarily representing workers, and the Socialist Party which, after the Events, came to represent a large fraction of the middle strata. However, it still underestimates the radicalism of the demands of the most politicized supporters of the movement. The "entente" they were looking forward to was not merely political, but social and economic as well. It was to be based on the transformation of the division of labor in a self-managed society.

SELF-MANAGEMENT: STRATEGY AND GOAL

"Humanity will be able to live in freedom only when the last capitalist has been hanged with the entrails of the last bureaucrat" (Graffiti from the walls of Paris, 1968).

The history of revolutions is a record of anticipated futures that never came to pass. These are branches off the main line of history that punctuate it with repeated images of freedom. The collective imagination of those in revolt recalls and reworks these images in accordance with the varying conditions of time and place. In opposition to the accepted wisdom—that society is fate, that the individual must adapt to survive—revolutions demand that society be adapted to the individuals. This demand opens a vertiginous abyss beneath the feet of whole peoples who the day before trod the solid ground of everyday life.

Even in defeat the memory of revolution remains as indelible evidence that history might be made by human beings instead of merely suffered. Sometimes this memory informs a peoples' daily practice of politics for long periods between revolutions, so that the broken thread is not wholly lost and can be rejoined to later upsurges as revolutions relay each other across the decades and the generations. This has been true of France for nearly two centuries. The May Events and its aftermath, down to the present day, cannot be understood in forgetfulness of this fact.

Walter Benjamin once wrote that revolution is "a tiger's leap into the past." He called on the historian of revolution to "blast open the continuum of history" and reestablish the broken links between revolutionary experiences back through the centuries (Benjamin, 1968: 261-262). The element of repetition and continuity was certainly present in the May Events. Superficially, the link was everywhere in the cobblestone barricades that recalled so many earlier Parisian insurrections. More significant was the pattern of workers' activities. Every workers' revolution since 1905 has proceeded from a general strike to the formation of "soviets," workers' councils poised to seize power from the state. In the May Events too a general strike and even a few soviets trooped back upon the stage of history to perform again the play begun and interrupted so many times in so many countries in this century.

But was the general strike of May and June truly revolutionary? Was it an economic or a political movement, a movement for wage increases or for socialism? Did it have a practical strategy? Were its various components united? Posed in this form the questions are unanswerable. The mass strike, considered as a recurring pattern of working-class resistance, is always both economic and political, and so were the Events (Luxemburg, 1970: 186). No revolutionary movement sets out from a coherent plan. Instead they are driven forward toward solutions to the problems they themselves create when they break with past ways of getting things done. In these respects the May Events were fairly typical of the early stages of many an urban revolution.

Whether the May Events qualify as a full fledged revolution or not, something very extraordinary happened in its penultimate moment, the moment in which workers and students demanded the resignation of a government that could no longer even control the state bureaucracy, much less run the country. In this moment of hesitation at the end of May the nation hung in suspense while the workers and the government weighed their chances. In this moment the movement became something more than a mere summation of particular struggles for immediate interests. Massive disobedience to authority in every sphere, whatever its immediate occasion, set off a chain reaction in the crucible of which a political will was formed. What did that will demand? The answer to this question will require a brief historical detour.

Without generations of socialist propaganda by the "official" French Left, and in particular the French Communist Party, the May Events would certainly not have had such broad support from workers. And yet the communists had nothing to offer the movement in 1968. The most important difference between the communists and the movement concerned the attitude toward the state. By May 1968 the French Communist Party was fully committed to an electoral strategy. Its goal was to put together an "antimonopoly alliance" capable of winning a parliamentary majority and creating "an advanced democracy as a step toward socialism." But at this time the French communists were among the most loyal supporters of the Soviet Union. Their intended allies, moderate socialist parties representing employees, small businessmen and farmers, were unalterably opposed to the Russian model of socialism. The Party denied dictatorial intentions and insisted that it was committed to democracy. Yet it never criticized the absence of this desirable system in the Soviet Union, a lapse that left its sincerity open to question.

Furthermore, communist strategy identified socialism with a program of extensive nationalizations which, the students charged, would leave the bureaucratic apparatus of the state and the corporations intact and concentrate ever more power at the top. Meanwhile, moderate socialists saw their role as maintaining the separation of the economy and the state that has always been the foundation of the liberal conception of freedom. The resulting alliance would seem to be self-cancelling.

The problem was in fact insoluble as it was posed by these parties. The old freedoms are withering in any case through the growing identification of giant corporations and the state, the organized planning of the economy by monopolies and oligopolies, the increasing bureaucratization of major social institutions, and the ever more effective manipulation of consumers and voters by the mass media. The communist strategy would seem to change only the men at the top, but not the oppressive structure. Nationalization of the economy would simply complete the technocratic project of monopoly capitalism itself, whatever its social content.

The mainstream of the student movement rejected the entire political strategy of these left parties. The error, they argued, lay in situating the struggle on the electoral plane, taking the state as the object and not the enemy in the struggle, conserving bureaucratic forms of administration, and conceiving socialism and democracy exclusively in terms of the degree of state intervention in the economy. Instead, the students demanded an end to the technocratic division of labor as the basis for a radically new model of socialist society.

Furthermore, the revolutionaries argued, given the institutionalized power of modern capitalism in every sphere of daily life, given its control of mass culture, an electoral victory of the left would be, if not impossible, at the very least a feeble substitute for a revolution attacking the sources of social reproduction. As one leaflet notes,

> In the present situation . . . the system's integrative models of mass consumption and the search for social advancement . . . represent in reality the modern form of oppression which is no longer materialized exclusively in the State. The instrument of capitalist power thus no longer resides so much in this latter [the state] as in the submission of workers to models of consumer society and to all the differentiated forms of authority that insure its functioning ("Quel est le Sens des Elections Qui Nous Sont Imposé").

This analysis has not been refuted by the later history of the French left.

It was for such reasons that the activists of May demanded a socialism arising from a mass revolutionary movement, one that would not simply change the men at the top, but which would shatter the hierarchy and replace it with a new principle of social coordination. Socialism was to emerge not from an electoral victory, but through the transformation of the general strike into an "active strike" in which the workers would set their factories back in motion on their own account. (Something like this actually occurred in a number of localities (Guin, 1969).) Then, with the economy turning again, but for the workers and not for their former bosses, the state would quickly succumb. A parallel power would arise in each town and village as workers coordinated their efforts with each other and the farmers. Socialism would be initiated from below and not handed down from above in nationalizations.

Self-management, one of the goals of this revolution, would also serve as a strategy in the struggle against capitalism. This strategy had a triple edge. First, it would end the lethargy and atomization of the general strike, facilitate the independent organization of the workers as a powerful political force, and make it very difficult for the government to mobilize against the secession of whole industries and regions. Second, the active strike was supposed to alter the balance of ideological power between capital and labor by showing the obsolescence of capitalist ownership. If workers did not need the capitalists to run the economy, the entire population would be encouraged to follow them. Third, it would insure a passage from capitalism to socialism on the basis of popular action and in a form that would limit the power of the state after the revolution, safeguarding the new society from Stalinism and techno-bureaucratic oppression. The strategy is explained in the leaflet reproduced on the next page (*"Nous Continuons la Lutte"*.)

In France industrial democracy has an anarchist ring. In fact, the revival of the black flag during May was an astonishing reminder of a whole French anarchist tradition long thought to be dead outside a few musty sects. Everyone was aware of this historical reference, and yet the concept of self-management, which suggests this comparison in the French context, was not the product of the surviving anarchist sects but of the actual struggle pursued to its logical conclusion.

In this respect the May Events are better compared with the last great wave of European revolutions that followed World War I, in which millions of workers across Europe more or less spontaneously formed workers' councils to bring industrialism under the direct control of the immediate producers. Everywhere but in Russia these revolutions were defeated, and we know the fate of workers' councils in the Soviet Union. What we cannot say for sure is that they would have failed so completely in richer countries such as Germany which also had revolutions in this period and might have offered the council communist program a more suitable terrain than Russia.[9] Soon Stalinism was to bury the issue in any case.

As a result, industrialism has continued to develop on the track originally set by its capitalist origins. Its central problem is still control of the labor force which, lacking ownership or identification with the firm, has no very clear reason to favor its success. The instruments of that control, management and technological design, have rooted the system so deeply in consciousness and practice that it seems the outcome of progress as such. The fact that the system has been shaped not only by technical necessities but also by the tensions of the class struggle has been forgotten.

Council communism proposed to base management and technology not on the needs of capital but on those of workers, as expressed by votes in firm-based elections. Of course the practical details were never settled, but it is at least plausible that the relatively well educated

---

[9] For a discussion of Karl Korsch's contemporary council communist theory of socialization and translations of texts, see Kellner (1977)

WE ARE CONTINUING THE STRUGGLE

The movement cannot endorse an operation of the "popular front" type or a transitional government. The material concessions that we could obtain would in no way modify the scandalous character of the present society. Besides, they would be quickly absorbed by a rise in the cost of living organized by management.

This is why the ultimate weapon of the workers struggling for revolution is DIRECT MANAGEMENT of their means of coordination and production.

Another step must be taken!!!

Comrades, the occupation of the factories must now signify that you are capable of making them function without the bourgeois framework which exploited you. It is necessary now to permit the revolutionary movement to live, to develop itself, to organize production under your control. You thereby deprive capitalism of its instruments of oppression. Assure production, distribution: the whole working class must show that a workers' power in possession of its means of production, can establish a real socialist economy.

The goal of SELF-MANAGEMENT AS AN ECONOMIC AND SOCIAL SYSTEM is to fully realize free participation in production and consumption through individual and collective responsibility. It is thus a system created above all for man, to serve him and not to oppress him.

Practically, self-management consists in the worker comrades operating their factories by and for themselves and, consequently, the suppression of the hierarchy of salaries as well as the notions of wage earner and boss. It is up to them to constitute the workers' councils, which they elect to carry out the decisions of the whole.

These councils must be in close relation with the councils of other enterprises on the regional, national and international plane.

The members of these workers' councils are elected at a specified time and their tasks are rotated. It is necessary in practice to avoid recreating a bureaucracy which would tend to set up a leadership and an oppressive power.

DEMONSTRATE THAT WORKERS' MANAGEMENT OF THE ECONOMY IS THE POWER TO DO BETTER FOR EVERYONE WHAT THE CAPITALISTS DID SCANDALOUSLY FOR A FEW.

employees of an advanced capitalist country could substitute themselves for stockholders in guiding the policies implemented by the firm. Certainly, they would be better informed and closer to the issues than most stockholders. The long-run transformation of industrialism implied by this change would be far more significant than anything that could be accomplished by the substitution of state bureaucrats for capitalists at the helm of a structurally rather similar system.[10]

The May Events revived this forgotten council communist tradition under the name "self-management." The target of protest in this new situation was not just capitalist control of the economy, but more generally technocratic control of society, the spread of an administrative power based on technical mediation. What is of course far from clear is whether the movement, had it lasted longer, could have coordinated these two struggles, the anti-technocratic movement of the students and the middle strata with the workers' movement against capitalism. And no doubt council communism, with its worker-centric view of power, would have run up against difficulties mastering a social order based on so many diverse forms of technical mediation supported by so many different kinds of administrations. Some of these problems are discussed in more detail in chapter 6.

Nevertheless, this movement could be seen as a radical return to the idea of *social* revolution, of a revolution that displaces the state from the center of the stage to allow initiative from below to substitute itself for political domination from a fixed center. Black flags flew alongside red ones in France during May, but the synthesis of the two was widely understood as a revival of the submerged libertarian trend in Marxism itself, in opposition to all established models of socialism.[11]

To call the May Events a "revolution," it is not necessary to show that the government could have been overthrown by an insurrection at this point. The defining characteristic of a revolution is not that it is stronger than the state, but that it abruptly calls the existing society into question in the minds of millions and effectively presses them into action. A revolution is an attempt by these millions to influence the resolution of a profound social crisis by violent or illegal means, reestablishing the community on new bases. This is precisely what happened during May. Social forms were as though liquefied into the individuals

---

[10] For important recent contributions to the still inconclusive debate over the possibility of socialism, see Schweickart (1993) and Stiglitz (1994).

[11] For a discussion of these tensions in Marxism, see Thomas (1994).

whose coordination within their framework had made possible the old society. This was what an earlier French revolutionary, Saint-Just, called "the public moment," the moment in which the social contract is reviewed and reconstituted in action (Saint-Just, 1963: 20).

THE AFTERMATH

While the May Events did not succeed in overthrowing the state, they accomplished something else of importance, an anti-technocratic redefinition of the idea of progress that continues to live in a variety of forms to this day. Like other similar movements around the world, the May Events set in motion a process of cultural change which transformed the image of resistance, shifted the focus of opposition from exploitation to alienation, and prepared the rejection of Stalinist authoritarianism in the new social movements. It was to this deeper cultural change that Sartre referred when he said of the May Events that they "enlarged the field of the possible."

The new left inaugurated a period of cultural change that renewed the social imagination. The feeling of impotence before the vast forces of progress cultivated by the postwar technocracy gave way to activism in many domains. Ambitious goals formulated in absolute revolutionary terms in the 1960s were gradually retranslated into more modest but realizable reforms. Without the struggles of those years in the background it is difficult to imagine the growth of client-centered professionalism, changed medical practices in fields such as childbirth and experimentation on human subjects, participatory management and design, communication applications of computers, and environmentally conscious technological advance.

It is fashionable now to dismiss the new left as an aberration. This attitude depends on a narrow view of its causes and consequences. If the new left was merely an outburst of adolescent narcissism, then indeed it hardly deserves our further attention. But the evidence against this summary judgment is all around us, so obvious it is usually overlooked. In the domain that interests us here, these movements were precursors that announced the limits of technocratic power. In the chapters that follow I will attempt to elaborate a theoretical account of technology that can make sense of the hope expressed by those students who, in 1968, proclaimed against all odds that "Progress will be what we want it to be."

Part I.

THE POLITICIZING OF TECHNOLOGY

3.
Environmentalism and the Politics of Technology

INTRODUCTION: TRADEOFF OR TRANSFORMATION

Early environmentalists attempted to awaken concern about a wide range of problems, from pesticides to population control, without always discriminating priorities among them. The critics may have ranked the issues differently, but as members of a beleaguered minority dismissed as cranks by majority opinion, they rarely had the time or inclination for quarrels amongst themselves. As is often the case with stigmatized out-groups, harmony prevailed precisely in proportion to the burden of exclusion carried by those brave enough to join.

That happy state of affairs did not survive the first successes of the environmental movement in the early 1970s. Significant disagreements emerged which persist to this day. One of the early signs of the depth of the split appeared in 1971 as Paul Ehrlich and Barry Commoner debated the relative importance of population and pollution control.

Paul Ehrlich was not the first to discover the population explosion—the honor is usually granted Malthus—but he has done more than anyone else in the United States to spread the notion. A professor of Population Studies at Stanford University, Ehrlich has been a tireless Cassandra of demographic disaster. Books such as *The Population Bomb* (1968) and *How To Be a Survivor* (1971), speeches on dozens of college campuses, and his campaign for Zero Population Growth reached a wide audience and helped to make ecology a legitimate public issue. Indeed, Albert Gore is quoted approvingly on the jacket of one of his latest books. However, because Ehrlich has always considered population control to be the key environmental issue, his politics have been curiously ambiguous. He has identified himself with diverse and seemingly conflicting causes: no-growth economics, Chinese population policy, counter-cultural anti-consumerism, opposition to Mexican immigration and high minority birthrates.

Barry Commoner is the Director of the Center for the Biology of Natural Systems at Queens College. He too began an intense campaign for the environment in the late 1960s and early 1970s, culminating in his run for President on the Citizen's Party ticket in 1980. His 1971 bestseller, *The Closing Circle*, began a long polemic with the advocates of population control by arguing for a class politics of the environment. He soon became the chief public advocate of socialist environmentalism. More recently, he has played a leading role in the National Toxics Campaign. One aspect of his program, the emphasis on technical change, has become standard fare in the environmental movement.

The scientific substance of the debate between these two spokesmen for the environment concerns the causes of and the solution to the environmental crisis. The cause: experts are divided, some asserting that the principal source of the crisis is overpopulation, others blaming it on polluting technologies. The first argue that "the causal chain of deterioration is easily followed to its source. Too many cars, too many factories, too much pesticide, . . . too little water, too much carbon dioxide—all can be traced easily to *too many people*" (Ehrlich, 1968: 66-67). The second protest that "environmental degradation is not simply the outcome of some general expansive process, growth of population, or demand for goods, but of certain very specific changes in the ways goods are produced which are themselves governed by powerful economic and political considerations" (Commoner, 1973a: 53).

The solution: the same division appears, reflecting radically opposed policies corresponding to different class and national interests. Not surprisingly, the prosperous nations and social strata that consume such disproportionate quantities of resources are most worried about running short. Accordingly, environmentalists representing them tend to advocate controls over population and economic growth. On the other side, it is to be expected that the poor, who hope to gain from economic growth but who in the meantime cannot easily escape the health hazards and pollution with which it is now associated, should be most attracted to theories that criticize not growth *per se* but its unintended consequences. Their representatives in the environmental movement therefore worry most about polluting technologies and the exhaustion of "garbage dumps" which they too claim is upon us.

Thus the Commoner-Ehrlich debate quickly moved beyond scientific disagreement to embrace two radically different rhetorics and strategies. Their argument, which took place at the very beginning of widespread public concern over the environment, adumbrated the main themes of later controversies over humanism and anti-humanism, democracy and dictatorship, North/South disputes, and so on. These themes are reflected today in the very different emphases of "deep ecology" organizations such as Earth First! and environmentally conscious trade unions such as the Oil, Chemical and Atomic Workers. In Germany, some of the same disagreements are reflected in the split within the Green party between the "Fundis" (fundamentalists) and the "Realos" (realists), the former demanding an end to industrial and population growth, while the latter pursue red-green alliances with labor to reform industrialism. Thus Ehrlich and Commoner did indeed prove to be prophets, but not so much of the environment as of the controversies in the movement to save it.

At the core of the disagreement are very different views on the nature of technology. Fundamentalist environmentalism emphasizes control of growth because it can conceive of no change in the industrial order that would render it ecologically compatible (Ullrich, 1979). Technological determinism thus leads straight to a Malthusian position for which environmental and economic values must be traded off against each other. This is Ehrlich's position. Commoner's contrary view depends on a nondeterminist philosophy of technology which admits the possibility of radical technical transformation. Only on this condition can growth and the environment be reconciled. In this chapter, I review their early debate and some of their more recent positions with a view to gaining historical perspective on these environmental controversies.[1]

AN END TO HISTORY

There is something surprising about these disagreements. After all, scientists are supposed to be better at building consensus than the rest of us. But there is a precedent for the conflictual outcome: the scientists' movement for nuclear disarmament that followed World War II. That earlier experience turns out to be particularly relevant to environmentalism since some of the leading environmentalists were participants in it, while others imitated it in their activities and writings.

The original scientists' movement arose from the anguished realization that the creation of the atomic bomb contradicted the supposedly

---

[1] Recent books by Ehrlich and Commoner restate their original positions somewhat softened by time, bringing the debate up to date. See Ehrlich and Ehrlich (1990); Commoner (1990). I will be commenting on them where they are relevant, however I do not pretend to offer a full picture of these new books which, while sometimes more measured than the authors' earlier work, do not have the seminal importance of their initial contributions to defining the ideological polarities of the environmental movement.

humanitarian mission of research. Yet the very fact that science had proved itself capable of such a feat promised scientists a larger voice in the disposition of the forces they had unleashed than they had ever enjoyed as benefactors of humankind. The opportunity to speak with new authority was immediately seized by veterans of the Manhattan Project.[2]

Physicists, many of whom had been sympathetic to socialism in the depression years, quickly dropped public concern for class issues and set themselves up as spokesmen for Science, a new force in human affairs with as yet unsuspected promise and power. The new scientific statesmanship hoped to gain a hearing by emphasizing the apocalyptic nature of the forces science had unleashed, and organizing a united front of scientists to put the new authority of research to good use. It called on the human species to address the issue of survival, and to subordinate all particular individual, social and national interests to this larger issue.

The scientists' movement brought a fear and a hope: the fear of the mortality of the human species, the hope of world government and an end to the use of force in the affairs of nations in response to the dangers of the nuclear age. Some scientists suggested that all nuclear secrets be immediately shared with the Soviet Union as a *quid pro quo* for Soviet renunciation of the bomb. Others wanted the United States to surrender its nuclear arsenal to the United Nations, and to renounce production of such weapons.

Of course none of this occurred. Instead, cold war competition between the Soviet Union and the United States began surreptitiously in Hiroshima, and since then we have all grown accustomed to living under a nuclear sword of Damocles. It soon became clear that far from resolving outstanding world problems, the fear of nuclear pan-destruction simply changed the stakes of the contest. A generation earlier, Nobel had similarly imagined that the discovery of the awful weapon dynamite would finally put an end to war.

With ecology the biological sciences are now supposed to open an escape hatch from the divisions of nation and class that drive human history. Like a natural disaster of planetary scope, the environmental crisis could unify humankind beyond historic rivalries in a more fundamental confrontation with nature itself. Accordingly, the environmental movement began as a politics of species survival, frightening people on to the

---

[2] A detailed account of the scientists' movement is contained in Smith (1965).

common ground of a "no deposit, no return" earth.

Ehrlich, for example, attempted to give environmentalism the trappings of a new scientists' movement, as is apparent from the title of his 1968 best seller: *The Population Bomb.* (His most recent book is called *The Population Explosion.*) In fact, he won the sympathy of the *Bulletin of the Atomic Scientists*, founded in 1945 to work for public understanding of the nuclear threat. Like the postwar scientists' movement, his strategy rested on augmenting the authority of the scientific community to the measure of the crisis it identified. He was therefore particularly anxious to preserve a united front of scientific opinion, and proposed a public compromise with Commoner while behind the scenes they could sort out their technical disagreements in their own good time.

Now, it turns out that Commoner was an activist in the original scientists' movement as a senatorial assistant after the War. He later fought for the Nuclear Test Ban Treaty and founded a journal called *Nuclear Information.* But while Ehrlich attempted to revive something resembling the old scientists' movement on the basis of an apocalyptic rhetoric, Commoner had moved on to a very different position. He focused on the social tensions emerging around environmentalism, and attempted to articulate them in class terms. As far as he was concerned, there could be no true environmental consensus. The millennial conflict of rich and poor invaded this new common ground as it has every similar locale on which humanity has attempted to set up camp.

RACE AND NATION

Ehrlich's views, as presented in *The Population Bomb,* have the virtue of being simple, clear and easy to dramatize. Like any other exponential curve in a finite environment, that which traces the population explosion must finally level off. "Basically, then, there are only two kinds of solutions to the population problem. One is a 'birth rate solution,' in which we find ways to lower the birth rate. The other is a 'death rate solution,' in which ways to raise the death rate—war, famine, pestilence—*find us*" (Ehrlich, 1968: 34).

Writing in 1968, Ehrlich argued that the latter process had already begun. He suggested three likely futures for the human race over the coming decades. His most optimistic projection included the death of "only" 500 million people in a ten-year "die-back" to a new balance of population and resources. This conclusion followed from Ehrlich's belief that in 1958 "the stork passed the plow" in the developing countries. The biological limits of agricultural production having been reached, the future looked grim indeed.

With disaster on the way, Ehrlich wondered whether after the "time of famines" the human race would be able finally to achieve a "birth rate solution" to its problems. He argued that human society could be saved only by a combination of moral, financial and especially coercive legal incentives, applied on an international scale by the US or a world government.

But as the global implications of the politics of the environment became clearer, Malthusianism itself appeared to be the real catastrophe awaiting racial minorities and the Third World. Ehrlich repeatedly said that he hoped to involve "everyone" in the work of environmental salvation. But his coalition got off to a bad start in at least one important area: blacks rejected Zero Population Growth, which many of them saw as a racist attack on their survival. Ehrlich denied that his was a movement of prosperous, well educated whites anxious to shift the ecological burden to poor blacks. He proposed, for example, that a "baby tax" to discourage reproduction be accompanied by special exemptions for minorities. "The best way to avoid any hint of genocide is to control the population of the dominant group" (Ehrlich and Harriman, 1971: 23). Why, nevertheless, was the Zero Population Growth movement unable to calm the fears of blacks? Perhaps part of the answer is to be sought in this newspaper advertisement for birth control: "Our city slums are packed with youngsters —thousands of them idle, victims of discontent and drug addiction. And millions more will pour into the streets in the next few years at the present rate of procreation. You go out after dark at your own peril. Last year one out of every four hundred Americans was murdered, raped or robbed. *Birth control is an answer.*"[3]

This "crime in the streets," "law and order" approach selected the audience it wished to reach, and certainly it was not blacks, who were used to being blamed for all these urban ills. Indeed, blacks would seem to be the enemy, the human horde that must be stemmed. By whom? Evidently by those who "go out after dark at [their] own peril," a phrase that in the context of this ad seems to identify the respectable white population.

It is no wonder that blacks were frightened by a propaganda the ultimate implication of which was their forcible sterilization (a practice which, if rare, was by no means unknown in the US). The attitude of

---

[3] Quoted in Commoner (1971: 232).

some zero population growth advocates toward the Third World indicates, furthermore, that these fears may indeed have been justified. For, when the crowded slum was in a foreign country there was no hesitation at all about invoking force in the name of population control.

In *The Population Bomb* Ehrlich stated his agreement with Paul and William Paddock, the authors of a book called *Famine—1975!* (Paddock and Paddock, 1967). The Paddocks proposed a "triage" approach to food aid based on traditional army medical policy. Those countries which have enough resources need not be helped because they can help themselves. Those on the borderline, which can survive but only with help, should be aided to the maximum. "Finally," Ehrlich noted in his summary of the Paddocks' proposal, "there is the last tragic category—those countries that are so far behind in the population-food game that there is no hope that our food aid will see them through to self-sufficiency. The Paddocks say that India is probably in this category. If it is, then under the triage system, she should receive no more food." And he added, "In my opinion, there is no rational choice *except* to adopt some form of the Paddocks' strategy as far as food distribution is concerned" (Ehrlich, 1968: 160-161).

While countries like India would be abandoned, the others would be required to introduce strict, involuntary population control as a condition for receiving food. Ehrlich comments:

> Coercion? Perhaps, but coercion in a good cause. I am sometimes astounded at the attitudes of Americans who are horrified at the prospect of our government insisting on population control as the price of food aid. All too often the very same people are fully in support of applying military force against those who disagree with our form of government or our foreign policy. We must be relentless in pushing for population control around the world (Ehrlich, 1968: 166).

If this remark is already "brutal and heartless" (the words are Ehrlich's own), what are we to say of Garret Hardin's still more eloquent defense of the same position: "How can we help a foreign country to escape overpopulation? Clearly the worst thing we can do is send food. The child who is saved today becomes a breeder tomorrow. We send food out of compassion, but if we desired to increase the misery in an overpopulated nation, could we find a more effective way of doing so? Atomic bombs would be kinder."[4] And Hardin concludes, "Fortunate minorities must act as the trustees of a civilization that is threatened by uninformed good intentions (Hardin, 1971: 1792)."

Ehrlich was more squeamish in *How To Be a Survivor*. There he proposed a massive aid program for the Third World, remarking that US leadership of the world struggle to lower birth rates "means leadership by example" (Ehrlich and Harriman, 1971: 17). And he went on to say that "The population problem cannot be 'solved' by withholding medical services or food and letting people die of disease or starvation" (Ehrlich and Harriman, 1971: 52). He still believed that force would be the surest instrument of rational demographic policies, but he no longer suggested that the United States should exercise this force alone. Instead, he called for "mutual coercion, mutually agreed upon."[5] A world government is needed to wield power over human numbers.

At this point we come full circle: in 1946 J. Robert Oppenheimer wrote, "Many have said that without world government there could be no permanent peace, and that without peace there would be atomic warfare. I think one must agree with this" (Oppenheimer, 1955: 12). In its conception of salvation through world government, the postwar scientists' movement echoed the humanistic opposition to war going back to Kant. The resurgence of such a conception in an environmental movement based on a similar ideological infrastructure is not surprising. This outcome is implicit in the whole approach, which consists in identifying a common survival interest of the species superseding all particular interests.

However, in contact with vulgar realities, the universalistic scheme of world government suffered a peculiar degeneration in the late 1940s which may shed some light on the ambiguities of the new environmentalist formulations. Worried about the implications of a nonwhite majority in a world state, scientists proposed measures that today we would certainly condemn as racist, such as votes weighted in favor of rich white nations.[6]

---

[4] Note once again the metaphoric equivalence of the population "bomb" and the atomic bomb, characteristic of this trend.

[5] The phrase is Hardin's (1970: 45).

[6] Vide R. Niebuhr in *The Bulletin of the Atomic Scientists*, Oct. 1949, p. 289; E. Teller in *The Bulletin of the Atomic Scientists*, Dec. 1947, p. 355, and, Sept. 1948, p. 204; E. M. Friedwald in *The Bulletin of the Atomic Scientists*, Dec. 1948, p. 363.

Are these twisted proposals irrelevant relics of a bygone era? Or are they typical consequences of the waves of impotent universalism breaking over the shoals of powerful particularisms? World government in the interests of population control is fraught with dangers anticipated in the earlier disappointing experience with the concept. This is because mutual coercion is the prerogative of approximately equal powers. But only the developed countries have the capacity to enforce their will. Furthermore, it is primarily in these countries that there is significant popular support for coercing poor nations into population control programs. The kind of world government which would use force to impose demographic controls would be a government *of* the developing countries *by* the developed ones.

MALTHUSIAN IDEOLOGY

As a Malthusian, Ehrlich emphasized the objective, natural limits of the biosphere, the absolute scarcities which confront the human race. His work popularized this approach, which quickly found echoes in a multitude of proclamations and essays announcing a new age of limits.

In 1972 the Club of Rome released a frightening doomsday study. *The Limits to Growth* concludes that "the basic mode of the world system is exponential growth of population and capital, followed by collapse" (Meadows et al., 1972: 142). *The Limits to Growth* predicts that rising population and industrial capacity will lead to increased demand for ever scarcer raw materials. Within a century, left to its own devices, world industry will be spending so much on these increasingly costly resources that it will be unable to renew depreciated capital. Finally, the industrial base will collapse along with services and agriculture, causing a drastic drop in population as the human race returns to barbarism. Could it be that the modern industrial system is destined to be a brief—and tragically flawed—experiment rather than the triumphant apotheosis of the species?

At about the same time in England, the editors of *The Ecologist* published a document entitled *Blueprint for Survival*, endorsed by "33 leading scientists." The *Blueprint* called on Britons to slow their economic growth and halve their population to avoid "the breakdown of society and irreversible disruption of the life-support systems on this planet" (*Blueprint for Survival*, 1974).[7]

---

[7] Cf. also, Mansholt (1972).

Still more radical were the arguments in Robert Heilbroner's *An Inquiry into the Human Prospect*. Heilbroner foresaw the end of liberal democracy in the turbulent era of environmental crisis. "From the facts of population pressure," he writes in retrospect, "I inferred the rise of 'military-socialist' governments as the only kinds of regimes capable of establishing viable economic and social systems" (Heilbroner, 1974: 156). Retribalization appealed to him as a long-term alternative to a fatally flawed industrialism (Heilbroner, 1974: 141).

The continuity with present positions is clear, although some recent interventions carry us well beyond even the wildest speculations of the 1970s to the very borderline of madness. For example, the *Earth First! Journal* published a discussion of the beneficial environmental effects of AIDS. One anonymous author wrote, "If radical environmentalists were to invent a disease to bring human population back to ecological sanity, it would probably be something like AIDS. As radical environmentalists, we can see AIDS not as a problem, but as a necessary solution (one you probably wouldn't want to try yourself)" (Miss Ann Thropy, 1987: 32).

Ehrlich's most recent book is far more moderate, perhaps in tacit recognition of the failure of his earlier alarmist predictions. (I say "tacit" because, rather surprisingly, despite the enormity of the errors in his earlier estimates of food and resource limits he writes as though *The Population Bomb* had been confirmed on the whole by events.) He no longer emphasizes overpopulation exclusively, nor endorses coercive population control. Yet population politics is still his central concern. After discussing the many sources of environmental catastrophe, he concludes, "ending population growth and starting a slow decline is not a panacea; it would primarily provide humanity with the opportunity of solving its other problems" (Ehrlich and Ehrlich, 1990: 157).

All these Malthusian positions treat society as a natural object ruled by deterministic laws. Ehrlich, for example, claims that the "population bomb" is a biological process—human reproduction—gone wild. Technology too is naturalized by the assumption that economic growth implies more technology of the sort we use now. Short shrift is made of proposals for using less harmful technologies, substituting plentiful or renewable resources for diminishing ones such as petroleum, and achieving a more ecologically compatible conception of prosperity. Hence an increase in human numbers and wealth must bring about a corresponding increase in pollution and resource depletion.

Without these deterministic premises, the analogy between the population bomb and the atom bomb is weak and the rationale for a politics of survival breaks down. Why? Because the atom bomb is a unique technological advance with consequences that are not subject to a technological fix. But what if, unlike the atom bomb, the industrial system can be radically transformed? As we will see, Commoner argues that both our technological means and our economic goals can evolve to include health and environmental considerations currently ignored or undervalued. Change may occur in both the problems to which modern industrial technology is addressed and the solutions it offers, reconciling growth with the environment. No similarly benign option exists in the case of nuclear weapons.

THE BIOLOGICAL OR THE SOCIAL

For Commoner, environmental problems of all sorts, including overpopulation, are effects of social causes inherent in capitalism and colonialism. For example, population growth in the Third World is due not to the natural fertility of the species, but to poverty and high infant mortality rates. European population growth rates declined as prosperity increased in a process known as the "demographic transition." Colonial exploitation of the Third World blocked the demographic transition there, resulting in the current imbalance. If social factors influence reproductive behavior, we need to create conditions in which those factors favor slower population growth in the poorer countries. This will require, not "coercion in a good cause" but massive economic aid. Since the population problem is primarily social rather than biological, a social solution is appropriate.

Unfortunately, Ehrlich and Commoner's recent books do little to advance the argument. Now of course both authors have the benefit of twenty years more demographic experience. And while both profess to believe in voluntary birth control and agree on some basic facts, such as the likely point at which world population will level off (10 billion), they seem not to have noticed the developments most damaging to their own arguments. Ehrlich, for example, still expects "the stork to pass the plow," just a bit later than 1968 or 1975. And Commoner does not discuss the important implications of Chinese birth control policies and women's issues for the demographic transition argument on which he continues to rely.

As for the pollution problem, the disagreement can be clearly stated in terms of Ehrlich's own formula for calculating environmental impact as a product of population size, affluence—that is, the amount of goods per capita, and the propensity of productive technology to pollute. Ehrlich assumed that the first of these factors is the decisive one, concluding therefore that the pollution problem is derivative of the population problem. But Commoner argued from a close study of the relative impact of the three factors that "most of the sharp increases in pollution levels is due not so much to population or affluence as to changes in productive technology" (Commoner, 1971: 175).

Commoner noted that US pollution increased from 200 to 2000% in the twenty years from 1946-1966, while population went up only 42%. His conclusion: "Population growth in the United States has only a minor influence on the intensification of environmental pollution" (Commoner, 1971: 231). The real culprit is the massive transformation of industrial and agricultural technology since World War II. "Productive technologies with intense impacts on the environment have displaced less destructive ones," for example, the substitution of detergents for soap, synthetic fibers for cotton and wool, plastics for wood, the increased use of aluminum, air conditioners, more and more powerful automobiles, and escalating fertilizer and pesticide use on farms (Commoner, 1971: 175). The result of these changes is an immense increase in the environmental impact of modern societies, to the point where we are approaching the breakdown of the biological processes which have continuously renewed the air, soil and water for millions of years (Commoner, 1971:13). Thus not biological and technological determinism, but economics lies at the root of the environmental crisis.

What needs to be done? Commoner proposed transforming modern technology "to meet the inescapable demands of the ecosystem" (Commoner, 1971: 282). He placed a price tag on this program, and a high one at that, estimating that "most of the nation's resources for capital investment would need to be engaged in the task of ecological reconstruction for at least a generation" (Commoner, 1971: 284). For many years, in numerous articles and books, Commoner argued that only a democratic socialist economic system could address environmental problems effectively. His latest book, like Ehrlich's, is somewhat more cautious. He still believes that the pursuit of short-term profits motivates bad technical decisions. And now, after the experience of the last twenty years, he is more convinced than ever that mere tinkering with pollution controls is insufficient. Instead, environmentally unsound technologies should be abolished outright and replaced with better ones.

But Commoner has been chastened by the fall of communism in the Soviet Union and Eastern Europe, and the breakdown of old assumptions about planning and markets that, like most other leftists, he took for granted in earlier days. Now he writes that the market "is a

useful means of facilitating the flow of goods from producer to consumer; but it becomes a social evil when it is allowed to govern the technology of production" (Commoner, 1990: 223). Technological design
must be freed from the profit system.

THE QUESTION OF DIMINISHING RETURNS

Now the political stakes in the debate are clear. Behind the contention
over scientific issues, behind the dispute over the resource depletion and
environmental degradation, behind the methodological disagreement
about the biological or social character of the factors leading to the crisis,
lies, quite simply, the old debate over capitalism and socialism! But was
Commoner right to link the fresh young environmental movement with
the tired old struggle for socialism? After all, environmental problems
appear to be indifferent to socioeconomic system. Commoner's critics
saw little more than outmoded demagogy in his attempt to Marxify
ecology. Ehrlich was particularly disturbed; he feared Commoner's politics would shatter the unity, beyond class and ideology, of his movement
for survival. As he put it, "There is no point in waving a red flag in front
of the bulls" (Ehrlich and Harriman, 1971: 136).

Ehrlich claimed that Commoner's politics was based on bad science.[8] Commoner was supposed to have underestimated the significance
of population growth because he ignored the nonlinear relation between
population size and pollution. Under the "law of diminishing returns,"
small increases in population might be responsible for disproportion-
ately large increases in pollution. Commoner, Ehrlich charged, crudely
compared a small population increase with a large pollution increase and
concluded that other factors must be decisive. In fact, the variables may
interact in such a way that even a mere 42% increase in population can
cause the 200 to 2000% rise in pollution cited by Commoner.

Take the case of food production. High levels of productivity may
be obtained from good soil with only a little fertilizer. But there is just so
much good soil. Once population grows beyond certain limits, farmers
must plant mediocre soil as well in order to produce food for everyone.

---

[8] See Commoner, et al. (1972: 23ff). The two articles published here, a review of *The
Closing Circle* by Ehrlich and Holdren, accompanied by Commoner's rejoinder, culmi-
nate the debate. A somewhat different version of the piece by Ehrlich and Holdren was
published in the May, 1972 issue of the *Bulletin*, which also contains a re-rebuttal by
Ehrlich and Holdren (1972). See also Ehrlich's letter to *The New York Times*, Feb. 6,
1972. This section summarizes the central argument of these publications.

And at this point fertilizer use increases dramatically as bad land is primed into giving reasonable yields. With increased fertilizer use comes increased water pollution. This, according to Ehrlich, is precisely what is happening in the US.

This critique is similar to the method of *The Limits to Growth*. First a natural limit on a presumably unsubstitutable resource is postulated. Second, the environmental consequences per unit of technological activity are estimated at roughly current levels. Third, a level of per capita demand is assumed, and multiplied by actual and projected population size. As exhaustion of the resource approaches, efficiency declines, costs and pollution rise, and eventually the very survival of the population dependent on it is threatened.

Commoner replied that the problem of diminishing returns is simply irrelevant in the case of major technological developments since World War II. Furthermore, he argued, in actual practice returns "diminish" less for environmental than for economic reasons, reflecting not natural resource limits but socially relative mechanisms of accounting and pricing. What, in Ehrlich's example of farming, *compels* the farmer to use excessive fertilizer? Certainly not some absolute scarcity of land; at the time of the debate there was still plenty of good land left in the United States, but the government actually paid farmers *not* to use it in order to maintain farm prices. This is what compelled farmers to push land in use to the limits of its capacity in order to make a profit. And at these limits, something like a problem of diminishing returns occurs as ever greater increments of fertilizer are required to produce a constant increase in the productivity of the soil. But this problem is strictly accountable to restrictions on planted acreage.

On balance, Commoner seems to get the better of this argument. It is, of course, possible to construct ideal models of the "world system" in which everything is held constant while population and resources are extrapolated to an inevitable clash. But this is not the real world, in which limits turn out to be relative to a multiplicity of factors, many of them social.

This crucial issue continues to divide Ehrlich and Commoner over twenty years after their original debate. Ehrlich still argues that overpopulation is at work in a wide variety of environmental problems and for the most part Commoner ignores the issue on the same grounds as before.

Ehrlich now defines "overpopulation" as an excess of inhabitants over the "carrying capacity" of the land they inhabit. There is no absolute limit to the number of people a given territory can support since environmental impact is relative to affluence and technology as well as to human numbers. But he criticizes those like Commoner who emphasize the possibility of accommodating larger numbers with improved technology: "overpopulation is defined by the animals that occupy the turf, behaving as they naturally behave, not by a hypothetical group that might be substituted for them" (Ehrlich and Ehrlich, 1990: 40).

Fair enough, but Ehrlich frequently ignores the disproportionate impact of the sort of basic technological change Commoner advocates, and treats population control as the obvious solution to the problem of overpopulation. He relies once again on the supposed nonlinear relation between population and pollution to explain why small reductions in population would have significant beneficial impacts. Once again we hear about diminishing returns, without the evidence that would convince us that population control is really crucial to addressing most environmental problems (Ehrlich and Ehrlich, 1990: 137).

Ehrlich's definition of overpopulation and the diminishing returns hypothesis work together to depoliticize environmental issues. He wants to argue for a politics of survival beyond all historic considerations of class and national interest, but in fact he presupposes a specific constellation of interests, that of modern capitalism and neo-imperialism with their technology: "the animals that occupy the turf, behaving as they naturally behave." This is why he ends up seeking a biological solution. Although there are flaws in his approach that will be discussed later, Commoner achieves a more realistic assessment of the problems with a more socially conscious method.

THE PERSONAL OR THE POLITICAL

An approach to environmental problems which treats technology as a thing of nature, fixed and unalterable, ends up by treating nature as a social object wherever it is subject to technical control. In the case of population politics, the locus of control is human reproduction, which individuals and governments can manipulate through voluntary contraception and involuntary sterilization.

By contrast, an approach which emphasizes the social sources of the problems will prefer to act on the biological mediations indirectly, through the social mechanisms governing institutional and mass behavior. The intended result may be the same, a better proportion between population and resources and a less polluting society, however the means to the end will be quite different.

From a purely *technical* point of view, rapid, drastic and necessarily coercive reduction in the number of people is environmentally equivalent to changing the technology used by a much larger population. For example, Los Angeles smog could be halved by halving the population—hence also automobile use—in the city. But the same result could also be achieved at present population levels by halving emissions from the cars in use, or by substituting mass transit for half the cars. Even though the environmental result is similar in these cases, there is no *moral* equivalence between such very different policies as requiring smog control devices on cars and legally limiting families to a single child.

Commoner concluded that the choice between these two routes is "a political one which reflects one's view of the relative importance of social control over personal acts and social processes" (Commoner, 1971: 233). Here is the nub of the disagreement. When the emphasis is placed on population, "social control over personal acts" appears as the solution. This approach is at once more individualistic and more repressive than emphasizing the reform of the "social processes" which, Commoner claimed, ultimately determine both birth rates and technological choices.

Indeed, the dilemma of population politics is the absence of any significant realm of action other than appeals to individual conscience and government enforced limits on family size. There is not much to be done at the political level; one cannot very well demonstrate against babies, nor even against parents. Unless the state intervenes (as it has in China), the issue is a private one, each couple choosing individually how many children it wants. This explains why Ehrlich's political program wavered between moralistic voluntarism and more or less harsh state action (Ehrlich, 1968: 175).[9] The resulting strategy offered a way in which people could, without exercising social control over social processes, nevertheless mitigate the effects of an ecologically unsound technology by personally shouldering the burden and the costs.

The significance of the debate now becomes clear. People may, in Commoner's words, choose a "new ecology-minded personal lifestyle. . . designed to minimize the two factors that intensify pollution that are under personal control: consumption and population size" (Commoner, 1971: 209). Or, "insofar as [they] are unwilling to undertake this personal action, they will need to seek relief by altering the economic, social and

---

[9] Ehrlich (1968: 175). See also Hill (1970).

political priorities that govern the disposition of the nation's resources" (Commoner, 1971: 212). Commoner himself chose political rather than personal action, control over institutions rather than over individuals.

Is a synthesis impossible? Can we not at the very least exercise voluntary control over personal behavior as well as political control over institutions? Ehrlich attempted just such a synthesis of the personal and the political in his 1971 book *How To Be a Survivor*. There he broadened his approach to include not only population control, but general egalitarian social reform, anti-imperialism, technological reform, and a reduction through "de-development" of the excessively high living standard of the "overdeveloped" countries.

But synthesis is not easy; the divisive class and national issues cut directly across it, revealing it to be an eclectic combination of incompatible strategies. For example, it must have been difficult to approach workers and the poor with a slogan such as: "Try to live below your means! It will be good for your family's economic situation, and it may also help to save the world" (Ehrlich and Harriman, 1971: 149). In a society based on economic inequality, one cannot hope to organize a strong political movement around voluntary self-deprivation. The alternative, invoking the power of the state to lower living standards, has usually served not higher moral ends but the interests of economic and political elites.

Meanwhile, business opposed much of Ehrlich's program. At first it felt threatened by environmentalism. Its initial strategy consisted in distracting people from a crisis in which it did not believe, or in ridiculing environmentalists. One mainstream commentator wrote skeptically on *The Limits to Growth*, "Conceivably, if you believe their predictions of extremely short time spans before the exhaustion of resources, there are many speculative killings to be made" (Silk, 1972: 35).

Then, in 1971 the American Can Company extended its voluntaristic anti-littering campaign to take in the whole environmental crisis. Keep America Beautiful, Inc. proclaimed: "People start pollution. People can stop it." Hundreds of millions of dollars of free advertising space were devoted to diverting environmental pressures away from business and toward individual action.[10] This campaign was largely successful; soon the American public agreed with Pogo, the comic strip character who said, "We have met the enemy and he is us."

---

[10] "Group Seeks to Shift Protests on Pollution" (1971).

The businessmen who sponsored this campaign, and President Nixon who praised their civic consciousness, had no illusions about the implications of the environmental movement. They did not believe that it promised a universal good in which all could share equally. Rather, they hoped that the political energy mobilized by the increasingly articulate critics of capitalist environmental practice could be focused on private options, leaving basic economic institutions unchanged. Indeed, not only unchanged, but in a position to cash in on those great "speculative killings" in which, by this time, quite a few informed investors had come to believe.[11]

This anecdote begins to reveal the divisive potential of the environmental crisis. There is in Commoner's words, "more than logic and ecology at work here." If the debate heats up it is because human survival is a political issue: we are all concerned, but not all in the same way. As Commoner put it:

> Is it in fact true that environmental improvement is a good so universal in its value that it can override vested interests that contend so bitterly over other issues—such as jobs? The answer, I am convinced, is no. There is usually no way to work out an evenhanded distribution of the cost of environmental improvement; something has to give (Commoner, 1972b: 33).

CLASS STRUGGLE REVISITED

It should be clear by now that Commoner *wanted* the environmental movement to be "progressive" in the traditional sense of the term. He hoped it would become a factor in the struggle not only for nature, but also for human beings, not only for survival, but also for a more egalitarian society. But this is not a sentimental question; Commoner had to prove that his radicalism was not gratuitous, that the allies he had chosen were indeed likely to work for environmental reform. Here is his basic argument.

Pollution is a major short-term cost cutter. For an initial "free period" during which the environment tolerates degradation,

---

[11] As Henry Ford II wrote (1970: 62): "The successful companies in the last third of the twentieth century will be the ones that look at changes in their environment as opportunities to get a jump on the competition."

Pollutants accumulate in the ecosystem or in a victim's body, but not all the resultant costs are immediately felt. Part of the value represented by the free abuse of the environment is available to mitigate the economic conflict between capital and labor. The benefit *appears* to accrue to both parties and the conflict between them is reduced. But in fact pollution represents a debt to nature that must be repaid. Later, when the environmental bill is paid, it is met by labor more than by capital; the buffer is suddenly removed and conflict between these two economic sectors is revealed in full force (Commoner, 1971: 271).

Thus environmental politics is a zero-sum game in which the distribution of costs affects classes differently, according to their position in the economic system. Starting from this premise, Commoner constructed what are, in effect, ideal-typical models of class-determined attitudes toward the environment.

The capitalist's relation to the environment is shaped by his short-term focus on profits and his ability to shift costs away from himself on to others. Environmental constraints often conflict with popular marketing strategies, such as increasing automotive horsepower, or threaten potentially profitable investment opportunities. Pollution appears as an externality in all his calculations, an externality largely suffered by others because he has the means to escape its worst effects privately, by buying air-conditioning for his house and car, living in the suburbs or the country, vacationing in unspoiled regions, and so on.

Conclusion: capitalism will resist environmental controls until they become unavoidable and then attempt to get others to bear the burden. This theoretical prediction has been a fairly good description of business attitudes in the United States.

Workers' objective position with respect to the environment is quite different because for them pollution is not an exogenous but an endogenous factor. Workers in the plant suffer the effects of pollution far more than executives in administrative offices. Even during the "free period" workers and the poor "pay" for pollution through inconvenience and disease. As these costs rise, the issue is brought home in their daily lives. Here is the vital difference between the lower and upper classes in their relation to the environment.

This was the basis for Commoner's faith that workers, or at least their unions, would eventually lead militant opposition to environmental degradation. "The need for a new alliance is clear. Neither worker nor environmentalist can reach their separate goals without joining in a common one: to reconstruct the nation's productive system so that it conforms to the imperatives of the environment which supports it, meets the needs of the workers who operate it, and secures the future of the people who have built it" (Commoner, 1973b: 20).

Fine sentiments, but while Commoner offered good reasons for workers to become active in the environmental movement, it has become clear that he overlooked the ambiguity of labor's situation. Labor can, as he suggested, fight to insure that the burden of environmental restoration is more fairly shared by improving the conditions under which it works and lives. However, it can also resist the unequal burden capitalist environmentalism imposes on it by resisting all environmental expenditures, shortsighted though this policy may be. Which path it will choose depends on the power of consumer society to shape the model of welfare at the expense of non-market goods such as safer working conditions and clean air and water. The failure of the struggle for shorter hours in the 1930s offers an instructive and discouraging precedent. At that decisive juncture, the labor movement chose to privilege consumption over leisure (Hunnicutt, 1988).

When he wrote *The Closing Circle* Commoner was convinced that the intensified class conflict generated by the ecological crisis would be a great school in environmental policy. He believed that in this school American workers would learn to understand the economic mechanisms which cause the crisis and to reject equally the arguments of those who dismiss environmentalism and those who attempt to turn it into an issue of individual morality. In fact, labor environmentalism never played the central role he predicted. The failure of his strategy raises serious questions about his whole approach.

CULTURE AND CONSCIOUSNESS

The most obvious problem is Commoner's reliance on the traditional Marxist theory of class consciousness. One simply cannot predict the future beliefs of a class from its objective interests. The social theorist must explain the specific political and cultural factors that might, in any given case, distinguish the real consciousness of classes from the rational model constructed in theory. But Commoner omitted this second level of analysis, the level of political and cultural mediations.

The problem is especially serious because his theory of the environmental crisis hovered on the verge of a type of cultural criticism he opposed. He was so busy with his polemic against individualistic environmentalism that he rejected all concern with culture, which, he seemed to fear, would lead back to lifestyle politics.

But the changes in production for which Commoner called amounted to far more than the American Way of Life equipped with emission controls; they presupposed radical cultural changes. He came closest to facing this problem in the early 1970s in a discussion of the distinction between the formal measures of "affluence," such as GNP, and the actual goods and services enjoyed by the individuals. The good the consumer seeks, he argued, may be obtained in a variety of forms with very different environmental impacts (Commoner, Ehrlich and Holdren, 1972: 45-46).

What is at stake in such a distinction? Commoner noted that many safer materials and technologies such as soap, wood, and bottles were displaced after World War II by more polluting but also more profitable substitutes such as detergents, plastics, and cans. If consumers could obtain the same good in the old form as the new, then they would lose nothing by going back to safer alternatives. But the return to capital would be affected by this kind of environmental restoration.

However, the matter is considerably more complex. First, the older technologies are more labor intensive which suggests that labor too may have an interest in the application of the newer ones to the extent that wages depend on productivity. Commoner discounted a large part of the increased welfare workers are supposed to derive from such productivity increases, but in the final analysis the issue is not merely quantitative. Note, for example, his reference to the Lordstown strike in response to a question during Congressional testimony: "If you have followed the situation in some of the automobile plants in the last year or so, you probably realize that we may be reaching the human limit of automation. I think new ways of using human labor in a humane way ought to be looked into. In short, we should question the value of continued replacement of people by electronics" (Commoner, 1972a: 593). Here Commoner can be seen attempting to conjoin the environmental movement to a critical challenge to central values of capitalist culture, as it now exists both for capitalists *and* workers.

Second, the resubstitutions for which Commoner called would change the form in which consumers obtained familiar goods. For example, he did not oppose geographical mobility; he just wanted to achieve it through less polluting and wasteful means than the private automobile, and so on with a host of other commodities.

But utilitarian considerations have little to do with the choice of the form in which goods are delivered in a modern consumer society. Advertising invests forms with meanings that are often wholly unrelated to the ostensible function of the goods, but are nevertheless compelling for the consumers. Thus, the sexual and status connotations of automobile ownership, while doubtless less important than the transportation it provides, are not trivial. They would be lost in the switch-over to mass transit, a spare and utilitarian alternative by comparison. This fact in itself constitutes a significant cultural barrier to the changes Commoner advocated, but he had no way to discuss it because he worked exclusively at the level of imputed interests in abstract goods.[12]

Commoner was thus left in a dilemma. As a Marxist, he rejected the appeals to moral renunciation in which his adversaries specialized and attempted to attach environmentalism to the actual interests of the mass of humankind. But the logic of Commoner's attack on capitalism led him to question its model of welfare and suggest an alternative that was not supported by the everyday consciousness of any class in the society. What was at issue, then, in Commoner's program was not just an environmentally sound version of the present system, but a radical change in economic culture.

How much difference is there between Commoner's position, with its problematic connection to the conscious interests of workers, and a moral position that pretends to no such relation? This is a difficult question. To preserve the difference between renunciation and enlightened self-interest, it would be necessary to theorize a process of cultural change that pointed the way toward a model of welfare more consonant with environmental survival than the current one. On these terms, it might still be possible to argue for a relationship between environmentalism and (future) consciousness.

This is no merely verbal point: where a clean and healthful environment is considered not as an exogenous dumping ground but as a component of individual well-being, different environmental practices would be followed spontaneously by the individuals in their pursuit of welfare, and would not have to be imposed on them by "market incentives," or by political or moral coercion in opposition to their own perceived interests. And since technology is routinely adapted to changing social and economic conditions, there is no reason of principle why it should not be

---

[12] Significant attempts to theorize this problem, in an environmental perspective and in semiotic terms respectively, are Leiss (1976), and Baudrillard (1970).

redesigned to conform to the requirements of such a culture.

What is needed then is a theory not of individual lifestyle, nor only of social control over production, but also of cultural change. But Commoner was trapped in an overly rationalistic communication model that relied exclusively on scientific persuasion. His adversaries meanwhile seized on all the symbolic machinery of environmental consciousness-raising and turned it to account in the pursuit of policies he deplored.

Of course Commoner was right to reject the exaggerated environmental role they attributed to lifestyle politics. But personal involvement in environmentalism through gestures such as consumer boycotts, recycling, or conserving water are among the most effective means of cultural change available to the movement. Even if they have a limited impact on the environment, they change people and must not be rejected because they are no ultimate solution and have on occasion been accommodated to reactionary policies. Significantly, as Commoner has become involved with movements against toxics and for recycling, he too has come to recognize the importance of voluntarism in the environmental movement, not for the sake of self-imposed poverty, but as a source of cultural change.

THE LIMITS OF MORALITY

Ehrlich rejected Commoner's attempt to distinguish between the actual economic good individuals pursue and the specific form in which it is delivered technologically. This, he sarcastically dismissed as "redefining affluence," but in rejecting it he accepted uncritically the dominant model of welfare (Ehrlich and Holdren, 1972: 44). Ehrlich simply assumed the universality of the current definition of affluence and of the technology for achieving it.

These assumptions are also shared by *The Limits to Growth*, by Heilbroner and other environmental pessimists; they consider the environmental limits of what we currently take for wealth to be absolute limits on material progress as such. Neither different ends nor fundamentally improved technological means can mitigate the crisis. If contemporary standards of wealth and current technology are the best the human race can hope for, then all adjustments to environmental constraints appear as economic regression. But far from identifying the natural limits of the "world system," this position really only establishes the limits of a given type of capitalist economic and technical culture, which it defends against environmental obsolescence with the promise of spiritual compensations.

Ehrlich claimed that to save the environment wealthy societies would have to be "de-developed" through reducing living standards. Accordingly, he sought a coalition based on those with "a stronger interest in survival than in perpetuating over-consumption" (Ehrlich and Harriman, 1971: 155). Materialism must give way to spiritual values. The politics of ecology would seem to take place in a world of "over-consumers," some of whom are sufficiently enlightened to renounce their excesses.

De-development does not, however, sound like an easy sell in modern materialistic societies. Thus this form of environmentalism leads inexorably from moral self-control to legal coercion. As St. Paul wrote long ago, mankind is damned, not saved by the (moral) Law. The very need for self-control is a tribute to the power of temptation and the likelihood of sin. What can only be accomplished against the material impulses of the species will surely not be accomplished in the finite time spans of political action by a simple appeal to morality. Hence the recourse to law always lurks in the wings. In Heilbroner's *The Human Prospect,* for example, the state is explicitly charged with the salvation of humanity. Here the extreme consequence of the initial ideological choice is clearly drawn. The price of the perpetual maintenance of capitalist economic and technical culture in a world where they have become environmentally absurd is a forced regression along the continuum of freedom and satisfaction.

It is important to clarify the distinction between this approach and Commoner's. Ehrlich suggested a shift in the scene of fulfillment, from the material or economic domain, to the spiritual or ideological domain. His approach involved a tradeoff of economic for spiritual rewards. Commoner envisaged a resolution to the environmental crisis not through restricting the supply of material goods, but rather through changing the definition and delivery of them. Similar rewards would be offered in a different form, and there would be a greater appreciation of such currently undervalued goods as clean air or water. Thus Commoner remained within the traditional progressive framework. The difference is considerable, since modern culture orients the individual toward the spontaneous pursuit of material ends, while spiritual ones must be imposed or self-imposed by law or morality in opposition to the individual's own perceived interests.[13]

---

[13] For an illuminating discussion of the relation between material and spiritual values, see Gouldner (1970: 326-331).

Ehrlich's most recent book is not so ready to jettison democracy. But it is still confused on the question of affluence. At one point he indexes it to consumption, while at another he asserts that quality of life is at least partially independent of merely quantitative measures of consumption since it is relative to the actual usefulness of the goods consumed. This latter position is perilously close to the one he rejected as "redefining affluence" in his debate with Commoner. Now, he advocates reducing both consumption and the environmental impact of the technologies that provide consumer goods, both a no-growth economy and changes in production technology to accommodate environmentally sound development (Ehrlich and Ehrlich, 1990: 58, 228-29, 219, 139). Ehrlich still fails to focus the issue clearly and address the choices it implies.

Here we arrive back at Commoner's original premise: the environmental movement must choose between a repressive policy of increasing control over the individual, or a democratic policy of control over the social processes of production (and, I would add, culture.) On the former condition, the existing production system can be preserved, along with all the injustices associated with it, for a prolonged period in spite of the environmental crisis. On the latter condition, this production system must be radically changed through the development of new forms of social control.

CONCLUSION: BEYOND THE POLITICS OF SURVIVAL

The Commoner-Ehrlich debate provides a window on to the deep and apparently unavoidable conflicts inherent in environmental politics, conflicts that were already implicit in the earlier scientists' movement for nuclear disarmament. The contemporary political sensibility must be informed by the nuclear—now also environmental—age, from which we learn the threat to survival contained in the very nature of our civilization. A society that can destroy life on earth by the careless application of fluorocarbon deodorant sprays is indeed beyond the pale of any rational calculation of survival chances. History is over in principle in the sense that the old conflicts and ambitions must give way to a radically new type of human adventure, or else the species will surely die. Nevertheless, in practice the unfinished work of history continues, indeed intensifies the very horrors and upward struggles that threaten survival and yet promise also a precious spark of light to those hitherto excluded from the benefits of technical advance. Insensitivity to this ambiguity leads to a politics of despair that would freeze the current relations of force in the world—and with them the injustices they sustain—

as a condition for solving the problem of survival. That this is an impossible route to salvation is abundantly clear from the whole experience of the nuclear and environmental movements.

What we most need to learn from this experience is that action to end history is still action in history for historical objectives. Humanity is not yet the subject of the struggle to survive, and so this struggle too becomes a facet of the very class and national struggles the ultimate obsolescence of which it demonstrates. From this dialectic there is no escape.

The early seventies gave us a dress rehearsal of far deeper crises to come. If there was ever any doubt about the environmental crisis intensifying social and international conflict, that doubt should now be silenced. The environmental crisis, in short, brings not peace but a sword. And precisely for that reason it is not a unifying messianic force through which the human race could join in an ennobling struggle beyond the petty conflicts of history. Rather, it is a new terrain on which the old issues will be fought out, perhaps this time to a conclusion.

Part II.

DEMOCRATIC RATIONALIZATION

The three chapters of this section develop a theory of democratic technical change based on a revised constructivist approach. The first chapter addresses the determinist alternative and formulates a politically aware version of constructivism. This chapter draws the political conclusions from indeterminism: lay interventions into technology are shown to be "rational" and need not lead to costly tradeoffs of technical efficiency for "values." The second chapter develops a theory of democratic agency in the political sphere in opposition to the claim that technical progress leads inevitably to technocracy. The argument is based on a distinction between networks and systems. Networks of loosely connected persons and objects are traversed by multiple and often conflicting programs. The dominant program is generally recognized as defining for systems such as corporations and agencies. Democratic rationalization is the effect of subordinated programs realizing technical potentials ignored or rejected by these systems. The third chapter draws the conclusions for political theory from these considerations on rationality and agency. If technology is such a powerful institution, then surely it ought to be democratically controlled. But how should that control be exercised? What kind of legitimacy does citizen involvement in technology possess?

Part II.

DEMOCRATIC RATIONALIZATION

4. The Limits of Technical Rationality

TECHNOLOGY AND DEMOCRACY

A great deal of 20th century social thought has been based on a pessimistic view of modernity that achieved its classic expression in Max Weber's theory of rationalization. According to Weber, modernity is characterized by the increasing role of calculation and control in social life, a trend leading to what he called the "iron cage" of bureaucracy (Weber, 1958: 181-182). This notion of enslavement by a rational order inspires pessimistic philosophies of technology according to which human beings have become mere cogs in the social machinery, objects of technical control in much the same way as raw materials and the natural environment. While this view is overdrawn, it is true that as more and more of social life is structured by technically mediated organizations such as corporations, state agencies, prisons, and medical institutions, the technical hierarchy merges with the social and political hierarchy.

The idea and (for some) ideal of technocracy grows out of this new situation. Technocracy represents a generalization to society as a whole of the type of "neutral" instrumental rationality supposed to characterize the technical sphere. It assumes the existence of technological imperatives that need only be recognized to guide management of society as a system. Whether technocracy is welcomed or abhorred, these deterministic premises leave no room for democracy.

The title of this part of this book implies a provocative reversal of Weber's conclusions. "Democratic" rationalization is a contradiction in Weberian terms. On those terms, once tradition has been defeated by modernity, radical struggle for freedom and individuality degenerates into an affirmation of irrational life forces against the routine and drab predictability of a bureaucratic order. This is not a democratic program but a romantic anti-dystopian one, the sort of thing that is already foreshadowed in Dostoievsky's *Notes from Underground* and various back to nature ideologies. The new left and all its works have been condemned repeatedly on these grounds.

No doubt the new left is rightly criticized for the excesses of its romanticism, but the two preceding chapters of this book show that this is not the whole story. Modern societies experienced real crises in the late 1960s that marked a turning point in the willingness of the public to leave its affairs in the hands of experts. Out of that period came not just regressive fantasies but a new and more democratic conception of progress. I have attempted in several previous books to articulate that conception in a third position that is neither technocratic nor romantic. The crux of the argument is the claim that technology is ambivalent, that there is no unique correlation between technological advance and the distribution of social power. The ambivalence of technology can be summarized in the following two principles.

1. Conservation of hierarchy: social hierarchy can generally be preserved and reproduced as new technology is introduced. This principle explains the extraordinary continuity of power in advanced capitalist societies over the last several generations, made possible by technocratic strategies of modernization despite enormous technical changes.[1]

2. Democratic rationalization: new technology can also be used to undermine the existing social hierarchy or to force it to meet needs it has ignored. This principle explains the technical initiatives that often accompany the structural reforms pursued by union, environmental, and other social movements.

This second principle implies that there will generally be ways of rationalizing society that democratize rather than centralize control. We need not go underground or native to escape the iron cage. In this chapter and the next I will show that this is in fact the meaning of the emerging social movements to change technology in a variety of areas such as computers, medicine, and the environment.

But does it make sense to call the changes these movements advocate *rationalizations*? Are they not irrational precisely to the extent that they involve citizens in the affairs of experts? The strongest objections to democratizing technology come from those experts, who fear the loss of their hard-won freedom from lay interference. Can we reconcile public participation with the autonomy of professional technical work? Perhaps, as advocates of technocracy argue, we should strive not to politicize technology but to technicize politics in order to overcome the irrationality of public life. The counter-argument in favor of democratization must establish the rationality of informal public involvement in technical change.

---

[1] This principle explains why there can be no technical "fix" to fundamental social and political injustices. For examples, see Rybczynski (1991: chap. 5).

FROM DETERMINISM TO CONSTRUCTIVISM

Determinism Defined

Faith in progress has been supported for generations by two widely held deterministic beliefs: that technical necessity dictates the path of development, and that that path is discovered through the pursuit of efficiency.[2] So persuasive are these beliefs that even critics of progress such as Heidegger and Ellul share them. I will argue here that both beliefs are false, and that, furthermore, they have anti-democratic implications.

Determinism claims that technologies have an autonomous functional logic that can be explained without reference to society. Technology is presumably social only through the purpose it serves, and purposes are in the mind of the beholder. Technology would thus resemble science and mathematics by its intrinsic independence of the social world. Yet unlike science and mathematics, technology has immediate and powerful social impacts. Society's fate seems to be at least partially dependent on a nonsocial factor which influences it without suffering a reciprocal influence.

Determinism is based on two premises which I will call *unilinear progress* and *determination by the base*.

1) Technical progress appears to follow a unilinear course, a fixed track, from less to more advanced configurations. Each stage of technological development enables the next, and there are no branches off the main line. Societies may advance slowly or quickly, but the direction and definition of progress is not in question. Although this conclusion seems obvious from a backward glance at the history of any familiar technical object, in fact it is based on two claims of unequal plausibility: first, that technical progress proceeds from lower to higher levels of development; and second, that that development follows a single sequence of necessary stages. As we will see, the first claim is independent of the second and not necessarily deterministic.

2) Technological determinism also affirms that social institutions must adapt to the "imperatives" of the technological base. This view, which no doubt has its source in a certain reading of Marx, is long since the common sense of the social sciences. Adopting a technology necessarily constrains one to adopt certain practices that are connected with its employment. Railroads require scheduled travel. Once they are

---

[2] For an interesting recent collection of articles on determinism, see Smith and Marx (1994). The contribution of Philip Scranton seems closest in spirit to the theory presented here.

introduced people who formerly could live with rather approximate notions of time—the day marked out by church bells and the sun—need watches. So the imperative consequence of railroads is a new organization of social time. Similarly factories are hierarchical institutions and set the tone for social hierarchy throughout modern societies. Again, there is something plausible about this view, namely that devices and practices are congruent, but the stream of influence is not unidirectional.

These two theses of technological determinism present decontextualized, self-generating technology as the foundation of modern life. And since we in the advanced countries stand at the peak of technological development, the rest of the world can only follow our example. Determinism thus implies that our technology and its corresponding institutional structures are universal, indeed, planetary in scope. There may be many forms of tribal society, many feudalisms, even many forms of early capitalism, but there is only one modernity and it is exemplified in our society for good or ill. Late developers take note: as Marx once said, calling the attention of his backward German compatriots to British advances: "*De te fabula narratur*"— of you the tale is told (Marx, 1906: 13).

Underdetermination

The implications of determinism appear so obvious that it is surprising to discover that neither of its two premises withstand close scrutiny. Yet contemporary sociology undermines the idea of unilinear progress while historical precedents are unkind to determination by the base.

Recent constructivist sociology of technology grows out of the new social studies of science. The "strong program" in sociology of knowledge challenges the exemption of scientific theories from the sort of sociological examination to which we submit nonscientific beliefs. The "principle of symmetry" holds that all contending beliefs are subject to the same type of social explanation regardless of their truth or falsity. This view derives from the thesis of underdetermination, the so-called Duhem-Quine principle in philosophy of science, which refers to the inevitable lack of logically compelling reasons for preferring one competing scientific theory to another (Bloor, 1991). Rationality, in other words, does not constitute a separate and self-sufficient domain of human activity.

A similar approach to the study of technology denies that a purely rational criterion such as technical effectiveness suffices to account for the success of some innovations and the failure of others. Of course it remains true that some things really work and others do not: successful design respects technical principles. But there are often several possible designs with which to achieve similar objectives and no decisive technical reason to prefer one to the others. Here, underdetermination means that technical principles alone are insufficient to determine the design of actual devices.

What then does decide the issue? A commonplace reply is "economic efficiency." But the problem is trickier than it seems at first. Before the efficiency of a process can be measured, both the type and quality of output have to be fixed. Thus economic choices are necessarily secondary to clear definitions of both the problems to which technology is addressed and the solutions it provides. But clarity on these matters is often the outcome rather than the presupposition of technical development. For example, MS DOS lost the competition with the Windows graphical interface, but not before the very nature of computing was transformed by a change in the user base and in the types of tasks to which computers were dedicated. A system that was more efficient for programming and accounting tasks proved less than ideal for secretaries and hobbyists interested in ease of use. Thus economics cannot explain but rather follows the trajectory of development.

Constructivism argues, I think correctly, *that the choice between alternatives ultimately depends neither on technical nor economic efficiency, but on the "fit" between devices and the interests and beliefs of the various social groups that influence the design process.* What singles out an artifact is its relationship to the social environment, not some intrinsic property.

Pinch and Bijker illustrate this approach with the early evolution of the bicycle (Pinch and Bijker, 1987). In the late 19th Century, before the present form of the bicycle was fixed, design was pulled in several different directions. The object we take to be a self-evident "black box" actually started out as two very different devices, a sportsman's racer and a means of transportation. Some customers perceived bicycling as a competitive sport, while others had an essentially utilitarian interest in getting from here to there. Designs corresponding to the first definition had high front wheels that were rejected as unsafe by riders of the second type, who preferred designs with two equal-sized low wheels. The large diameter front wheel of the sportsman's racer was faster, but it was unstable. Equal-sized wheels made for a safer but less exciting ride. These two designs met different needs and were in fact different technologies with many shared elements. Pinch and Bijker call this original ambiguity of the object designated as a "bicycle," "interpretative flexibility."

Eventually the "safety" design won out, and it benefited from all the subsequent advances in the field. The entire later history of the bicycle down to the present day stems from that line of technical development. In retrospect, it seems as though the high wheelers were a clumsy and less efficient stage in a progressive development leading through the old "safety" bicycle to current designs. In fact the high wheeler and the safety shared the field for years and neither was a stage in the other's development. The high wheeler represented a possible alternative path of bicycle development that addressed different problems.

The bicycle example is reassuringly innocent as are, no doubt, the majority of technical decisions. But what if the various technical solutions to a problem have different effects on the distribution of power and wealth? Then the choice between them is political and the political implications of that choice will be embodied in some sense in the technology. Of course the discovery of this connection did not await constructivism. Langdon Winner offers a particularly telling example of it (Winner, 1986: 22-23). Robert Moses' plans for an early New York expressway included overpasses that were a little too low for city buses. Poor people from Manhattan, who depended on bus transportation, were thereby discouraged from visiting the beaches on Long Island. In this case a simple design specification contained a racial and class bias. We could show something similar with many other technologies, the assembly line for example, which exemplifies capitalist notions of control of the work force. Reversing these biases would not return us to pure, neutral technology, but would simply alter its valuative content in a direction more in accord with our own preferences and therefore less visible to us.

Determinism ignores these complications and works with decontextualized temporal cross-sections in the life of its objects. It claims implausibly to be able to get from one such momentary configuration of the object to the next on purely technical terms. But in the real world all sorts of attitudes and desires crystallize around technical objects and influence their development. Differences in the way social groups interpret and use the objects are not merely extrinsic but make a difference in the nature of the objects themselves. Technology cannot be determining because the "different interpretations by social groups of the content of artefacts lead via different chains of problems and solutions to different further developments" (Pinch and Bijker, 1987: 42). *What* the object *is* for the groups that ultimately decide its fate determines what it *becomes* as it is modified. If this is true, then technological development is a social process and can only be understood as such.

Chart 2: How Artifacts Have Politics

Selection Criteria	Partially Substitutable Artifacts	Shared Effects (e.g.uses)	Unique Effects

Artifacts 1-4 share certain effects but each also has its own unique effects which distinguish it from the others. Effects in this sense include uses, contextual requirements that must be met to employ the artifacts, and their unintended consequences. Criteria 1-4 all select the shared effects of the artifacts and each also valorizes one or another of the unique effects. Where different unique effects have different political consequences, competing groups will have preferred criteria corresponding to the fit between their goals and the various artifacts. The criteria can also be combined in the course of the evolution of the artifacts through design changes that adapt one of them to also delivering the unique effects of one or several others. In a political context such combinations correspond to alliances.

Determinism is a species of Whig history which makes it seem as though the end of the story were inevitable from the very beginning. It projects the abstract technical logic of the finished object back into its origins as a cause of development, confounding our understanding of the past and stifling the imagination of a different future. Constructivism can open up that future, although its practitioners have hesitated so far to engage the larger social issues implied in their method.

Indeterminism

If the thesis of unilinear progress falls, the collapse of the notion of determination by the technological base cannot be far behind. Yet it is still frequently invoked in contemporary political debates. I shall return to these debates later in this chapter. For now, let us consider the remarkable anticipation of current conservative rhetoric in the struggle over the length of the workday and child labor in mid-19th Century England. Factory owners and economists denounced regulation as inflationary; industrial production supposedly required children and the long workday. One member of parliament declared that regulation is "a false principle of humanity, which in the end is certain to defeat itself." The new rules were so radical, he concluded, as to constitute "in principle an argument to get rid of the whole system of factory labor" (*Hansard's Debates*: 1844 (22 Feb–22 April), 1123, 1120). Similar protestations are heard today on behalf of industries threatened with what they call environmental "Luddism."

Yet what actually happened once limitations were imposed on the workday and children expelled from the factory? Did the violated imperatives of technology exact a price? Not at all. Regulation led to an intensification of factory labor that was incompatible with the earlier conditions in any case. Children ceased to be workers and were redefined socially as learners and consumers. Consequently, they entered the labor market with higher levels of skill and discipline that were soon presupposed by technological design and work organization. As a result no one is nostalgic for a return to the good old days when inflation was held down by child labor. That is simply not an option.[3]

This case shows the tremendous flexibility of technical systems. They are not rigidly constraining but on the contrary can adapt to a variety of social demands. The responsiveness of technology to social redefinition explains its adaptability. On this account technology is just another dependent social variable, albeit an increasingly important one, and not the key to the riddle of history.

Determinism, I have argued, is characterized by the principles of unilinear progress and determination by the base; if determinism is

---

[3] It is interesting (and distressing) to note the moral tensions around the use of child labor to manufacture imports such as sports shoes or circuit boards. In this as in so many other domains, globalization makes it possible to evade regulations that cannot be challenged on home territory. Predictably, political protests here against child labor abroad are weaker than would be resistance to reintroducing child labor at home.

wrong, then research must be guided by two contrary principles. In the first place, technological development is not unilinear but branches in many directions, and could reach generally higher levels along several different tracks. And, secondly, social development is not determined by technological development but depends on both technical and social factors.

The political significance of this position should also be clear by now. In a society where determinism stands guard on the frontiers of democracy, indeterminism is political. If technology has many unexplored potentialities, no technological imperatives dictate the current social hierarchy. Rather, technology is a site of social struggle, in Latour's phrase, a "parliament of things" on which political alternatives contend.

CRITICAL CONSTRUCTIVISM

Technology Study

The picture sketched so far requires a significant change in our definition of technology. It can no longer be considered as a collection of devices, nor, more generally, as the sum of rational means. These definitions imply that technology is essentially nonsocial.

Perhaps the prevalence of such tendentious definitions explains why technology is not generally considered an appropriate field of humanistic study; we are assured that its essence lies in a technically explainable function rather than a hermeneutically interpretable meaning. At most, humanistic methods might illuminate extrinsic aspects of technology, such as packaging and advertising, or popular reactions to controversial innovations such as nuclear power or surrogate motherhood. Of course, if one ignores most of its connections to society, it is no wonder technology appears to be self-generating. Technological determinism draws its force from this attitude.

The constructivist position has very different implications for the humanistic study of technology. They can be summarized in the following three points:

1. Technical design is not determined by a general criterion such as efficiency, but by a social process which differentiates technical alternatives according to a variety of case-specific criteria;

2. That social process is not about fulfilling "natural" human needs, but concerns the cultural definition of needs and therefore of the problems to which technology is addressed;

3. Competing definitions reflect conflicting visions of modern society realized in different technical choices.

The first point widens the investigation of social alliances and conflicts to include technical issues which, typically, have been treated as the object of a unique consensus. The other two points imply that culture and ideology enter history as effective forces not only in politics, but also in the technical sphere. These three points thus establish the legitimacy of applying the same methods to technology that are employed to study social institutions, customs, beliefs, and art. With such a hermeneutic approach, the definition of technology expands to embrace its social meaning and its cultural horizon.

Function or Meaning

The role of social meaning is clear in the case of the bicycle. The very definition of the object was at stake in a contest of interpretations: was it to be a sportsman's toy or a means of transportation? It might be objected that this is merely a disagreement over function with no hermeneutic significance. Once a function is selected, the engineer has the last word on its implementation and the humanist interpreter is out of luck. This is the view of most engineers and managers; they are at home with "function" but have no place for "meaning."

In chapter 9 I will propose a very different model of the essence of technology based not on the distinction of the social and the technical, but crosscutting the customary boundaries between them. In this conception, technology's essence is not an abstraction from the contingencies of function, a causal structure that remains the same through the endless uses to which devices are subjected in the various systems that incorporate them. Rather, the essence of technology is abstracted from a larger social context within which functionality plays a specific limited role. Technologies do of course have a causal aspect, but they also have a symbolic aspect that is determining for their use and evolution. From that standpoint, I would like to introduce Bruno Latour's and Jean Baudrillard's quite different but complementary proposals for what I will call a *hermeneutics of technology*.

Latour argues that norms are not merely subjective human intentions but that they are also realized in devices. This is an aspect of what he calls the symmetry of humans and nonhumans which he adds to the constructivist symmetry of true and false theories, successful and unsuccessful devices.

According to Latour, technical devices embody norms that serve to enforce obligations. He presents the door closer as a simple example. A notice posted on a door can remind users to close it, or a mechanism can close it automatically. The door closer, in some sense, does the work of the notice but more efficiently. It materializes the moral obligation to close the door too easily ignored by passersby. That obligation is "delegated" to a device in Latour's sense of the term. According to Latour, the "morality" in this case can be allocated either to persons—by a notice—or to things—by a spring (Latour, 1992). This Latourian equivalent of Hegelian *Sittlichkeit* opens the technical world to investigation not simply as a collection of functioning devices determined by causal principles but also as the objectification of social values, as a cultural system.

Baudrillard suggests a useful approach to the study of the aesthetic and psychological dimensions of this "system of objects" (Baudrillard, 1968). He adapts the linguistic distinction between denotation and connotation to describe the difference between the functions of technical objects and their many other associations. For example, automobiles are means of transportation—a function; but they also signify the owner as more or less respectable, wealthy, and sexy—connotations. The engineer may think these connotations are extrinsic to the device he or she is working on, but they too belong to its social reality.

Baudrillard's approach opens technology to quasi-literary analysis. Indeed, technologies are subject to interpretation in much the same way as texts, works of art, and actions (Ricoeur, 1979).[4] However, his model still remains caught in the functionalist paradigm insofar as it takes the distinction between denotation and connotation for granted. In reality, that distinction is a product not a premise of technical change. There is often no consensus on the precise function of new technologies. The personal computer is a case in point; it was launched on the market with infinite promise and no applications. The story of Chinese sea faring in the 15th century offers another marvelous example of prolonged suspense regarding function. The Chinese built the largest fleet composed of the biggest ships the world had ever seen, but could not agree on the purpose of their own naval achievements. Astonishingly, they dismantled the fleet and retreated into their borders, paving the way for the European conquest of Asia (Levathes, 1994: 20).

---

[4] Two interesting studies that illustrate this thesis around problems of lighting and electricity are Schivelbusch (1988) and Marvin (1988).

In the case of well established technologies, the distinction between function and connotation is usually fairly clear. There is a tendency to project this clarity back into the past and to imagine that the technical function of a device called it into being. However, as we have seen, technical functions are not pregiven but are discovered in the course of development and use. Gradually they are locked in by the evolution of the social and technical environment, as for example the transportation functions of the automobile have been institutionalized in low-density urban designs that create the demand for transportation automobiles satisfy. So long as no institutional lock-in ties it decisively to one of its several possible functions, these ambiguities in the definition of a new technology pose technical problems which must be resolved through interactions between designers, purchasers and users.

Technological Hegemony

Technical design responds not only to the social meaning of individual technical objects, but also incorporates broader assumptions about social values. The cultural horizon of technology therefore constitutes a second hermeneutic dimension. It is one of the foundations of modern forms of social hegemony. As I will use the term, hegemony is domination so deeply rooted in social life that it seems natural to those it dominates. One might also define it as that aspect of the distribution of social power which has the force of culture behind it.

The term "horizon" refers to culturally general assumptions that form the unquestioned background to every aspect of life. Some of these support the prevailing hegemony. For example, in feudal societies, the "chain of being" established hierarchy in the fabric of God's universe and protected the caste relations of the society from challenge. Under this horizon, peasants revolted in the name of the King, the only imaginable source of power. Technocratic rationalization plays an equivalent role today, and technological design is the key to its cultural power.

Technological development is constrained by cultural norms originating in economics, ideology, religion, and tradition. I discussed earlier how assumptions about the age composition of the labor force entered into the design of 19th century production technology. Such assumptions seem so natural and obvious they often lie below the threshold of conscious awareness. When one looks at old photos of child factory workers, one is struck by the adaptation of machines to their height (Newhall, 1964: 140). The images disturb us, but were no doubt taken for granted until child labor became controversial. Design specifications simply incorporated the sociological fact of child labor into the structure of devices. The impress of social relations can be traced in the technology.

The assembly line offers another telling instance (Braverman, 1974). Its technologically enforced labor discipline increases productivity and profits by increasing control through deskilling and pacing work. However, the assembly line only appears as technical progress in a specific social context. It would not look like an advance in an economy based on workers' councils in which labor discipline was largely self-imposed by the work group rather than imposed from above by management. In such a society engineers would seek different ways of increasing productivity. Here again design mirrors back the social order (Noble, 1984). Thus what Marcuse called "technological rationality" and Foucault the "regime of truth" is not merely a belief, an ideology, but is effectively incorporated into the machines themselves.

Technologies are selected by the dominant interests from among many possible configurations. Guiding the selection process are social codes established by the cultural and political struggles that define the horizon under which the technology will fall. Once introduced, technology offers a material validation of that cultural horizon. Apparently neutral technological rationality is enlisted in support of a hegemony through the bias it acquires in the process of technical development. The more technology society employs, the more significant is this support. The legitimating effectiveness of technology depends on unconsciousness of the cultural-political horizon under which it was designed. A critical theory of technology can uncover that horizon, demystify the illusion of technical necessity, and expose the relativity of the prevailing technical choices.

Technical Regimes and Codes

Disputes over the definition of technologies are settled by privileging one among many possible configurations. This process, called closure, yields an "exemplar" for further development in its field (van den Belt and Rip, 1990: 140). The exemplar reacts back on the technical discipline from which it originated by establishing standard ways of looking at problems and solutions. These are variously described by social scientists as "technological frames" or "technological regimes" or "paradigms" (Bijker, 1987: 168; Nelson and Winter, 1982: 258-259; Dosi, 1982). Rip and Kemp, for example, define a regime as:

The whole complex of scientific knowledge, engineering practices, production process technologies, product characteristics, skills and procedures, and institutions and infrastructures that make up the totality of a technology. A technological regime is thus the technology-specific context of a technology which prestructures the kind of problem-solving activities that engineers are likely to do, a structure that both enables and constrains certain changes (Rip and Kemp, 1998: 340).

Such regimes incorporate many social factors expressed by technologists in purely technical language and practices. I call those aspects of technological regimes which can best be interpreted as direct reflections of significant social values the "technical code" of the technology. *Technical codes define the object in strictly technical terms in accordance with the social meaning it has acquired.* These codes are usually invisible because, like culture itself, they appear self-evident. For example, if tools and workplaces are designed today for adult hands and heights, that is only because children were expelled from industry long ago with design consequences we now take for granted. Technological regimes reflect this social decision unthinkingly, as is normal, and only social scientific investigation can uncover the source of the standards in which it is embodied.

Technical codes include important aspects of the basic definition of many technical objects insofar as these too become universal culturally accepted features of daily life. The telephone, the automobile, the refrigerator and a hundred other everyday devices have clear and unambiguous definitions in the dominant culture: we know exactly what they are insofar as we are acculturated members of our society. Each new instance of these standard technologies must conform to its defining code to be recognizable and acceptable. But there is nothing obvious about this outcome from a historical point of view. Each of these objects was selected from a series of alternatives by a code reflecting specific social values.

The bicycle reached this point in the 1890s. A technical code defining the bicycle as a safe means of transportation required a seat positioned well behind a small front wheel. The bicycle produced according to this code, known at the time as a "safety," became the forebear of all future designs. The safety connoted women and mature riders, trips to the store, and so on, rather than racing and sport. Eventually the safety was able to incorporate the racing connotations of the bicycle in specialized designs and the old high wheeler was laid to rest. Note that in this typical case the choice of the exemplary design reflected the privilege granted the specific code defining for it, i.e., designating objects as "safe" or "unsafe." The high wheelers could only have won out by a similar privileging of "fast" and "slow."

Because technologies have such vast social implications, technical designs are often involved in disputes between ideological visions. The outcome of these disputes, a hegemonic order of some sort, brings technology into conformity with the dominant social forces, insuring the "isomorphism, the formal congruence between the technical logics of the apparatus and the social logics within which it is diffused" (Bidou, et al., 1988: 71). These hermeneutic congruencies offer a way to explain the impact of the larger sociocultural environment on the mechanisms of closure, a still relatively undeveloped field of technology studies.

Kuhnian Perspectives on Technical Change

This analysis leads to an obvious question: if all this is true, why aren't we more aware of the public interventions that have shaped technology in the past? Why does it appear apolitical? It is the very success of these interventions that gives rise to this illusion. Success means that technical regimes change to reflect interests excluded at earlier stages in the design process. But the eventual internalization of these interests in design masks their source in public protest. The waves close over forgotten struggles and the technologists return to the comforting belief in their own autonomy which seems to be verified by the conditions of everyday technical work.

The notion of the "neutrality" of technology is a standard defensive reaction on the part of professions and organizations confronted by public protest and attempting to protect their autonomy. But in reality technical professions are never autonomous; in defending their traditions, they actually defend the outcomes of earlier controversies rather than a supposedly pure technical rationality. Informal public intervention is thus already an implicit factor in design whatever technologists and managers may believe.

Lay initiatives usually influence technical rationality without destroying it. In fact, public intervention may actually improve technology by addressing problems ignored by vested interests entrenched in the design process. If the technical professions can be described as autonomous, it is not because they are truly independent of politics but rather because they usually succeed in translating political demands into technically rational terms.

With some modifications, Kuhn's famous distinction between revolutionary and normal science can be reformulated to explain these aspects of the design process (Kuhn, 1962). The alternation of professional and public dominance in technical fields is one of several patterns that correspond roughly to the distinction between normal and revolutionary scientific change. There is, however, a significant difference between science and technology. Natural science eventually becomes far more independent of public opinion than technology. As a result, democratic interventions into scientific change are unusual, and revolutions explode around tensions within the disciplines. Of course even mature science is responsive to politics and culture, but their influence is usually felt indirectly through administrative decisions and changes in education. By contrast, ordinary people are constantly involved in technical activity, the more so as technology advances. It is true that they may be objects rather than subjects of the technologies that affect them, but in any case their closeness offers them a unique vantage point. Situated knowledges arising from that vantage point can become the basis for public interventions even in a mature technological system.

These situated knowledges are usually viewed with skepticism by experts guided by the pursuit of efficiency within the framework of the established technical codes. But in Kuhnian terms, efficiency only applies within a paradigm; it cannot judge between paradigms. To the extent that technical cultures are based on efficiency, they constitute the equivalent of Kuhn's normal science and as such they lack the categories with which to comprehend the paradigmatic changes that will transform them in the course of events. And since democratic interventions are often responsible for such changes, they too remain opaque to the dominant technical culture.

Reflexive Design

The subordination of technology to society is not merely a matter of assigning functions to devices, a self-evident form of dependency. It goes far beyond that to affect the very definition of the functions that ought to be fulfilled, and the quality of the environment associated with the devices that fulfill them, both in production and use. But if that is the case, wouldn't technologists themselves benefit from bringing these issues to the surface in their work? A reflexive design process could take into account the social dimensions of technology at the start instead of waiting to be enlightened by public turmoil or sociological research.

No doubt there are many undocumented cases of reflexive design often stimulated by marketing considerations. I am aware of its growing importance through experience in the field of computer mediated communications. Different types of interface reflect different conceptions of the virtual world in which users must function as they interact online. At first interface designers sought universal solutions to the problems of online communications, but as time went on they began to adjust interfaces to specific group and task requirements. Thus was born the fields of "groupware," and "computer supported cooperative work" (cscw). From 1984 to 1987, I was personally involved in studying groupware on a series of grants from the US Department of Education, the French Telecom, and the Digital Equipment Corporation (dec). The aim of the research was to find a meta-design to guide the design of online environments for different types of social groups.

dec got involved in connection with its networking business. The company recognized that in hooking up computers it was also linking their users in new patterns of interaction and collaboration that would require appropriate software support. We called this the "Social Factors" project. In contrast with human factors, i.e. the adaptation of technology to generic constraints, social factors would adapt computer-created social environments to group needs (Feenberg, 1986b; Feenberg, 1993).

But of course, the reification of a certain conception of group needs in software risks fixing patterns of behavior and authority that might be more easily contested or subverted in less structured face-to-face settings. Thus social factors quickly lead to political factors. This is the burden of Lucy Suchman's piquantly entitled article "Do Categories Have Politics?" (Suchman, 1994). In this article Suchman, who works with software designers at Xerox parc, developed a political critique of the authoritarian implications of a specific type of cscw software design.

Examples like this give a hint of the deeper significance of the new theories of technology. The issue is not simply "society's responsibility" for controlling technology, but extends to a reflexive transformation of technical disciplines themselves as the design process becomes socially conscious.

PROGRESS AND RATIONALITY

The Tradeoff Model
The anti-deterministic arguments of the previous sections of this chapter undermine one basis of the technical professions' claims to

autonomy. If they have succeeded in incorporating public concerns in the past, why reject participation on principle today? However, even if the democratic position is granted this much, it is still possible to argue that participation has unreasonable costs. Thus the autonomy thesis still has another leg to stand on. This is the notion that technical rationality can supply the most efficient solution to economic problems when it suffers the least interference. On this basis one might argue that there is an inevitable tradeoff between ideology and technology.

This discussion takes us back over the ground covered in the chapters of Part I. The claims of technical purity were denied most vigorously by anti-technocratic movements such as the May Events that challenged the direction of progress. And the environmental debate turns ultimately on whether environmental goals are compatible with technological advance. Is a democratic alternative to technocracy conceivable? Can a technological society pursue environmental goals without sacrificing prosperity? Many would answer these questions in the negative, claiming that public involvement in technology risks slowing progress to a halt, that democratization and environmental reform are tantamount to Luddite reaction. In this section I will address this objection through an analysis of the limits of technical rationality in social policy.

Let me begin by acknowledging that public fear of technology sometimes results in costly changes or even abandonment of controversial innovations. And of course there is the famous NIMBY ("not in my back yard") syndrome that has greeted nuclear power, toxic waste incinerators, genetic engineering facilities, and other harbingers of a future lived on a higher plane of anxiety.

I call the public's response to new and imponderable risks it is not equipped to evaluate "rational dread." Childhood dread of the monster under the bed can usually be stilled by more information—a simple glance may suffice. But the dread of modern technologies such as atomic energy resists informational strategies. On the contrary, often more information leads to still greater concern. To make matters worse, the hope that expert advice could unburden the public has long since been disappointed as general skepticism overtakes the authority of knowledge. The problem is occasionally resolved by forcing a return to an already accepted level of risk rather than achieving habituation to the higher level involved in new technologies.

The American nuclear power industry has indeed been the victim of just such a response (Morone and Woodhouse, 1989). The significance of this case cannot be overestimated: the nuclear industry was one of the major technological projects of modern times. Nuclear power promised to free industrial society from dependency on the fragile bottleneck of fossil fuels. But the industry became fixated on unsafe designs in the 1960s and was unable to adapt to the standards of the 1970s and 1980s. In the head on confrontation with public opinion that followed, technology lost, at least in the US. Today conversion initiatives multiply as the owners of old nuclear plants switch back to fossil fuels.

What is the moral of this story? One can conclude with bitter irony that technology is in fact democratically controlled because "the very irrationality that has come to dominate the nuclear debate confirms that the public will is still what counts" (Florman, 1981: 69). But it is a good question where the "irrationality" lay, in the government and utility industries which pushed for impracticable goals or in the public which called them to account out of unverified fears. Clearly, we would be much better off if the many billions of research dollars spent to develop nuclear power had been employed in other ventures, for example, in the fields of solar energy and energy storage.[5]

In any case, this example is not typical. Fear usually does not kill new technology; for the most part, it simply changes the regulatory environment and the orientation of development. Automotive safety and emissions is a good example. Regulation gradually effected changes that were well within the technical capabilities of manufacturers. The results are much safer and less polluting vehicles, not the disaster foreseen by the foes of government "interference."

These issues appear with particular force in the environmental movement. Arguably, this is the single most important domain of democratic intervention into technology. Environmentalists want to reduce harmful and costly side effects of technology to protect nature and human health. This program can be implemented in different ways. As Commoner has argued, in a capitalist society there is a tendency to deflect criticism from technological processes to products and people, from a priori prevention to a posteriori cleanup. These preferred strategies are generally costly and reduce efficiency, with unfortunate political consequences.

Restoring the environment after it has been damaged is a form of collective consumption financed by taxes or higher prices. Because this approach to environmentalism dominates public awareness, it is

---

[5] For a sensible approach to the problem of the rationality of risk assessment, see Schrader-Frechette (1991).

generally perceived as a cost involving tradeoffs, and not as a rationaliza-tion with long-term benefits. But in a modern society, obsessed by eco-nomic well-being, that perception is damning. Economists and busi-nessmen are fond of explaining the price we must pay in inflation and unemployment for worshipping at Nature's shrine instead of Mammon's. Poverty awaits those who will not adjust their social and political expectations to technological imperatives.

This tradeoff model has environmentalists grasping at straws for a strategy. As we saw in the previous chapter, Ehrlich held out the pious hope that people would turn from material to spiritual values in the face of the mounting problems of industrial society. Heilbroner expected enlightened dictators to bite the bullet of technological reform even if a greedy populace shirked its duty. It is difficult to decide which of these solutions is more improbable, but both are incompatible with basic democratic values.

The tradeoff model confronts us with dilemmas—environmentally sound technology vs. prosperity, workers' control vs. productivity, etc.—where what we need are syntheses. Unless the problems of modern industrialism can be solved in ways that both enhance public welfare and win public support, there is little reason for hope.

But how can technological reform be reconciled with prosperity when it places a variety of new limits on the economy? The child labor case shows how apparent dilemmas arise on the boundaries of cultural change, specifically where major technological regimes are in transition. In such situations, social groups excluded from the original design net-work articulate their unrepresented interests politically. New values the outsiders believe would enhance their welfare appear as mere ideology to insiders who are adequately represented by the existing designs.

This is a difference of perspective, not of nature. Yet the illusion of essential conflict is renewed whenever social changes affect technology. At first, satisfying the demands of new groups after the fact has visible costs and, if it is done clumsily, will indeed reduce efficiency until better designs are found. But usually better designs can be found and apparent barriers to growth dissolve in the face of technological change.

This situation indicates the essential difference between economic exchange and technique. Exchange is all about tradeoffs: more of A means less of B. But the aim of technical advance is precisely to avoid such dilemmas by devising what the French philosopher of technology, Gilbert Simondon, called "concrete" designs that optimize several vari-ables at once. A single cleverly conceived mechanism then corresponds to many different social demands, one structure to many functions. As I will explain in the next chapter, design is not a zero-sum economic game but an ambivalent cultural process that serves a multiplicity of values and social groups without necessarily sacrificing efficiency.

Regulation of Technology

That these conflicts over social control of risk are not new can be seen from the interesting case of the "bursting boilers" (Burke, 1972). Steamboat boilers were the first technology the US Government subjected to safety regulation. Over 5000 people were killed or injured in hundreds of steamboat explosions from 1816, when regulation was first proposed, to 1852, when it was actually implemented. Is this many casualties or few? Consumers evidently were not too alarmed to continue traveling by riverboat in ever increasing numbers. Understandably, ship owners interpreted this as a vote of confidence and protested the excessive cost of safer designs. Yet politicians also won votes demanding safety.

The accident rate fell dramatically once technical improvements were mandated. Legislation would hardly have been necessary to achieve this had these improvements been technically determined. But in fact boiler design was relative to a social judgment about safety. That judgment could have been made on market grounds, as the shippers wished, or politically, with differing results. In either case, those results *constitute* a proper boiler. What a boiler "is" was thus defined through a long process of political struggle culminating finally in uniform codes issued by the American Society of Mechanical Engineers.

This example shows how the technical code responds to the changing cultural horizon of the society. Quite down-to-earth technical parameters such as the choice and processing of materials are *socially* specified by the code. The illusion of technical necessity arises from the fact that the code is thus literally "cast in iron," (at least in the case of boilers.)

Conservative anti-regulatory social philosophies are based on this illusion. They forget that the design process always already incorporates standards of safety and environmental compatibility; similarly, all technologies support some basic level of user or worker initiative and skill. A properly made technical object simply *must* meet these standards to be recognized as such. Conformity is no ideological extravagance but an intrinsic production cost. Raising the standards means altering the definition of the object, not paying a price for an alternative good or value as the tradeoff model holds.

The Fetishism of Efficiency

But what of the much discussed cost/benefit ratio of design changes such as those mandated by environmental or other similar legislation? These calculations have some application to transitional situations, before technical advances responding to new demands fundamentally alter the terms of the problem. But it is important not to overestimate their scientific value simply because they are expressed in numbers. All too often, the results depend on economists' very rough estimates of the monetary value of such things as a day of trout fishing or an asthma attack.[6] If made without prejudice, these estimates may well help to prioritize policy alternatives, but one cannot legitimately generalize from such pragmatic applications to a universal theory of the costs of regulation.

Such fetishism of efficiency ignores our ordinary understanding of the concept which is primarily of relevance to social philosophy. In that everyday sense, efficiency concerns those values with which economic actors are routinely concerned. The plumber may compare plastic to copper pipe as to their efficiency; he may even consider septic tanks vs. sewer hookups. But he is not expected to calculate the value of the night soil modern plumbing wastes. Such unproblematic aspects of technology can be safely ignored.[7]

In theory one can decompose any technical object and account for each of its elements in terms of the costs it imposes and the goals it meets, whether it be safety, speed, reliability, etc., but in practice no one is interested in opening the "black box" to see what is inside. For example, once the boiler code is established, such things as the thickness of a wall or the design of a safety valve appear as essential to the object. The cost of these features is not broken out as the specific "price" of safety and compared unfavorably with a more "efficient" but less secure design. Violating the code in order to lower costs is a crime, not a tradeoff.

Design is only controversial while it is in flux. Resolved conflicts over technology are quickly forgotten. Their outcomes, a welter of

---

[6] There are actually fairly sophisticated ways of estimating the value of a day of trout fishing. But what is the "cost" of an asthma attack? I recall once reading to my two asthmatic children the news summary of an economist's argument against revising the Clean Air Act. On hearing that the economist had valued asthma attacks at an average of $25 each, my children were outraged. But would it really improve matters much to multiply the numbers by two, five, or ten? The inherent flaws of this method of evaluating regulations far outweigh the advantages where significant health issues are concerned.

[7] This limitation is related to the concept of satisficing. See Elster (1983:138ff).

taken-for-granted technical and legal standards, are embodied in a stable code, and form the background against which economic actors manipulate the unstable portions of the environment in the pursuit of efficiency. The code itself is not normally varied in real world economic calculations, and as further advance occurs on the basis of it, movement backward no longer seems technically feasible.

Anticipating the stabilization of a new code, one can often ignore contemporary arguments that will soon be silenced by the emergence of a new horizon of efficiency calculations. This is what happened with boiler design and child labor; presumably, current debates on the environment will have a similar history and we will someday mock those who object to cleaner air and water as a "false principle of humanity" that violates technological imperatives.

There is a larger issue here. Non-economic values intersect the economy in the technical code. The examples we are dealing with illustrate this point clearly. The legal standards that regulate workers' economic activity have a significant impact on every aspect of their lives. In the child labor case, regulation widened educational opportunities with consequences that are not primarily economic in character. In the riverboat case, the choice of high levels of security was no tradeoff of one good for another, but a non-economic decision about the value of human life and the responsibilities of government.

Technology is thus not merely a means to an end; technical design standards define major portions of the social environment, such as urban and built spaces, workplaces, medical activities and expectations, life patterns, and so on. The economic significance of technical change often pales beside its wider human implications in framing a way of life. In such cases, regulation defines the cultural framework *of* the economy; it is not an act *in* the economy.

The Concept of Potentiality

The false dilemmas of technical politics arise from a peculiarity of change in the technical sphere. Technical resources can be configured in many different patterns. Any given configuration realizes a certain fraction of the well-being potentially available at the achieved technical level. Unrealized technical potential stands as a measure of the existing system. Where the contrast between what is and what might be becomes a political issue, technical resources are reconfigured in response to public pressure.

Looking back, the new configuration may seem obvious, but looking forward it is often very difficult to imagine radical technical solutions to contemporary problems. Worse still, without a clear idea of a solution, it is difficult even to formulate the problems clearly in their technical aspect. Thus often only after innovations have been introduced does it become entirely clear to what demand they respond.

Not only is it difficult to anticipate future technical arrangements, it is all too easy to think up utopias that cannot be realized under the existing ones. Thoroughgoing social changes are often inspired by such large ideological visions. In such cases, the long-term success of the new vision depends on its ability to deliver a better life over an extended period. That in turn depends on the technical changes necessary for its realization. Once success has been achieved, it is possible to look back and argue that the older way of life obstructed progress. In anticipation, theory may situate itself imaginatively on the boundary of the new civilizational configuration that will give a concrete content to its speculations, judging this society from the standpoint of a possible successor. However, so long as its hopes remain contingent for their realization on still unimagined technical advances, they can only take an ethical or ideological form. Their concrete formulation depends ultimately on the advances that will someday realize them by locking in the sort of irreversible sequence we call progress. As progress unfolds on the basis of the constrained choices that have shaped technology in the past, lines of development emerge with a clear direction. What were once values posited in the struggle for the future, become facts inherited from the past as the technical and institutional premises of further advance.

In economics the failure to actualize the full potential of a resource is called "suboptimization." Where suboptimizations are rooted in the technical code, we are dealing not with a specific or local failure but with the generalized wastefulness of a whole technological system. In economic terms, unrealized civilizational potentialities appear as systematic underemployment of major resources due to the restrictions the dominant economic culture places on technical and human development. A new culture is needed to shift patterns of investment and consumption and to open up the imagination to technical advances that transform the horizon of economic action.

The speculative claims of morality become ordinary facts of life through such civilizational advances. The child labor example illustrates these points clearly. Reforms based on ethical demands led to social changes so profound that eventually those demands became self-evident facts of life. At the time, businessmen worried about the economic costs of the reforms, but today these costs seem trivial, even irrelevant, in the light of the enormous human gain that results from the modern practices of child rearing and education. Of course time is of the essence in such cases. The point of view of contemporaries is not arbitrary, just subject to radical reinterpretation in a wider historical context. Something similar seems to be occurring today in the movements for environmental reform and for the equality of women and racial minorities.

Where the struggle for new ideals succeeds in restructuring society around a new culture, it will not be perceived as trading off wealth against morality, but as realizing the economic potentialities associated with its ethical claims. The dilemma of virtue and prosperity is not absolute, but can be mediated in the course of technological development. This was Commoner's position as we saw in the last chapter. He resisted the suggestion that environmental protection is incompatible with prosperity, and attempted to redefine social wealth in more inclusive terms. To some extent this redefinition has actually taken hold. As it sinks down into the structure of technology itself, through advances that adapt technical systems to the natural environment, it will become "obvious" that environmentalism represents progress.

Because economic culture is not fixed once and for all, and because a population's socially relative goals may be served by a variety of technological means, it is possible to link ideals and interests in a progressive process of technical change. In that process potentialities that appear at first in ethical or ideological form are eventually realized in an effective consciousness of self-interest. This link makes possible a radical democratic politics of technology.

Part II.

DEMOCRATIC RATIONALIZATION

5. The Problem of Agency

Beyond Technocracy

In the previous chapter, I argued that neither deterministic technological imperatives nor even the weaker tradeoff model can provide a basis for technocratic ideology. Yet it is undeniable that advanced societies exhibit the great concentrations of power in technically mediated organizations Weber foresaw. Thus despite its theoretical problems, the technocracy thesis will not go away. There really is something unique about the place of technical expertise in the administration of modern societies, something that goes beyond traditional bureaucracy, something that is deeply connected to the inexorable spread of what James Beniger calls the "control revolution" (Beniger, 1986).

Despite occasional resistance the design of technical institutions disqualifies modern men and women for meaningful political participation. The division of labor becomes the model for the division of society into rulers and ruled. As in the factory or hospital or school, urban centers, media, even unions are reconstructed around the paradigm of technical administration. Expertise legitimates power in society at large, and "citizenship" consists in the recognition of its claims and conscientious performance in mindless subordinate roles. The public sphere withers; a literal reign of silence is instituted as one-way communication replaces dialogue and debate throughout society.

The resulting weakness of democratic interventions into technology is symptomatic. The fundamental problem of democracy today is quite simply the survival of agency in this increasingly technocratic universe. This is the central problem the Frankfurt School thematized in Adorno's concept of "total administration," Marcuse's "one-dimensionality," and Habermas's "technization of the lifeworld." On the right, where agency is identified with the market and the fetus, it is easy to come up with a program for addressing this problem. The left has greater difficulties.

The politics of sexual and racial identity returns agency to the individual but at a level that leaves basic technocratic structures untouched. Without denying the importance of these issues, I would like to stimulate reflection on the renewal of agency in the technical sphere. This chapter will attempt to explain the nature of the democratic rationalizations that undermine technocracy from within.

Technocratic Legitimation

How is the efficiency of a technocratic order translated into legitimacy, in other words, how does technocratic ideology silence opposition to the technical processing and control of human beings? There is of course a whole literature on media manipulation, but we need to dig deeper to find the sources of the plausibility of the media image of benign and rational technocratic authority. There must be something happening in the social lifeworld that explains the effectiveness of technocratic ideology.

Latour's delegation theory suggests an approach. Recall that on Latour's account norms are "delegated" to devices that enforce moral obligations by their very structure and functioning. Latour's example of the automatic door closer may seem trivial. No doubt "Close the door" is better described as a "convention" than as a "moral principle." But when devices determine social roles, their normativity cannot be so easily dismissed. Latour writes,

> I will call...the behavior imposed back onto the human by non-human delegates *prescription*. Prescription is the moral and ethical dimension of mechanisms. In spite of the constant weeping of moralists, no human is as relentlessly moral as a machine....We have been able to delegate to nonhumans not only force as we have known it for centuries but also values, duties, and ethics. It is because of this morality that we, humans, behave so ethically, no matter how weak and wicked we feel we are (Latour, 1992: 232).

Social cohesion depends on technical prescriptions since traditions, laws, and verbal agreements are insufficient by themselves to hold together a complex society. Thus the social bond is mediated by technical objects as well as by human communication, and that mediation supports a *sui generis* form of normativity.

The prescriptions contained in devices define a division of labor. The distinction of white and blue collar, conception and execution, command and obedience, agent and client is already prefigured in technological design. In most organizations role definitions are the subject of a generalized consensus and work norms are associated with these definitions. The technical choices that establish roles are simultaneously normative choices that are imposed on everyone who chooses to belong to the organization. To find out the meaning of good work, look at the technical requirements of the assembly line: it not only paces work on management's terms, it also defines good work as keeping up with the pace it sets. This example can be generalized and not only to other types of production technology. In medicine, education, and administration, technical devices prescribe norms to which the individual is tacitly committed by organizational belonging. Technocracy is the use of technical delegations to conserve and legitimate an expanding system of hierarchical control.

Technocracy need not impose a specific value-based ideology vulnerable to critique on factual grounds. Rather, it relies on the consensus that emerges spontaneously out of the technical roles and tasks in modern organizations. Controversies are routinely settled by reference to that consensus. Meanwhile, the underlying technical framework is sheltered from challenge. Technocracy thus succeeds in masking its valuative bias behind the facade of pure technical rationality.

Once a system of centralized administration is established, it is difficult to imagine working any other way, and those in charge must perpetuate it as the condition of their own effectiveness. Thus actors in command of technically mediated institutions, whether private or public, capitalist or communist, subordinate their technical choices to the implicit meta-goal of reproducing their operational autonomy. As large-scale organizations come to dominate much of the social process, specialized functions of hierarchical institutions such as factories, workplaces or prisons are generalized to everyday social life. It is this which ultimately explains why despite diminishing educational and cultural inequalities, social evolution continues on an authoritarian track. Rationalization theory and its various descendants—critiques of enlightenment, power/knowledge, technocracy—can be restated on these terms without deterministic implications.

The Recovery of Agency

The student movements and the counterculture of the 1960s demanded self-management and participatory democracy as antidotes to what they saw as technocracy triumphant. Modern society was thought to suffer not from economic exploitation but from technical domination. This background explains the popularity of Marcuse's *One-Dimensional Man* and other similarly pessimistic social critiques. But these gloomy accounts of modern life left little or no room for change. The conceptual line between the left dystopian critique and the positivist celebration of technocracy was surprisingly thin. Theoretically, the critique was very nearly self-cancelling.

In practice dystopianism was so influential in stimulating opposition to the closed system it described that thirty years later its exaggerations are obvious. While the technocratic tendency of modern societies is no illusion, it is nowhere near as total as its adversaries once feared. Political action is still possible and indeed has on occasion been effective despite the obstacles.

These issues were prominent in the political debates of the 1960s, when for the first time the left called technical progress into question. In that period the idea of resistance was shaped by such large-scale movements as the May Events of 1968, the antiwar movement, and the urban riots in American cities. Technology appeared to be an enemy comparable to the state; hence anti-technocratic struggle was sometimes conceived on the model of political revolution. Actions such as burying a car in celebration of Earth Day and the destruction of a mainframe computer at a Canadian University carried this position to its logical conclusion. When revolution failed, some of the rebels actually returned to the land to escape the mechanical embrace of the "System."

Times have changed. There is a certain continuity in the themes of contemporary political movements, which still focus on race, gender, and the environment, but activism today is far more modest in its ambitions. We have come to recognize politics in smaller interventions in social life, sometimes called "micropolitics," a situational politics based on local knowledge and action. Micropolitics has no general strategy and offers no global challenge to the society. It involves many diverse but converging activities with long-term subversive impacts. This approach is particularly relevant in the technical sphere where it is difficult to conceive totalizing strategies of change.

Certainly communist societies failed in this project. Soviet Communism was unable to move from its original modernizing strategy to a transition to socialism. Mao's Cultural Revolution is now generally regarded as a technical disaster. Nor were radical critics in the West more successful in defining a total response. Marcuse's absolute refusal is a tragic moral posture, not an effective political stance. Heidegger's outright rejection of agency is not a true alternative to instrumental control but merely its abstract negation. Political events have long since overtaken these negative postures. What we have learned is that even if no totalizing approach makes sense, the tensions in the industrial system can be grasped on a local basis from "within," by individuals immediately engaged in technically mediated activities and able to actualize ambivalent potentialities suppressed by the prevailing technological rationality.

I call this "democratic rationalization." It starts out from the consequences of technology itself, from the ways in which it mobilizes the population around technical mediations. In the new technical politics, the social groups so constituted turn back reflexively on the framework that defines and organizes them: "we," as patients, users of a domestic computer system, participants in a division of labor, neighbors of a polluting plant, are the actors. It is this sort of agency that holds the promise of a democratization of technology. Technical politics foreshadows a world in which technology, as a kind of social "legislation" affecting every aspect of our lives, will emerge from these new types of public consultation.

A NONINSTRUMENTALIST THEORY OF AGENCY

Cultural Studies and Critical Theory

My goal is to develop an account of collective action in the technical sphere, one which can explain actual democratic struggles over technology occurring today. By starting out inductively, with these struggles as a touchstone, I hope to avoid several problems that plague discussions of technology and politics. All too often, these discussions tacitly presuppose that technical democratization is an administrative problem within the established framework of our society. The existing machinery of voting and regulation is taken as the model of democracy, and the goal is to incorporate technological decisions into the system. Indeed, more and more individual instances occur in which voting and regulation play an important role, but when generalized as a quasi-constitutional guarantee of technical democratization, the impractical nature of these reform schemes is all too obvious. "We the People" are simply not mobilized as a whole around technical issues to a degree that would make a constitutional approach plausible.

What is more, there are reasons of principle to think that technical democratization cannot proceed primarily through such formal means. The state and its administrations are products of centuries of centralization of power in bureaucratic structures that are congruent with a specific technical code. To the extent that that code is inherently authoritarian, it must be changed from below, not from above, and that requires active citizen involvement. We do have examples of that and we need to understand what is going on in such cases. For that purpose ultimate questions of democratic sovereignty are less interesting than the nature of the concrete democratic subjects that emerge in the midst of technical networks in opposition to technocratic forms of control. I will show here how recent technology studies can be reconfigured to recognize the role of technical micropolitics in democratic technical change.

Cultural studies offers one source for a democratic approach to technology. Cultural studies began by contesting the unilateral emphasis on the power of the media in earlier work on mass culture. Under the influence of Raymond Williams, Gramsci and French post-structuralism, the Birmingham School argued that consumers of mass culture are not passive objects of manipulation but that they interpret and appropriate the messages directed at them and in the process transform their meaning. They characterized the power structure of advanced societies as a contestable "hegemony" rather than as the "total administration" from which Critical Theory appeared to offer no escape.[1] I have introduced the notion of technological hegemony for a similar purpose: so that ordinary users can count as potential actors in the transformation of the system.

Cultural studies was important in bringing such ideas to the attention of a wide academic audience, but this was hardly the first interactive account of popular agency in technologically advanced society. American scholars influenced by the Frankfurt School in the 1960s reacted early against the excessive claims of the one-dimensionality thesis. While

---

[1] For a valuable survey of recent cultural theories, see Kellner (1995: chap. 1). His approach to the media, which draws on both cultural theory and the Frankfurt School, has influenced mine.

Marcuse maintained that transcending demands would have to come from "without" (art, philosophical critique, the instincts, the Third World), activist theoreticians sought an account of resistance as an immanent reflex of the system. It seemed inexplicable on Marcusean terms that such vast movements of protest had arisen in societies on the verge of complete integration. In response to this challenge, Stanley Aronowitz published *False Promises* in 1973, one of several attempts in that period to recover agency within a Critical Theory framework. This Frankfurt School connection is significant for our project.

The cultural studies approach has been applied to technology by Roger Silverstone (Silverstone et al., 1992, Silverstone and Haddon, 1996). He and his collaborators have developed a reception theory of the appropriation of technology in the household. Just as TV viewers impose their own interpretations on the shows they watch, so users can resignify and even modify the devices they use in accordance with their own codes and values. This process, called "domestication," yields a technical object adapted to the home environment.

Undoubtedly, the phenomena Silverstone identifies do exist. However, the domestication model appears a bit too cozy as a general description of user appropriations. Silverstone emphasizes the "conservative" implications of domestication, and compares it to a process of "taming" wild devices as they are adapted to the home (Silverstone and Haddon, 1996: 60). But what of cases, such as online communication, where users do not bring technology in from the outside but act through it on the public world? What of cases, such as nuclear power, where the relevant actors are not situated in the home at all? Is "domestication," with all its conservative implications, the right term for these?

Merete Lie and Knut Sorensen (1996) have indeed attempted to extend the range of the term. Rejecting Critical Theory for failing to comprehend and inspire agency in the technical sphere, they turn to cultural studies for a more dynamic model of technical change. They hope to join domestication theory to social constructivism in a synthesis explaining the active role of users in design. But to accomplish this ambitious goal they were obliged to modify the original theory in a significant way: they "disentangled it from its location in homogeneous and relatively stable, moral economies of households" (Lie and Sorensen, 1996: 13). The results of this modification are encouraging; their book offers a number of concrete examples in which the limitations of the Silverstone's approach are overcome to some extent. But domestication in this new meaning can apparently describe such things as our relationship to nuclear power plants and hazardous chemicals (Lie and Sorensen, 1996: 12). At this point a certain doubt about the viability of the concept intrudes.

The doubt does not concern the basic thrust of the theory of user agency but merely the domestic metaphor. That metaphor connotes the narrow confines of the home however it is reformulated, and thus privileges adaptation and habituation in a way that short circuits the appeal to agency. Perhaps we can get used to nuclear power plants in our neighborhood much as we get used to a television in the dining room, but it is far from clear in what sense significant agency is involved in either case. An adequate concept of agency need not sacrifice the results of domestication research to employ a different metaphor. I have attempted to do so below in my discussion of creative appropriations of computer and medical technology. Nor are these reservations about the concept of "domestication" intended to devalue activity in the home. The point is not to distinguish appropriative acts by the scene on which they take place but rather by the consequences they portend for society at large.

I have proposed the term "democratic rationalization" to signify user interventions that challenge undemocratic power structures rooted in modern technology. With this concept I intend to emphasize the public implications of user agency. I would like to reserve it for cases that have such implications so as not to confuse it with other types of adaptations of and to technology.

Democratic rationalizations differ from domestications in Silverstone's sense in three other respects. First, they are not conservative but prefigurative; they open up a possible future rather than protecting traditional values from technology. Second, they do not represent the "moral economy of the household," but a wide range of modern concerns, including human rights, health, the environment, and the quality of work. And third, democratic rationalizations usually involve innovative communicative strategies, necessary to thematizing these concerns as public issues in a technocratic society.

The theory of democratic rationalization continues the argument of the Frankfurt School, informed by the new emphasis on agency in the technical sphere. The problem is still the struggle against technocracy and its claim to an exclusive monopoly on rationality. But the solution now is to find radical political resources immanent to technologically advanced societies. Since so much of the power structure of these societies is simply an authoritarian overlay of the technical system, change in that system can destabilize that structure.

This argument recalls Ulrich Beck's theory of the "risk society" and the associated notion of "sub-politics." The risk society "arises in... autonomized modernization processes which are blind and deaf to their own effects and threats" (Beck, et al., 1994: 6). These negative potentials of industrialism result from the one-sided pursuit of goals such as profits and growth in complete indifference to externalities and the environment. In this new situation, which Beck calls "reflexive modernization," the political is transformed. Normal politics increasingly loses its political character as it becomes a form of system management, while new "sub-political" forces emerge in the interstices of the society, contesting the consequences of reflexive modernization in many spheres, and most especially in relation to technology and the environment where the contradictions appear with particular clarity. Sub-politics, like my concept of democratic rationalization, represents a wider range of human and natural concerns the system excludes in its fragmented pursuit of mastery (Feenberg, 1991: chap. 8).

Beck concludes that were technology to free itself from the narrow military and economic institutions that now control it and to emerge as an autonomous subsystem in its own right, it would be exposed in its contingency and opened to

> fantastic constructivism, self-doubt and technology pluralism, on the one side; on the other, new negotiating and mediating institutions and democratic co-determination, where economic considerations rank below others. This would be possible only...if technology were declared an official concern—as has happened with education in the twentieth century—and financed from public means. Out of the question? It is conceivable in any case and thus a proof that technology—the quintessence of modernity—is organized in an antiquated way (Beck, et al., 1994: 28).

Counter-hegemony

The concept of democratic rationalization makes the link between cultural studies of technology and the problematic of modernity focused by Critical Theory. The issue of technocracy can now be engaged with new conceptual means that open possibilities foreclosed unilaterally by the earlier pessimistic critiques.

The middle writings of Michel Foucault and two other French thinkers, Michel de Certeau and Bruno Latour offer fruitful starting points for this revision of Critical Theory. Here I am returning to some of the same sources drawn on by cultural studies but from a rather different angle. By way of introducing the contributions of these thinkers, I will briefly discuss Foucault's method in his writings of the period of *Discipline and Punish* (1977) and the first volume of *The History of Sexuality* (1976). His approach can be summarized in four methodological principles:

1. Traditional sovereign power, such as that of a ruling monarch, must be distinguished from disciplinary and biopower exercised by a modern bureaucratic order.

2. Scientific disciplines must be studied not in terms of their relation to a universal value such as truth, but under the local horizon of the social practices, artifacts, and power relations with which they are associated.

3. The source of resistances must be sought not in what are usually called "interests," but in the structure of the power relationship itself; resistances are an immanent reflex of the exercise of power.

4. Subjugated knowledges arising in association with resistances are a possible base for a recodification of the social order.

Sovereign power is embodied in a person, for example, the king, whose actions are perceived as proceeding from a preeminent social position. In modern societies, however, power becomes detached from individual persons and even institutions. It is embodied now in practices that are in some sense prior to and founding for the subjects who wield it in empirical interactions. This agonistic conception of society transposes some of the pathos of subjectivity to practices, patterns of action that do the work human actors perform in traditional social theory. Practices organize, they control, they proliferate, and they even "subjectify"—stimulate the production of subjectivity in human beings submitted to them.

Practices of power are strategies without strategists, strategies that work against the inevitable resistance of the human materials they strive to control and form. Resistance to the strategies of power is a spontaneous dimension of the power relation itself. Practices designed to discipline human beings, to turn them into productive agents, must impose themselves on unwilling bodies through repetition, reward and punishment. The practices of biopower that aim to organize sexuality and reproduction in the interests of the state must channel and stimulate the effects they seek in conflict with an original presocial sexuality. Interestingly for a philosophy of technology, Foucault finds these various modern practices embodied in artifacts such as the Panopticon as well as in the scientific-technical discourses that accompany their deployment in modern societies.

Foucault's conception of power and resistance depersonalizes both, and detaches them from agents such as states and classes. They have now become a system out of which agents emerge. The systemic character of power makes it possible to link it with truth in new ways. A system of power reveals the world in something like the Heideggerian sense (Dreyfus, 1992). It opens a certain angle of vision and defines a corresponding realm of objects. This foundational work of power does not contradict the pursuit of truth but makes it possible by orienting research in a specific direction. Regimes of truth are power-dependent epistemic horizons that characterize particular periods and disciplines. Modern hegemonies are rooted in truth in this sense, and not in violence and display in the manner of the old sovereign powers.

To regimes of truth correspond subjugated knowledges that express the point of view of the dominated. Subjugated knowledges are "situated" in a subordinate position in the technical hierarchy. They lack the disciplinary organization of the sciences, and yet they offer access to an aspect of the truth that is the specific blind spot of these sciences. A critique of the panoptic order of modern society emerges from the subjugated standpoint of its victims. A "recodification" of the system is possible through the incorporation of the resistances articulated in subjugated knowledges. Foucault writes,

> I would say that the State consists in the codification of a whole number of power relations which render its functioning possible, and that Revolution is a different type of codification of the same relations. This implies that there are many different kinds of revolution, roughly speaking as many kinds as there are possible subversive recodifications of power relations...(Foucault, 1980: 122-123).

Logically implied but insufficiently elaborated, this notion of counterhegemony offers the hope of radical change without reliance on traditional agent-based models such as the class struggle, which Foucault believes have outlived their usefulness.

Strategies and Tactics

Michel de Certeau took Foucault's work in this period as inspiration for a variation on the same themes. In this section I will show how his modification of Foucault's position can serve the philosophy of technology.

De Certeau found games to be a useful model of society. Games define the players' range of action without determining their moves. As we will see, this metaphor can also be applied to technology, which sets up a framework of permitted and forbidden "moves" in much the way games do. The technical code is the most general rule of the game, biasing the play toward the dominant contestant.

De Certeau defines "strategies" as institutionalized controls embodied in modern social organizations such as corporations or agencies. These organizations accumulate a "capital" of power through continuous action on the members of society. The process of accumulation builds a new kind of social space, an "interiority" within which elites are able to constitute themselves as such and from out of which they act on a social "exteriority." De Certeau writes,

> I call *strategy* the calculation (or manipulation) of the balance of forces which becomes possible once a subject of will and power (a firm, an army, a city, a scientific institution) is isolatable. Strategy presupposes a place that can be circumscribed as one's *own* (*un propre*) and that can serve as the base from which to direct relations with an *exteriority* consisting of targets or threats (clients, competitors, enemies, the countryside around the town, research goals and objects, etc.)....One might call this a Cartesian gesture: circumscribing one's own in a world bewitched by the invisible powers of the Other. [It is] the gesture of scientific, political and military modernity (De Certeau, 1980: 85).

The Cartesian gesture defines a specific type of rationality, a rationality of planning and control that operates on the world from without. With de Certeau we worry less about the supposedly relativistic implications of the Foucauldian analysis of regimes of truth and focus instead on a question of more interest to philosophy of technology: the nature of the link between technological thinking and modern administration. (Still lacking, however, is an account of the role of technology itself, which I will develop in the next section.)

De Certeau also takes up the problem of resistance. Most social groups lack a strategic organizational base. They are located in the "exterior" and can only react "tactically" to strategies they cannot escape. Although they remain more or less within the framework of the dominant strategy, they respond to it with subtly deviant actions that alter its significance. Tactics thus differ from outright opposition in that they subvert the dominant codes from within by introducing various unexpected delays, combinations, and ironies into the application of strategies. "A thousand ways of *playing/outplaying the other's game*, that is to say, the space others have instituted, characterize the subtle, tenacious, resistant activity of groups which, for lack of a base, must maneuver in a network of established forces and representations" (De Certeau, 1980: 59–60).

According to de Certeau, the tension between strategies and tactics is due to the multiplicity of codes that coexist in any society. Hegemonic codes lay down the framework within which the marginal ones play a tactical role. What de Certeau calls "exorbitant" practices are the equivalent of a dominant language. Everyone must speak it, but marginal practices, like local slang, can give it a special twist. Tactics thus belong to strategies the way speech belongs to language. The technical code of society is the rule of an exorbitant practice, a syntax which is subject to unintended usages that may subvert the framework it determines. [2]

I argued at the beginning of this chapter that technocratic domination is rooted in operational autonomy. In de Certeau's terms, this would be the growth of strategic power. That power expresses itself in plans which inevitably require implementation by those situated in the tactical exteriority. But no plan is perfect; all implementation involves unplanned actions in what I call the "margin of maneuver" of those charged with carrying it out. In all technically mediated organizations margin of maneuver is at work, modifying work pace, misappropriating resources, improvising solutions to problems, and so on. Technical tactics belong to strategies as implementation belongs to planning.

---

[2] Phenomenological and situational theories of action developed for the study of interface design offer models of the difference de Certeau sketches in these reflections. (See Winograd and Flores (1987) and Suchman (1987)). However, unlike de Certeau, the authors of these theories do not generalize the distinction they make between "plans" and "situated actions" to the level of society as a whole. For more on this subject, see Feenberg (1991: chap. 5).

Margin of maneuver has no necessary political implications. It is inherently ambiguous, required for implementation in conformity with the dominant technical code, but also containing potentials incompatible with that code. Successful administration today consists in suppressing those dangerous potentials in the preservation of operational autonomy. But under some conditions, the dominated may succeed in altering the framework, forcing management to accept changes that diminish its autonomy. In this context, the claim that the technical base of the society is ambivalent means that it can be modified through tactical responses that permanently open the strategic interiority to the flow of subordinates' initiatives. This implies changes in the strategies encoded in the division of labor and technology. As I explain in the next chapter, I call this "deep democratization" to distinguish it from theories of decentralization and local control. Democratization can be conceptualized on these terms as an immanent potentiality of technologically advanced societies.

THE THIRD SYMMETRY

Actor Network Theory

De Certeau's theory of practice was developed in an intellectual milieu shared to some extent by Bruno Latour and Michel Callon, whose actor network theory I turn to now. Not surprisingly, there are intriguing similarities between these approaches. Together, they provide the basis for a theory of democratic interventions in the technical sphere.

Latour invites us to study technology as the embodiment of "programs," i.e. intentional structures with a close resemblance to de Certeau's strategies. Technical objects are not "things" in the usual sense, but nodes in a network that contains both people and devices in interlocking roles. Actor network theory argues that the social alliances in which technology is constructed are bound together by the very artifacts they create. Thus social groups do not precede and constitute technology, but emerge with it. This is another aspect of the symmetry of humans and nonhumans which, Latour believes, distinguishes his theory from the usual formulations of constructivism.

Latour argues that just as authors and readers meet on the printed page, so the builders and users of machines are joined in the application. Machines are comparable to texts because they too inscribe a "story," i.e. a prescribed sequence of events which the user initiates and undergoes.

This analogy then authorizes a semiotics of technology drawing on concepts developed in linguistics, several of which play an important role in the theory.

In the first place, Latour adapts the concept of "shifting out," or change of scene, to describe the process of "delegating" functions to humans or nonhumans through technological design. Just as characters in stories move from one space or time to another at the whim of the author, so elements of technological "programs" are shifted from one "matter" to another. In Latour's example of an automatic door opener, the imperative "close the door" is shifted out from a message posted on the wall to a spring, from the ethical to the mechanical domain.

Secondly, he adapts the distinction between the syntagmatic and paradigmatic dimensions of the phrase to sociotechnical networks. No elaborate account of this distinction is needed here. As Latour explains it, the syntagmatic dimension refers to the additive process of enrolling elements in the technical network, and the paradigmatic dimension describes the various shifts or delegations through which these elements are effectively bound together (Latour, 1992: 250-251).

Images of Resistance

Callon notes that networks are constructed by "simplifying" their members, that is, by enrolling them under a definite aspect that serves the program while ignoring other aspects that do not. In line with this notion, John Law calls network builders "heterogeneous engineers" because they manage the simplification and linking of many different types of human and nonhuman elements (Law, 1987). But, Callon adds, "the actor network should not...be confused with a network linking in some predictable fashion elements that are perfectly well defined and stable, for the entities it is composed of, whether natural or social, could at any moment redefine their identity and mutual relationships in some new way and bring new elements into the network" (Callon, 1987: 93). In short, the simplification might fail and the suppressed qualities reemerge. Latour calls the disaggregating forces the network must resist or turn aside, its "anti-program."

At one point in his account, Latour illustrates the idea of the anti-program with Frankenstein's monster. Like the objects enrolled in technical networks, the monster has an "independent life" that threatens its builder. Latour quickly turns from the "worn-out commonplace made up by bleeding-heart moralists" frightened by "autonomous" technology

(Latour, 1992: 251-252). Yet there is more to the commonplace than he admits. As we have seen, the notion of a technical system implies near total control from a center, a place of power. This pretension is belied by the analytic practice of actor network theory, much as Frankenstein's monster belied the pretensions of his creator and "redefine[d his] identity and mutual relationships." But then the image of poor Frankenstein, unable to control his monster, is not merely grist for the mill of soft-hearted culture critics. It stands for the inherent limits of technical power.

Perhaps Shelley romanticizes the problem in a way which excuses Latour's harsh judgment. Let us try another literary example, the myth of the "sorcerer's apprentice" who sets in motion a process that gets out of control. H.G. Wells composed an astonishingly prescient version of the myth in *The Food of the Gods*, a tale of two early bioengineers who invent a miracle food that causes animals and plants to grow to eight times their normal size (Wells, 1967). Sloppy experiments conducted on a farm near London result in the birth of giant wasps, rats, and even people. The trait is inheritable, and soon the world is irreversibly changed by "bigness insurgent."

In Latour's terms, the delegation of the original program to sacks, walls, and guardians broke down as rats got at the food, and the network was unexpectedly prolonged (in its syntagmatic dimension) through its nonhuman rather than its human members. Of course from the standpoint of the preexisting experimental program the network was supposed to serve, this amounts to chaos, but if one views the matter objectively, i.e. *not* from the standpoint of the two scientists and their failed strategy, the network can be seen to grow. And this makes it possible for new actors to pursue new programs.

In fact Wells shows us a new system emerging out of the elements of the old one as a result of the unforeseen breakdowns, partial disaggregation, and tactical reappropriations. Wells likes the results and so makes the products of the disaster—his "Children of the food"—new heterogeneous engineers with their own program for reestablishing order, their order, an order of giants. *The Food of the Gods* is a metaphor for the replacement of the narrow old-European world by a dynamic industrialism, but it can also serve here to illustrate a certain similarity between de Certeau's tactics and Latour's anti-programs.

System, Network, Lifeworld

In this story we have an example of the fragility of technical systems. Where the "simplification" of human subordinates breaks down, a specific type of network instability results. This has political implications which make perfect sense in de Certeau's terms. As he argues, systems are vulnerable to tactical transformation. The anti-program is thus not merely a source of disorder but can recodify the network around new programs that realize unsuspected potentialities.

To understand these potentialities, we need to return to the problem of function once again. What is the reality of this all too obvious concept that emerges spontaneously from our daily technical practice? As I will explain in more detail in chapter 9, function resembles price as a fetishistic form of objectivity. Like price, function is a relational term which we attribute to the object as a real quality. In reality, the function of any technology is relative to the organizations that create and control it and assign it a purpose. It has a function as part of a "system" in the systems-theoretic sense of the term.

Now, "system" is surely one of the slipperier concepts in social science. In one common usage, systems are defined as goal-oriented complexes of interacting elements. In the biological and social world, these appear as self-reproducing structures, such as organisms or corporations. In nature, the criteria that delimit the structure appear to be objective. We can identify internal processes, such as immunological response, that effectively distinguish an organism from its environment and even from diseases that attack it internally. Of course viruses, parasites, and cancer pose a problem for this model, but they are the exception in the biological realm rather than the rule. But the boundaries between social systems and their environments are not so sharp. Indeed, in the social realm viruses, parasites, and cancers offer fruitful metaphors to many processes of change and have often been so employed, if usually in a pejorative vein.

For example, officially the stockholders own the company and appoint a management responsible to themselves. The company as system would seem to be constituted around the intentions of its owners, embodied in system maintenance procedures by its managers. However, the official system is not the only "self-reproducing complex of interacting elements" in play. What of the workers and their union which treats the company as a very different kind of system in which management is a parasite? What of the community in which the company is located which considers it as a cancerous subsystem of a larger urban system? Are workers and community leaders mere "environment" or are they competing systematizers operating on the same terrain as management?

Of course management would like to achieve complete autonomy. It may try to sharpen the system boundaries, as it understands them, by fighting union viruses and political parasites. But in the social domain what we call a "system" is actually a series of layers that coincide at some points, diverge at others. It only looks like a coherent whole when seen from one or another limited viewpoint, corresponding to one or another of its many layers. From an objective perspective, external to any specific engagement with the company, we can reasonably ask to whom it really belongs. Its shareholders, the victims of its products, its workers, the community? And is it the same system, independent of the answer to this question? Political struggles, strikes, technical innovations, movements of capital, legislation and courts, not law-governed natural processes, decide the outcome. And very different outcomes are possible; witness the social charter of the European Community which grants rights to workers and communities unheard of in the United States.

But this is to say that social systems are very much in the eye of the beholder. Systems, as self-reproducing wholes, are fragile subsets of much more loosely organized complexes of interacting elements that may support several overlapping systemic projects. I call these larger complexes "networks." To identify these networks with the "environment" in the systems-theoretic sense of the term is to prejudge the issue of system boundaries, to privilege arbitrarily the system managers' point of view over the decentered complexity of the real world. So long as system managers are successful, this prejudgement appears reasonable.[3] But among the elements of the networks are human beings whose participation has a symbolic as well as a causal dimension. They are capable of representing the system and acting on it from out of a lifeworld it does not encompass. They may prey on the system and destroy it like bacilli in the bloodstream, but they are also capable of reorganizing the network in conflict with system managers and producing a new configuration of the resources it contains. They are, in other words, *involved* in a way that makes nonsense of the organic metaphor of living creature and environment.

---

[3] Similarly, the very possibility of scientific idealization rests on the emergence of a system standpoint that selects out a narrowly defined domain of objects and tasks. Technical disciplines are similarly narrow in scope. But the less differentiated world of real technology includes elements excluded by theory. That real world of technology is a network, not a system, but a network that encompasses systems within it. For a related discussion of this general distinction, cf. Dodier (1995: 88-91).

System managers become aware of this wider background of their activities through unintended consequences and system breakdowns that highlight incompletely controlled or integrated elements of the network. The functional translation of the problems revealed in these breakdowns is an essential step in restructuring the system. Success in this enterprise tends to obscure the fact that any given function is a selection from the full range of possibilities revealed in the breakdown, including some which contradict system maintenance.

This wider range of "potentialities" may include positive elements that can only be systematized through new or modified technological designs, or even through the creation of new organizations with new leaders and goals. Such radical transitions cannot be conceptualized from a purely functional point of view, always relative to a given system and its line of development.

In sum, the system concept reflects the spontaneous representations of owners, managers or organizers in charge of an apparatus that implements their program. They have a natural tendency to bound the apparatus conceptually in terms of their strategies, and to consider everything which is not under their control as "environment." But this teleological understanding of systems violates Latour's principle of symmetry. The intentions of managers are no more fundamental than the vagaries of people (and things) enrolled unintentionally in the network of which the "system" is a subset. A network theory of the technical politics in which these unofficial actors engage needs new categories that do not depend on the self-understanding of managers.

Chief among these new categories is a third principle of symmetry I will add to the symmetry of successful and unsuccessful theories and devices, introduced by constructivism, and the symmetry of humans and nonhumans, proposed by actor network theory. We must supplement these with the symmetry of program and anti-program, at least in those cases where the anti-program is taken up by actors able to build a new system around it. This third symmetry is the basis of a democratic politics of technological rationalization. If sociology of technology can recognize it as more than a deviation from system norms, a much needed theory of the democratic politics of technology can be created. In the concluding section of this chapter, I will sketch some starting points for such a theory.

DEMOCRATIC RATIONALIZATIONS

Technical Micropolitics

The micropolitics of technology gives rise to movements so different from traditional politics they are easily misinterpreted. Neither ideologies nor clienteles hold them together, but the very technical networks they challenge. The goals of these struggles are also new. Democratization of modern technically mediated organizations is not fundamentally about the distribution of wealth nor even formal administrative authority, but concerns the structure of communicative practices.

Who are the public actors involved in this new type of politics? Not citizens as such, but individuals who are directly affected by a particular technical decision. Only in the local situation are nonprofessionals likely to be motivated to learn enough about a technical issue to intervene. Lay activists who are bound together by a shared problem such as a threat to their neighborhood or an incurable chronic illness develop a situated knowledge as they confront the issues. They may provoke technical controversies in an attempt to influence public opinion.

This has been the main approach of environmental movements which, over and over, have begun in local protests and spread from there to shape public opinion and change laws and regulations. Normally only technical professionals would pay attention to the industrial processes environmentalists challenge, but today we believe in the right of the public to prevent such processes from doing harm. To be a citizen is to be a *potential* victim. This is why information plays such a critical role in environmental politics: the key struggles are often decided in the communicative realm by making private information public, revealing secrets, introducing controversy into supposedly neutral scientific fields, and so on. Once corporations and government agencies are forced to operate under public scrutiny, it becomes much more difficult to support dangerous technologies such as nuclear power.

In other cases, professionals themselves may open what Arnold Pacey calls an "innovative dialogue" with those affected by their activities (Pacey, 1983: chap. 8). We have seen that this was the goal of much of the French middle strata in the May Events. Similar struggles were waged over a much longer period by radical professionals in the United States with, unfortunately, less support from below and little success (Hoffman, 1989). In Scandinavia an attempt was made to institutionalize innovative dialogue through union-sponsored experiments in user participation in design (Ehn, 1989). The literature on agricultural aid to the Third World is full of similar accounts of collaboration between experts and end users of the technical systems they devise (Richards, 1985).

In still other cases users appropriate technologies creatively, re-inventing existing devices through innovative applications. The computer field offers striking illustrations of this new politics of technology. Progress of a generalized sort in speed, power, and memory goes on apace while corporate planners struggle with the question of what it is all for. The institutional separation of innovation from social demand has gone so far that technical development finds no obvious path from engineering idea to marketable application. Instead, R&D opens branches, and the determination of the "right" branch is not within the competence of engineers because it is not inscribed in their narrowly conceived field of activity. This is the context in which amateur hackers and ordinary users were able to transform the computer from an information processor into a communications medium. Users altered the design of the French Minitel system and the Internet through a posteriori interventions, adding human communication functions to systems that were originally destined to handle data (Charon, 1987).

Technical controversies, innovative dialogues, and creative appropriations such as these have become inescapable features of contemporary political life. They open technical issues to general democratic debate and lay out the parameters for official "technology assessment" (Cambrosio and Limoges, 1991). I develop these examples in more detail in the remainder of this section.

Controversy: Environmentalism

Ecological networks emerge into public view, and indeed are often constituted as objects of science, on the borders of technological systems. There, where unintended consequences meet citizen outrage, a new kind of politics has been born, and this in turn has provided a stimulus to the study of the subtle interconnections of people and things.

From the human standpoint, ecological issues are primarily medical, but from the standpoint of industry the stakes are the autonomy of enterprise. Since the earliest forms of regulation, autonomy has had a price. Those who use potentially dangerous technologies have been forced to conform with technical codes that prescribe a certain minimum level of protection of nature and human health. At first regulation is generally experienced as an external intrusion, as it was by steamboat owners in the case of the bursting boilers. But managers eventually learn that they can best preserve the integrity of their system by defining its boundaries narrowly to limit violations of these codes.

Unfortunately, there are other more devious ways of preserving autonomy. Control of the risky elements in the network and control of information about the network can be traded off "paradigmatically" for a time in public debate. Hiding a health hazard, or better yet defining it out of existence, and removing it physically, are functionally equivalent strategies from a systems perspective at least for a definite period. And, centralized technical decision making, working to fulfill simple mandates such as profits or growth, generates strong pressure to narrow the range of concerns incorporated into design, if necessary by controlling information to protect system boundaries (de la Bruhèze, 1992: 141).

This observation indicates the ambiguous role of technocratic management of environmental and related issues such as occupational health and product safety. On the one hand, technocracy brings expertise to bear on the problems, but on the other hand, monopolizing information offers a cheap alternative to actually solving them. Technocracy is thus not the boon to technical advance it claims to be, but on the contrary is often guilty of obstructing the innovations needed to solve problems that it does its best to hide.

Information control strategies come up against the widespread access to expertise and publicity in democratic societies. Controversies draw attention to violations of the rights and health of those affected by the enterprise. As information control becomes more difficult, boundary-drawing must be shifted out to the level of devices and procedures and the problems solved at the technical level. This has two principal effects. On the one hand, crude simplifications that threaten conformity with the code may eventually have to be abandoned, the complex and uncontrollable character of certain elements admitted, and substitutes found. In favorable cases advances may resolve the problems without loss of efficiency. On the other hand, the resort to technical solutions tends to discredit earlier alibis for indifference to the problems, not just by refuting them but by revealing them as ideological. Who today believes that the accident at Three Mile Island proved the *safety* of nuclear power as industry advocates claimed at the time? Who does not see in this claim a self-serving excuse for a deplorable indifference to safety?

Innovative Dialogue and Participatory Design

The agents of such transformations of networks are an interesting lot, insufficiently studied by sociology of technology. Foucault called them "specific intellectuals" to distinguish them from the type of literary intellectual who traditionally spoke in the name of universal values (Foucault, 1980: 127-129). Specific intellectuals constitute a new class of heterogeneous engineers whose tactical labors extend the recognized boundaries of networks, often against the will of managers, through initiating innovative dialogues with a public audience (Pacey, 1983: chap. 8).

In some cases the very same innovators who create the technology later denounce its effects and subvert the boundary-drawing strategies of corporations or agencies employing their inventions. The most famous such instance was the atom bomb. It was built by scientists with the idea that it could be used like an ordinary weapon in World War II, and indeed it was so used during the brief period when the US was the only nuclear power. The military wished to retain this reassuring conception of the bomb. But, anticipating the arms race and its apocalyptic implications, the bomb's inventors redefined it as a threat to the survival of Americans. The scientists' movement established itself as the representative of a larger planetary network encompassing not only bombs and Russians, but bombs, Russians and Americans as well. To influence policy, scientists published journals and organized movements of ordinary citizens concerned about nuclear war (Smith, 1965).

Environmental disputes benefit from similar defections and splits among biologists, and similarly point out the illusory nature of the reassuring system boundaries managers attempt to draw. Environmentalists bring out contradictions between different technical codes—medical, engineering, agricultural, etc.—while redefining networks to include hitherto excluded members. Where excluded members mobilize, political movements of a new type emerge that promise to create a lively technical public sphere. As we saw in chapter 3, scientists often play a central role in these movements, awakening communities to unnoticed dangers and formulating local knowledge in a technical language that has legitimacy in the public sphere.

These examples generalize Pacey's "innovative dialogue" far beyond its intended range. He is interested in the impact of lay people on specific technical innovations. The nuclear and environmental cases are less about innovation in the usual sense than about the emergence of new types of post-technocratic relationships between experts and the public affected by their activities. But these relationships are turning out to be an important source of innovation in the environmental arena. I therefore feel justified in coopting Pacey's concept for my purposes.

His own examples come primarily from the field of development aid. There cross-cultural interactions overlie the already complicated relationship between technical experts and lay people. Much like those unfriendly computer interfaces that emerge straight from an engineering environment alien to ordinary users, development projects are typically conceived far from the site of application in terms of a technocratic culture alien to local peoples. The results can be disastrous. But unlike computer interface designers, who usually do not live with the victims of their mistakes, development experts are sent out to implement the projects they design. They are sometimes so disturbed by what they see, they seek local help to modify and adapt their projects. Narratives of these incidents generally follow a pattern: from initial failure to collaboration to at least temporary success. Thereafter two outcomes are possible: either the new approach is marginalized as standard approaches to modernization finally prevail through heavier investments or more effective suppression of local resistances; or—more positively—what is learned from the locals is internalized in the modernizing technical code.

The first outcome is illustrated by a project which sent Norwegian boat builders to Tanzania to teach coastal peoples how to make European-style boats. "This ill-fated project ended with the beaches of Mbegani and Bagamoyo strewn with rusting unused boats that local fisherman could not repair because they lacked the necessary equipment and supplies" (Swantz and Tripp, 1996: 53-54). Eventually, one of the Norwegian experts turned to skilled local boat builders for ideas on how to proceed. Together they modified a traditional design, substituting planks for the carved hull and improving its size and stability. After some years of success, the authorities managed to introduce more modern designs and the early innovative dialogue was interrupted, not without offering an example of fruitful collaboration.

The second, more promising pattern is exemplified by the Green Revolution according to some experts on African agriculture. One writer describes how early hybrid seeds developed under ideal conditions failed to pay off on African farms. The results were better with "farmer-managed trials, where farmers are allowed to try out the technology themselves, to see how it performs in their social and economic circumstances" (Harrison, 1987: 100). Another Africa specialist concludes from many examples that "the research effort must be a partnership between 'formal' science on the one hand and 'community ecological knowledge' on the other" (Richards, 1985: 141).[4]

Similar experiments have taken place in Western industry with mixed results. The most famous and best documented examples of such "participatory design" occurred in Scandinavia, where a strong union movement and sympathetic government provides a background of support. The much studied UTOPIA project in Sweden brought software engineers together with newspaper workers to develop innovative ways of computerizing the printing process. Although the software worked at its place of origin, it could not be sold elsewhere and the project did not become the model its originators had envisaged. Nevertheless, the principle of effective communication and collaboration was established and continues to interest both theoreticians of technology and some engineers, particularly in computer software design (Ehn, 1989; Sclove, 1995: chap. 11; Winograd, 1995: 118ff).

Innovative dialogue and participatory design promise a fundamental solution to the conflict between lay and expert. Just such a solution was prefigured in the May Events as members of professions and bureaucracies appealed to the people to work with them for deep democratization. In the long run, a technology continually revised and advanced through innovative dialogue would incorporate different values reflecting a broader range of interests and a more democratic vision. Undoubtedly, there are many obstacles to this outcome, but it is pointless to object a priori that experts are so bound to the alien project of "Western *episteme*," they can only distort the will of the laity (Marglin, 1996: 240). Such essentialist readings of the situation create an insoluble dilemma where there is an abundance of evidence for the possibility of collaboration and compromise.

Creative Appropriation: Reinventing Computers and Medicine

In an earlier book, *Alternative Modernity*, I devoted chapters to the discussion of democratic rationalization as it relates to computers and medicine.

---

[4] But some observers are not so sanguine. A specialist in Indian agriculture deplores the crude imposition of inappropriate Western methods and, while not disagreeing with the idea of innovative dialogue, complains that its time has not yet come (Visvanathan, 1996: 337).

These cases illustrate the power of users literally to "reinvent" the technologies with which they are engaged (Rogers, 1995: 174-180). Let me briefly summarize my conclusions as examples of the role of creative appropriations in the new politics of technology.

In the early 1980s, the French telephone company distributed millions of free terminals called Minitels, designed to look and feel like an adjunct to the domestic telephone, but intended to access information services (Feenberg, 1995: chap. 7). The telephonic disguise suggested to some users that they ought to be able to talk to each other on the network. Soon the Minitel underwent a further redefinition at their hands as they employed it for anonymous on-line chatting with other users in the search for amusement, companionship, and sex. Users "hacked" the network in which they were inserted and altered its functioning, introducing human communication where only the centralized distribution of information had been planned.

The design of the Minitel invited communications applications which the company's engineers had not intended when they set about improving the flow of information in French society. Those applications, in turn, connoted the Minitel as a means of personal encounter, the very opposite of the rationalistic project for which it was originally designed. The "cold" computer became a "hot" new medium.[5] A somewhat similar story could be told about the Internet although in this case there was no central control, but rather a cultural shift that occurred unexpectedly among the user community.

Here we have a dramatic illustration of the "interpretative flexibility" of technology. A concatenation of devices configured by its designers as the solution to one problem—the distribution of information—was perceived by its users as the solution to quite another problem—human communication. The new interpretation of the technology was soon incorporated into its structure through design changes and, ultimately, through a change in its very definition. Today, it would not occur to someone describing the principal functionalities of the computer to omit its role as a communications medium although communications applications were regarded as marginal by most experts only twenty years ago.

---

[5] There is no doubt an obscure connection between these events and the May Events of 1968, mediated by the "sexual revolution" which followed the defeat of the political revolution. As one former revolutionary become computer consultant put it, "In France telematic discourse has replaced political discourse."

At issue in this transformation is not just the computer's narrowly conceived technical function, but the very nature of the advanced society it makes possible. Are we citizens of an Information Age, rational consumers hungry for data, using computers to pursue strategies of personal optimization? Or are we postmodern individuals emerging from the breakdown of institutional and sentimental stability in a society fragmented "into flexible networks of language games" (Lyotard, 1979: 34)? In this case computer technology is not merely the servant of some predefined social purpose; it is an environment within which a way of life is elaborated.[6]

Just as a technocratic conception of the computer tends to occlude its communicative potentialities, so in medicine a parallel overemphasis on technique evokes new types of resistances. Today caring functions of medicine have become mere side effects of treatment, which is itself understood in exclusively technical terms. Patients become objects, more or less "compliant" to management by physicians. It was this system that was destabilized by the demands of the thousands of AIDS patients who flooded it in the 1980s (Feenberg, 1995: chap. 5; Epstein, 1996).

Experimental treatment was the key issue. Clinical research is one way in which a highly technologized medical system can care for those it cannot yet cure. But until quite recently access to medical experiments was severely restricted by paternalistic concern for patients' welfare. AIDS patients were finally able to change that. At the time their disease was first diagnosed, they belonged to social networks mobilized around gay rights that paralleled the networks of contagion in which they were caught; not only were they already networked, they were accustomed to creating controversy. Instead of participating in medicine individually as objects of a technical practice, they challenged it collectively and turned it to new purposes. Eventually, the FDA opened an innovative dialogue with AIDS activists and placed them on important regulatory committees (Epstein, 1996: 284ff). This struggle represents a counter-tendency to the technocratic organization of medicine, an attempt to recover its symbolic dimension and caring functions through democratic intervention.

---

[6] I will be returning to the question of human communication by computer in the context of my discussion of Albert Borgmann's work in chapter 8.

These cases illustrate an interesting pattern. Medical experimentation was defined in terms of the interests of scientific research and industrial product testing. The chief ethical problem it acknowledged was the protection of subjects from abuse and exploitation. The demands of the terminally ill for access to experimental drugs had no status. The French videotex system similarly emphasized professional interests such as access to data. Users' desire to communicate with each other was ignored. AIDS patients and network users intervened in each case to accommodate the system to excluded interests. As patients gained access to experiments, FDA regulations and experimental designs were forced to change. Similarly, the Minitel was transformed in response to its unexpected use for communication.

But are such movements truly emancipatory? Do they not simply deepen our involvement with technology in accord with the dystopian logic of modernity? The protest against dystopia draws its justification from the necessity of protecting certain dimensions of human life from technization. And it is true that advanced societies enroll their members in ever wider technical networks which, as dystopian pessimists claim, do indeed constrain behavior significantly. But absolute opposition to technology leaves no room for practical criticism and reform. Even as technology expands its reach, the networks are themselves exposed to transformation by the individuals they enroll. Human beings still represent the unrealized potential of their technologies. Their tactical resistances to established designs can impose new values on technical institutions and create a new type of modern society. Instead of a technocracy in which technology everywhere trumps human communication, we may yet build a democratic society in which technical advance serves communicative advance.

This is the essence of the new democratic politics of technology. The emphasis on communication in the environmental, AIDS and Minitel examples reveals the site of this new politics. Indeed, the role of communication in design can serve as a touchstone of democratic politics in the technological age. This is why I have been at pains to work out the relation between my position and Habermas's communication theory, despite the fact that he ignores technology. My critique of the Habermasian approach is developed in chapter 7.

But is it meaningful to talk about technology as more or less democratic? It might be objected that the argument so far merely shows that many types of human action play a role in technological development, a conclusion that is hardly revolutionary and which applies equally to development in domains we do not associate with democracy, such as sports, language, and religion. It is time now to justify the phrase "politics of technology" which I have used repeatedly in the course of my argument.

Part II.

DEMOCRATIC RATIONALIZATION

6. Democratizing Technology

TECHNOLOGY AND POWER

Technology is power in modern societies, a greater power in many domains than the political system itself. The masters of technical systems, corporate and military leaders, physicians and engineers, have far more control over patterns of urban growth, the design of dwellings and transportation systems, the selection of innovations, our experience as employees, patients, and consumers, than all the electoral institutions of our society put together.

But, if this is true, technology should be considered as a new kind of legislation, not so very different from other public decisions (Winner, 1995). The technical codes that shape our lives reflect particular social interests to which we have delegated the power to decide where and how we live, what kinds of food we eat, how we communicate, are entertained, healed, and so on. The legislative authority of technology increases constantly as it becomes more and more pervasive. But if technology is so powerful, why don't we apply the same democratic standards to it we apply to other political institutions? By those standards the design process as it now exists is clearly illegitimate.

Unfortunately, the obstacles to technical democracy are considerable and growing. They include the technocracy, which offers persuasive arguments for passivity. This vitiates all aspects of democratic life, but it is particularly worrisome in the emerging technical public sphere which contends directly with technocratic power without the benefit of democratic forms and traditions to maintain at least a facade of participation. The very right of the public to involve itself in technical matters is constantly called into question. In the technical sphere, it is commonly said, legitimacy is a function of efficiency rather than of the will of the people, or rather, efficiency *is* the will of the people in modern societies dedicated above all to material prosperity.

Political theory has yet to come to terms with these problems and often parrots technocratic alibis for undemocratic procedures in what are in fact contentious fields, such as medicine, transportation, urban design, and computerization of work, education, and other institutions. Meanwhile, we are treated to interminable and increasingly scholastic debates over such questions as the ultimate grounds, if any, of political obligation. Yet it is in the technical fields that the conditions for the exercise of rights are laid down and the good life effectively defined. As Langdon Winner writes,

> As our society adopts one sociotechnical system after another it answers some of the most important questions that political philosophers have ever asked about the proper order of human affairs. Should power be centralized or dispersed? What is the best size for units of social organization? What constitutes justifiable authority in human associations? Does a free society depend upon social uniformity or diversity? What are appropriate structures and processes of public deliberation and decision making? For the past century or longer our responses to such questions have often been instrumental ones, expressed in an instrumental language of efficiency and productivity, physically embodied in human/machine systems that seem to be nothing more than ways of providing goods and services (Winner, 1986: 49).

Admittedly, the reluctance of democratic theorists to discuss technology, much less to incorporate it into political theory, is not much abated by the anti-modern rhetoric of a few highly visible critics of technology. Nor do the wild projections of uncritical enthusiasts alter the scholarly inclination to ignore the whole technology business as a mare's nest. A much more nuanced approach is needed to bring the democratic theorists out of hiding and to involve them in the discussion.

COMMUNITARIAN DEMOCRACY

In the first part of this book, I argued that recent movements for technological change emerged within the context of the political Left. Thus it is not surprising that anti-technocratic movements of students and workers, like environmental movements, are often associated with the traditional Left critique of political representation. Concepts such as "self-management" and "participatory democracy" have been promoted as direct democratic alternatives to the prevailing political system. Motivating this preference for direct democracy is opposition to alienation, both capitalist and technocratic. But these movements are also haunted by a tension between their populism and the unavoidable reliance on expertise in any modern society. While a few activists hope for the end of specialization and a return to more primitive social arrangements compatible with pure direct democracy, most seek an uneasy compromise with the existing systems of representation. This approach converges with that of some recent democratic theory.

Political theorists have always been divided over the issue of direct versus representative democracy. The advocates of direct democracy, such as Rousseau, remind us of the importance of public participation, but it is the mainstream theories of representative democracy that have influenced actual political arrangements. Nevertheless, the argument for direct democracy is simple and compelling: representatives substitute themselves for the "people" and pervert their will. True personal freedom and independence can only be realized through active participation. Representation, even at its best, diminishes the citizens by confiscating their agency.

In response to such arguments, democratic theory usually pays lip service to the desirability of a lively public sphere. However, the fact that such a public sphere is, in the context of representative theory, an informal requirement of full democracy leads to a peculiar ambiguity: the constitutional conditions that make public participation possible also protect the privately owned mass media which everywhere substitute themselves for discussion and social action. Disarmed by its emphasis on representation and the central role of majorities in electoral politics, conventional democratic theory tends to devalue or ignore actual public participation by smaller numbers and tacitly to accept the mass mediated shadow for the substance of public life.

There has been a reaction against this impoverished version of democratic theory in recent years which has led to a reevaluation of participatory democracy. The new focus on participation is a more thoughtful version of the populism of the 1960s. The issue is no longer direct democracy versus representation. It is difficult to imagine an alternative to representation today. Even Rousseau believed that direct democracy was only possible in a small-scale setting such as a single city: Geneva was his model and at the time its population numbered a few thousand. Despite its obvious defects, representation is required wherever distances and large populations conspire against direct face-to-face deliberation. The contemporary response to this difficulty is to call for the multiplication of direct democratic forums in the context of a representative political system. The aim is to show, as Frank Cunningham puts it, that "different degrees of direct and representative practices should be regarded as complementary rather than exclusive, global alternatives" (Cunningham, 1987: 47). In formulations like this little remains of the ideal of direct democracy except its critique of the bureaucratic and procedural formalism of the modern state. But that is quite a bit, after all.

One of the most prominent advocates of the new populism is Benjamin Barber. Barber argues for a theory of "strong democracy," by which he means a participatory politics that relies primarily on local collective action (Barber, 1984). He describes the prevailing liberal democracy as "thin" by contrast. Thin democracy is mainly concerned with protecting individual rights and as a result it tends to demobilize and privatize the community. Only reinvigorated communities can arrest the slide of modern society into media-manipulated passivity. They must provide the scene for democratic learning processes and character formation. The electoral system has its uses but there is no way to delegate the experience of political participation which is essential to a truly democratic society. Thus Barber is not opposed to representation, he just believes it insufficient by itself to support democratic values and goals (Barber, 1984: xv).

Barber's theory offers a context for the sorts of movements discussed in the last chapter. All too often, public interventions into technology are dismissed as nonpolitical or, worse yet, undemocratic because they mobilize only small minorities. Such movements never satisfy thin democracy which emphasizes rights and representation to the exclusion of the central role of citizen action. Barber's strong democracy gets us closer to an adequate account. He is concerned with agency because of its importance in shaping the citizenry. Democratic interventions into technology, which frequently take a populist form, would seem to fit right in. However, Barber scarcely mentions technology, and his notion of leadership in a strong democratic society sidesteps the specifically technical problems of management and expertise. This lacuna is particularly apparent in his short discussion of workers' self-management, but it needs to be addressed in many domains, in medicine, education, urbanism, and so on (Barber, 1984: 305).

Richard Sclove has tried to rectify that oversight with a well developed defense of strong democracy in the technical sphere (Sclove, 1995: chap. 3). Like Barber, he does not advocate dismantling representative structures, but rather supplementing them with participatory institutions. Also, like Barber, he argues for increasing the autonomy of local communities and devolving as much authority on them as possible.

What he adds to Barber's argument is the notion that this is not merely a matter of political arrangements but also requires appropriate technology. It is the combination of these themes that Sclove sees as his basic contribution: "The theory of democracy and technology developed here contrasts with predecessor theories that emphasize either broadened participation in decision making or else evolving technologies that support democratic social relations, but that do not integrate these procedural and substantive concerns" (Sclove, 1995: 32-33).

Sclove argues for adjusting technological design to the requirements of strong democratic community. He suggests that design criteria be open to public discussion and decision. This technology-conscious revision of the idea of strong democracy draws support from some of the same phenomena discussed in the previous chapter, especially from the movement for participatory design which he analyzes at length as a harbinger of a different technological future compatible with democratic values (Sclove, 1995: chapter 11).

It is not just that user participation in design responds to the democratic ideal of widening opportunities to intervene in public life. Still more important for Sclove is the expected impact of lay participation on the elitist culture and design criteria of the technical professions. Here Sclove's argument converges with my own. We agree that where the public is involved in technological design, it will likely favor advances that enlarge opportunities to participate in the future over alternatives that enhance the operational autonomy of technical personnel.

But there are still problems with the populist approach. When technology is factored into the political equation, agency, representation, and locality all take on a new aspect that does not quite fit the strong democratic framework. For example, in modern technological societies the "people" are not just locally defined. They are also fragmented into subgroups organized by specific technical mediations. For the most part they can only act in the technical sphere through those subgroups, whether they be factory or clerical workers, students, patients, or soldiers. The geographically bounded units of traditional politics may eventually integrate the various technically mediated subgroups through legal or regulatory decisions. But usually where politics in the familiar sense of the term is involved at all, it draws the conclusions of an initial round of struggle that follows the links in technical networks. Unfortunately, all too often the fragmentation of technical publics renders them politically impotent and things never get this far.

The significance of this situation was already recognized by John Dewey, whose early articulation of the problems of combining participation and representation remain pertinent today. Indeed, on technology Barber's position represents a regression with respect to Dewey who, already in the 1920s argued for something like strong democracy, fully conscious of the difficulties posed by the "machine age." Dewey saw that the extreme mobility of a modern society was destructive of traditional forms of local community. Meanwhile, the new links being forged by the advancing technical system were still inarticulate. Dewey described the dilemma as follows:

> Indirect, extensive, enduring and serious consequences of conjoint and interacting behavior call a public into existence having a common interest in controlling these consequences. But the machine age has so enormously expanded, multiplied, intensified and complicated the scope of the indirect consequences, have formed such immense and consolidated unions in action, on an impersonal rather than a community basis, that the resultant public cannot identify and distinguish itself (Dewey, 1980: 126).

Dewey hoped that the free and cosmopolitan communication made possible by modern technology would to some extent mitigate this problem and revitalize local community. But the two terms of the dilemma—large-scale technical systems as the form of our technological future, and local community as the site of democratic deliberation—remained fixed for him.[1] Sclove's solution to the problem is more daring. Since we have now gone well beyond Dewey's rather uncritical confidence in science and technology, and have accepted their underdetermined, contingent character, why not decide politically that they be redesigned to fit local control? Sclove is not foolish enough to want to get rid of all large-scale systems, but he does believe that vastly increased local self-reliance lies in a technically feasible future (Sclove, 1995: 128). Hence his "democratic design criterion" F: "Seek relative self-reliance. Avoid technologies that promote dependence and loss of autonomy" (Sclove, 1995: 98).[2]

---

[1] For more on Dewey's theory of technology and community, see Hickman (1990).

[2] For a critique of decentralization politics that also contains an appreciation of its motives, see Winner (1986: chap. 5).

This ambitious solution to the incompatibility of technical and democratic forms is related to other problems with representation. Popular action in the technical sphere always presupposes a background of accomplishments embodied in specialized knowledge and technical leadership. Technical experts are not chosen by the people, but achieve their position through training and administrative procedures. Past popular action informs their traditions and culture, and insures that they serve many interests in carrying out their professional tasks, but present public participation generally comes from outside technical institutions.

Experts often resist these external interventions as undemocratic and claim to be the true representatives of a universal human interest in efficiency already embodied in their technical culture. In chapter 4 I challenged this view as a philosophy of technology, but it is also the legitimating basis of modern technical administration. And given the enormous authority administration wields over so many aspects of life, it certainly needs a legitimating basis of some sort.

But in reality, who or what does it represent? Must we choose between accepting administrative claims to universality or rejecting administration itself as a form of arbitrary domination? Sclove attempts to finesse this choice with a call for redesigning the technical infrastructure for local control, but what if we find this path of technical evolution implausible? Would we then have to conclude that public interventions into technology are either incompatible with modernity or fundamentally *undemocratic*.

This is the argument of pluralists such as Rein de Wilde who reject populism as a peculiarly American expression of the "democratic sublime" (de Wilde, 1997). In his view the most authentic form of representation is electoral and the subordination of technical and administrative personnel to normal parliamentary government is the only possible "democratization" of technology. Clearly, a far more developed account of the problem of representation is required to answer such arguments.

TIME, SPACE, AND REPRESENTATION

The problem we are up against has to do with the nature of representation in the technical sphere. If technology is political and its design a kind of legislation, then surely it must represent interests much as do ordinary political decisions and laws. But technical representation will be different from the kinds of electoral representation with which we are familiar just to the extent that the medium of technology is different from law. So far theorists of technical democratization have not directly addressed these differences. This may be one reason they have had little success in interesting political theorists in technology. If the issue of technical democratization is only approached within the populist framework, it is as easily dismissed as populism, which does not have a particularly wide audience in political theory.

As we have seen, the spatial parameters of societies have always been considered determining for the form of their governmental institutions. The face-to-face authority of the tribe or the assembly in earlier times gives way to the authority of the monarch or elected officials in large-scale societies. The extent of a territory is the measure of its inhabitants' dependence on political representation. As the global society outruns the attention and communication potentials of the assembled citizens, a correlated local sphere emerges as its complement. Representation is organized around territorial units which are small enough to reflect common interests that engage the concern and animate the discussions of local citizens. The representative is the bearer of these local concerns, responsible as an individual to the citizens. The representative's duty is to carry a message, to testify for the constituents, either for their real will or the ideal will postulated by the representative on moral or other grounds.

But space does not play the same role for technical authority. No matter how large the society, if its basic technologies are simple, they remain under individual control. Even where a few strategic technologies, such as irrigation, are controlled from a center, that control is generally not a material but a symbolic power base. It is doubtful that the farmers of ancient Mesopotamia obeyed because they feared the water being shut off; more likely, mastery of water manifested the divinity of their rulers and made obedience second nature. In a sense, then, premodern societies enjoyed a kind of direct democracy in the technical sphere where ordinary people controlled their own tools.

In an advanced technological society, this is no longer the case. The change has something to do with the new role of time in the technologically mediated social system. The accumulation of specialized knowledge and expertise implies a necessary specialization of personnel and function. The direct creation and appropriation of technology by users, characteristic of premodern societies, is no longer possible. Thus here it is temporal parameters rather than spatial ones that determine the shape of authority.

The technical system is not of course entirely closed. It is permeated by social influences which show up in designs that, as I have argued in chapters 4 and 5, have political implications. Design comes to reflect a heritage of properly technical choices biased by past circumstances. Thus in a very real sense, there is a technical historicity; technology is the bearer of a tradition that favors specific interests and specific ideas about the good life.

But unlike the spatial parameters of democracy, these temporal ones are not obvious. As we also saw in chapter 5, the differentiation of specializations gives specialists the illusion of pure, rational autonomy. This illusion masks a more complex reality. In reality, they represent the interests which presided over the underdetermined technical choices that lie in the past of their profession. The results are eventually embodied in technical codes which in turn shape the training of technical personnel. We have, in a sense, passed from an open direct democracy of technique to a covert representative form. But in what does that representation consist? How and by whom are local interests and decisions translated into technical codes capable of operating across time and space? Is there an equivalent in the technical domain of the global/local dichotomy and the associated notion of testimony?

Clearly, spatial locality is not primary. Labor unions have discovered that to their dismay as corporations use high-technology communication and transportation to ship production beyond their reach. Thus even where the technical "global" can still be understood in geographic terms, its identification with the entire surface of the planet renders local geographic units impotent to influence it. The spatialized global/local dichotomy on the basis of which political representation is organized cannot be directly transposed to the technical sphere.

The emergence of large-scale technical systems suggests an alternative principle of organization: the technical network itself. We have seen in chapter 5 how the network serves as the privileged site of protest and controversy. And of course we are all enrolled in so many networks, medical, urban, productive, and so on, that our various technical personas cover much of the political landscape.

If the technical "global" is taken to refer to the larger networks, then its "local" correlate becomes the basic institutional settings in which tactical resistances emerge. These may not have much relation to geographic localities. As patients, for example, the individuals may meet at a hospital, or even online as I will explain in chapter 8. As urban citizens, they may be united along the corridor of a proposed—and contested—freeway. Wholly new types of alliances can follow the pathways of the network between, for example, Nike wearers in the US and Asian shoemakers. Sometimes the usual relations of government and citizenry are reversed, and the creation of a government regulatory agency calls into being a subgroup of clients who, in acting together, acquire a technological surrogate of traditional citizenship (Frankenfeld, 1992: 464).

Where the individuals deliberate and act in those "local" technical settings, they reenact in the technical domain the very sort of populist participation so prized by advocates of strong democracy when it appears in local geographical settings. True, that deliberation may be highly mediated, and the action may be unexpected from a traditional standpoint, as in the case of consumer boycotts, but these interventions are the equivalent for a technologically advanced society of geographically local action in earlier times.

PARTICIPANT INTERESTS

What is it that unites the individuals in these new networked locales? Insofar as they are enrolled together, they have what I call "participant interests" in the design and configuration of the activities in which the networks engage them (Feenberg, 1995: 104ff). The concept of participant interests refers to the diverse personal impacts of technical activity: side-effects, both beneficial and harmful, social preconditions and consequences, effects on life conditions, and so on. Some of these are familiar, especially as they are articulated by unions in the sphere of production. As nodes in the technical networks of production, workers have participant interests in such things as health and safety on the job, educational qualifications and skill levels, and so on. Parallel phenomena characterize every type of network participation in every technical domain, although the emphasis differs from one domain to another.

Labor, for example, focuses most sharply on the impact of technology on job security, not an important consideration in other domains. Indeed, the labor movement is a rather limited case of technical politics, although it often functions as an implicit model of struggle over technology. The limits of this case are due to the peculiar evolution of the American labor movement, which agreed after World War II that most of the social and human context of production would lie outside the legitimate sphere of negotiation. Labor issues thus tend to be formulated in a way which abstracts from many of the most important implications of technology for workers.

This limitation dovetails with the tendency of economics and applied ethics to treat technology as a given, a constant, against the background of which individuals pursue their welfare and face ethical choices. But, as Hans Radder writes, "What is at least as important [as 'moral choices,' 'adverse side effects,' and 'costs and benefits'] in a normative evaluation of (proposed) technologies is the *quality* of the natural, personal, and sociocultural world in which the people involved will have to live in order to successfully realize the technologies in question" (Radder, 1996: 150). World-defining technical struggles emerge around these considerations. They are the technical equivalent of major legislative acts. As they become more commonplace, the democratic significance of technical politics will surely become clearer.

There is no more compelling example of this phenomenon than the movement of disabled people for barrier-free design (Sclove, 1995: 194-195). This is a case where a very simple design change, the sidewalk ramp, transforms the daily life of a large population. That design change was excluded by standard codes so long as disabilities were regarded as private problems. When the disabled finally demanded facilities for mainstream social participation, this immediately impacted many technical arrangements. The changed technical code of sidewalk construction is semantically "pure" of the ethical considerations that justify it and refers only to cement, but it does in fact represent a definite social group and its demands for a more accommodating world.

The example of the struggle over AIDS discussed in the last chapter is a more complex case, revealing how life inside a technical network gives rise to participant interests in changing a technically constituted world. Patient demands for a generalization of experimentation were a way of accommodating medicine to the needs of the terminally ill. Note that those demands involved significant modifications of the technical rules under which experiments were conducted. The use of placebos, the requirement that subjects have no prior history of experimental participation, and the limitation of participation to statistical minimums were some of the arrangements that were challenged.

These challenges were issued on ethical grounds, although they are hardly matters of right in the strong sense in which the Nuremberg Code defined absolute claims human subjects could make regardless of cost and consequence. It would make more sense, I think, to argue that these demands reflect participant interests which define a good medicine *ought* to deliver insofar as its legitimacy as a profession rests on helping the sick.

What was at stake in this case? On the side of patients, clearly, the main concern was survival, but it would be an error to reduce the entire movement to this one issue. Patients lived much of their lives in the world defined by medicine, yet the fact that they had an incurable disease seemed to disqualify them from attention and care. They did not accept this situation, but aimed to bring the organization of medicine into compliance with their human needs as participants in the medical world. To achieve this they proposed to transform experimental medicine into a standard form of care for the incurably ill, thus incorporating themselves fully into the system. That in turn implied a new ethical approach and corresponding design changes.

From the standpoint of researchers, the issue was posed differently. For them, experimentation was a means to knowledge, not medical care, limited by ethics out of respect for human rights. Since the patients shared both the cognitive goals of the researchers and their concern with the abuse of human subjects, compromise was possible. It required the translation of patients' ethical demands into appropriate technical form so that they could be satisfied in the course of knowledge production. Those demands were incorporated into the technical code of experimentation, i.e., formulated in technically rational terms as a guide to practice.

To achieve this, patients were drawn ever more deeply into the policy process and even the process of experimental design as they struggled to work out an acceptable compromise (Epstein, 1996). The outcome was the emergence of a new technical code supporting a significantly changed practice of experimental medicine that lay at the intersection of the participant interests of patients and the scientific concerns of researchers. Here we see the new role of ethics as a sort of switching post between the social and the technical.

DEEP DEMOCRATIZATION

Just as representative democracy deals effectively with space, so an equivalent form of representation can democratize temporally based technical power. But there are significant differences between representation in these two domains. Technical representation is not primarily about the selection of a trusted personnel, but involves the embodiment of social and political demands in technical codes. These codes crystallize a certain balance of social power. The problem of the loyalty of the representative, of his or her testimonial value, is far less significant in technical than in geographic representation. This is because entry into a technical profession involves socialization into its codes. A specialist who failed to represent the interests embedded in the code would be a technical failure as well. No similar check on personal idiosyncrasy and self-interest applies in the world of ordinary politics.

This is not to say that technical personnel are free of idiosyncrasy and self-interest, but these faults take a somewhat different form than on Capitol Hill. Expertise has historically served class power. The bias in favor of representing the interests of a narrow ruling group is strongly entrenched. An undemocratic technical system can offer privileges to its technical servants that might be threatened by a more democratic system. These are not problems that can be solved by throwing the bums out as we occasionally do on election day. The investment in technical competence is too high, the opportunity cost of doing without it too great, for such an approach to make sense. Instead, the most important means of assuring more democratic technical representation remains transformation of the technical codes and the educational process through which they are inculcated.

This may explain why the most commonplace forms of struggle in the technical domain are the democratic rationalizations described in the previous chapter, the various controversies, appropriations, and dialogues that modify technical codes. Sociologists and historians have paid attention to these emerging phenomena, but their place in democratic political theory has been explored only occasionally and then primarily in terms of the role of hearings and lay panels in resolving controversies (Fiorino, 1989). The difficulty of explaining their democratic significance is no excuse for writing political theory today as though technical advance had ceased in 1776.

Habermas is as plagued by this allergy to technology as other political theorists, as I will show in the next chapter, but his approach in his most recent work has implications for the problem of technical representation. Unlike many theorists, Habermas squarely faces the fact that the modern state is *also* an administrative complex and not just a constitution made flesh in the form of elected bodies. Taking administration into account, as Habermas does more or less on the terms of systems theory, adds a welcome element of realism. If the word "technology" is substituted for "administration" in many contexts of his argument, the resulting paraphrase makes good sense and supports the position taken here. (The differences between technology and administration will be taken up in the next chapter.)

Habermas argues that the classical democratic idea of the state as the transparent self-reflection of the will of the "people" runs up against the opacity of a vast administrative sector in modern societies. That sector is supposed to respond primarily to the norm of efficiency, but the complexity of its dealings is such that it necessarily transgresses the bounds of mere implementation. Administration is constantly obliged to go beyond the narrowly pragmatic choice of the most efficient means to explicitly legislated ends. As it engages with all sorts of inescapable issues that must be decided on normative grounds, its legitimacy comes into question. The medical example developed above is a clear case in point. The Food and Drug Administration was at the center of the controversy and could not escape its responsibilities by reference either to legislation or considerations of efficiency. State action, in this and many other instances, cannot be adequately conceived as the embodiment of the public will formulated in a central assembly, such as a legislature, capable of viewing and mastering the society as a whole. But how then can its decisions be legitimated?

Habermas's solution is participatory administration, administration open to influence from public inputs of one sort or another. These inputs would follow the fragmentary form of administrative action, intervening in specific cases as needed rather than proceeding deductively from general principles. Here is how he explains his position:

> Insofar as the administration cannot refrain from appealing to normative reasons when it implements open legal programs, it should be able to carry out these steps of administrative law making in forms of communication and according to procedures that satisfy the conditions of constitutional legitimacy. This implies a "democratization" of the administration that, going beyond special obligations to provide information, would supplement parliamentary and judicial controls on administration from within. But whether the participation of clients, the use of ombudspersons, quasi-judicial procedures, hearings, and the like, are appropriate for such a democratization, or whether other arrangements must be found for a domain so prone to interference and dependent on efficiency, is, as always with such innovations, a question of the interplay of institutional imagination and cautious experimentation. Of course, participatory administrative practices must not be considered simply as surrogates for legal protection but as procedures that are *ex ante* effective in legitimating decisions that, from a normative point of view, substitute for acts of legislation or adjudication (Habermas, 1996: 440-441).

Technical decision-making, like state administration, often goes well beyond mere questions of efficiency to shape the social environment and life patterns of the citizens. It too has normative implications and requires legitimating mechanisms based on public inputs if it is to be incorporated into the framework of a modern democracy. These mechanisms must assure its representative character and remove the suspicion that decisions arise in pure arbitrariness or covert interests. As we already begin to see, short of some such development in the technical sphere, technology will become the object of increasing mistrust and contestation. Democratic rationalizations are examples of such participatory legitimations.

These considerations on representation take us far from the preoccupation with community that often characterizes reflection on democratizing technology. It seems to me necessary to get away from unrealistic notions like the use of national electronic town hall meetings to decide technological questions, or redesigning technology so it fits neatly into the local framework of real town hall decision-making. Such schemes delegitimate by implication the forms of intervention open to us today which are not usually based on the principle of majority rule in a community setting.

But we should not completely abandon concern for classical democratic controls in the technical sphere. Clearly, where local control is possible, it is desirable. However, I fear this will be the case much less frequently than Sclove would have us believe. It is reasonable to be guided pragmatically on questions of local control of administration. We have other less ambitious models than strong democracy of alternatives to technocratic control, such as the collegial organization of certain professionals. These collegial forms of organization of teachers and physicians have distant roots in the old craft guilds. Like vocational investment in work, collegiality has been replaced by capitalist management practically everywhere and survives only in a few specialized and archaic settings such as universities and hospitals. Even there it is increasingly threatened. Not the essence of technology but the requirements of capitalist economics explain this outcome (Braverman, 1974; Noble, 1984). Refined and generalized, collegiality might be part of a strategy for reducing the operational autonomy of management and creating systematic openings for democratic rationalizations. The recovery of collegial forms would be a signficant step toward democratizing modern technically based societies.

There are other possibilities for electoral intervention. The summits of the technical bureaucracies could and should be chosen by conventional democratic means. Already stockholders elect the top managements of the enterprises they own. The boards of public corporations depend on elected officials. Electoral representation could be extended to offer citizenship to all participants in major technical institutions. In fact a radical version of this idea was proposed during the May Events under the name of "self-management." A disappointing vestige of the idea was realized by German and some Scandinavian unions, which won rights of "co-management," including participation of union representatives on boards of directors. But so far these reforms have had little impact on any advanced society.

I think there are two reasons for the relative failure of electoral control of technical institutions. In the first place, wherever some degree of control has been ceded, as in the case of German co-management, it is in a political context that admits of no major changes in technical codes. Thus co-management turns out mainly to be about preparing conventional labor negotiations, a useful function but not particularly relevant to democratizing technology.

It is not surprising that board membership is ineffective in a society where technical relations in production are uncontested. Indeed, the absence of such contestation is probably a condition for achieving board membership under capitalism. What is perhaps more worrisome is the lack of pressure to democratize public technical institutions in which everyone has a large stake, institutions such as utilities, medicine, and urban planning that are only loosely controlled by elected officials today, if at all. These institutions are not constrained by the logic of the market and could offer more receptive terrain for experimentation. But as Dewey foresaw, the dispersion of the technological citizenry, combined with a privatized culture and a media-dominated public process account for the passivity of a society which has not yet grasped how profoundly affected it is by technology. Only as that realization dawns are citizens likely to demand electoral checks on the policy-making bodies in control of technology.

Because technical leadership has a distinct place in the division of labor, it will always remain separate from the mass, and cannot be replaced by popular action. Nevertheless, the operational autonomy of experts and managers could be significantly reduced. Its maximization in the present system serves elite control. That control would be threatened if technical authority was accommodated to the gradual enlargement of subordinates' tactical initiative. As we saw, this was precisely what many members of the middle strata demanded in the course of the May Events. As distinct from "strong" democracy, I will call a movement for democratization "deep" where it includes a strategy combining the democratic rationalization of technical codes with electoral controls on technical institutions. Such a deep democratization would alter the structure and knowledge base of management and expertise. The exercise of authority would come to favor agency in technically mediated social domains. Deep democratization promises an alternative to technocracy. Instead of popular agency appearing as an anomaly and an interference, it would be normalized and incorporated into the standard procedures of technical design.

Part III.

TECHNOLOGY AND MODERNITY

Theories of modernity and empirical work on technology march forward in mutual ignorance. In these chapters I show how the two can be brought together in a new approach to the philosophy of technology. The first chapter of this section will reconsider the debate between Marcuse and Habermas concerning the nature of advanced technological societies. Marcuse placed technology at the center of his analysis while Habermas increasingly ignored it. Habermas's new framework is useful, but it can be improved by taking technology into account. Social constructivism, as developed here, provides a basis for a synthesis. The second chapter addresses the Heideggerian approach to technology and formulates a social-critical alternative. Heidegger, like contemporary philosophers of technology such as Albert Borgmann, are so hostile to technology as such they have nothing to say about particular technologies. Yet we know there are important distinctions to be made between types of technology and paths of development. Despite the limitations of these essentialist theories, they orient us usefully toward the problem of meaning in a technological society. The instrumentalization theory developed in the third chapter integrates the results of recent research in history and sociology of technology with a socially conscious revision of traditional philosophy of technology. I conclude with a constructivist interpretation of Simondon's concept of "concretization" as the basis for a revised account of technical progress.

Part III.

TECHNOLOGY AND MODERNITY

7. Critical Theories of Technology

INTRODUCTION: TWO TYPES OF CRITIQUE

The debate over technology between Marcuse and Habermas marked a significant turning point in the history of the Frankfurt School. After the 1960s Habermas's influence grew as Marcuse's declined and Critical Theory adopted a far less utopian stance. Recently there has been a revival of radical technology criticism in the environmental movement and under the influence of Foucault and constructivism. This chapter takes a new look at the earlier debate from the standpoint of these recent developments.

While aspects of Habermas's argument remain persuasive, his defense of modernity now seems to concede far too much to its claims to rationality. His essentialist picture of technology and other forms of technical action is less plausible after a decade of historicizing research in technology studies. I argue that Marcuse was right after all to claim that technology is socially determined even if he was unable to develop his insight fruitfully. In this chapter I propose an alternative which combines elements of both Marcuse's and Habermas's views. A synthesis is possible because the traditions of critique on which these thinkers draw are complementary. However, as we will see, neither comes out of the confrontation unscathed.

The substantivist *critique of technology as such* characterizes the Frankfurt School and especially its leading members, Adorno and Horkheimer. In *Dialectic of Enlightenment* (1972) they argue that instrumentality is in itself a form of domination, that controlling objects violates their integrity and distorts the inner nature of the dominating subject. If this is so, then technology is not neutral, and simply using it commits one to a valuative stance.

The critique of technology as such is familiar not only from the Frankfurt School but also from Heidegger (1977a), Jacques Ellul (1964), and a host of social critics who might be described unkindly as technophobic. They generally operate in a speculative framework. Heidegger's theory of technology is based on an ontological understanding of being; a dialectical theory of rationality does the same work for Adorno and Horkheimer. Their arguments usually end in retreat from the technical sphere into art, religion, or nature. These sweeping theories are not entirely convincing, and they are too indiscriminate in their condemnation of technology to guide efforts to reform it. Their strategy consists not in reforming technology but in bounding it. Nevertheless, they provide a useful antidote to positivist faith in inevitable progress. Albert Borgmann's critique of the computer, discussed in the next chapter, offers a contemporary example of this approach.

Habermas develops a modest demystified version of this position which is increasingly assimilated to a more general critique of bureaucracy.[1] Technical or in later writings, administrative, action has certain characteristics which are appropriate in some spheres of life, inappropriate in others. Habermas's approach implies that technology is neutral in its proper sphere, but outside that sphere it causes various social pathologies of modern societies. Although his position is powerfully argued, the idea that technology is neutral, even with Habermas's qualifications, is reminiscent of the naive instrumentalism so effectively laid to rest in recent years by social scientific technology studies.

Reform of technology is the concern of a second approach which I call *design critique*. Design critique holds that social interests or cultural values influence the realization of technical principles. In recent years, many social critics have offered general theories of modern technology. For some, it is Christian or masculinist values that have given us the impression that we can "conquer" nature, a belief that shows up in ecologically unsound technical designs; for others it is capitalist values that have turned technology into an instrument of domination of labor and exploitation of nature (White, 1972; Merchant, 1980; Braverman, 1974). In the terms of chapter 4, these are theories of technological hegemony, the values they criticize realized in biased technical codes.

---

[1] Thomas Krogh argues, in opposition to my complaint about the later Habermas's indifference to the issue of technology, that "the opposite is the case; the whole theory of media formation—perhaps the whole of volume two of [*Theorie des kommunikativen Handelns*]—is nothing but a theory of technology, technology taken in the wide sense we found in Luhmann..." (Krogh, 1998: 188). I would agree, nevertheless deploring the suppression of explicit reference to so important a matter and the consequences that has for theory.

These theories are sometimes over-generalized into versions of substantive critique. For example, if *all* technique is masculinist, then feminism would be irrelevant to the design of any particular device. But where essentialism is avoided and the critique confined to *our* technology, this approach promises a radically different future based on designs embodying a different technical code. On this account technology is social in much the same way as law, education or medicine, insofar as it is similarly influenced by interests and public processes. Critics of the Fordist labor process and environmentalists have challenged technical designs on these terms for many years (Hirschhorn, 1984; Zuboff, 1988; Commoner, 1971).

Although he was certainly influenced by Adorno and even Heidegger, Marcuse was not the romantic technophobe he is often taken for.[2] To be sure, he argues that instrumental reason is historically contingent, but unlike Adorno and Heidegger, he thinks human action can change the epochal structure of technological rationality and the designs which flow from it. A new type of reason would generate new and more benign scientific discoveries and technologies. Marcuse is an eloquent advocate of this ambitious position, but today the notion of a political transformation of science has a vanishingly small audience and discredits his whole approach.

The question I address here is: what can we learn from Marcuse and Habermas assuming that we are neither metaphysicians nor instrumentalists, that we reject both a romantic critique of science and the neutrality of technology?

In the following discussion, I work through the argument in three phases. I start with Habermas's critique of Marcuse in "Technology and Science as 'Ideology'" (1970), the locus classicus of this debate. Then I consider the deeper presentation of similar themes in Habermas's *The Theory of Communicative Action* (1984, 1987) where he reformulates his position in Weberian terms. Marcuse was not able to reply to these

---

[2] Marcuse was a colleague of Adorno and a student of Heidegger. For an account of his background, see Kellner (1984).

arguments so my procedure is anachronistic, but I will do my best to imagine how he might have responded on the basis of his own critique of Weber. Next, I discuss aspects of Habermas's theory that can be reconstructed to take the Marcusean critique into account. Finally, I offer my own alternative.[3]

FROM "SECRET HOPES" TO NEW SOBRIETY

"All Power to the Imagination"

Marcuse follows Adorno and Horkheimer's *Dialectic of Enlightenment* in arguing that technology bears the marks of a terrible history. Both inner and outer nature have been suppressed in the struggle for survival, at first against nature, and later against other human beings in class society. To carry any critical weight, this position must imply, if not an original unity of man and nature, at least the existence of some natural forces congruent with human needs. Like his Frankfurt School colleagues, Marcuse finds evidence in art that such forces have been sacrificed in the course of history. But today even consciousness of what has been lost is largely forgotten. Technical thinking has taken over in every sphere of life, human relations, politics, and so on.

Although *One-Dimensional Man* (1964) is often compared to *Dialectic of Enlightenment,* it is far less pessimistic. In putting forward a more hopeful view, Marcuse appears to be influenced by Heidegger, although he does not acknowledge this influence, perhaps because of their deep political disagreements. In Heideggerian terms, as Dreyfus explains them, Marcuse proposes a new disclosure of being through a revolutionary transformation of basic practices (Dreyfus, 1995). This would lead to a change in the very nature of instrumentality, which would be fundamentally modified by the abolition of class society and its associated performance principle. It would then be possible to create a new science and technology that would place us in harmony rather than in conflict with nature. Nature would be treated as another subject instead of as mere raw materials. Human beings would learn to achieve their aims through realizing nature's inherent potentialities instead of laying it waste for the sake of power and profit. Marcuse writes:

> Freedom indeed depends largely on technical progress, on the

---

[3] I discuss a number of related issues in the interpretation of Marcuse and Habermas in Feenberg (1995: chaps. 2 and 4).

advancement of science. But this fact easily obscures the essential precondition: in order to become vehicles of freedom, science and technology would have to change their present direction and goals; they would have to be reconstructed in accord with a new sensibility—the demands of the life instincts. Then one could speak of a technology of liberation, product of a scientific imagination free to project and design the forms of a human universe without exploitation and toil (Marcuse, 1969: 19).

Aesthetic practice offers Marcuse a model of a transformed instrumentality different from the "conquest" of nature characteristic of class society. Like the early twentieth-century avant-garde, especially the surrealists, Marcuse believed that the separation of art from daily life could be transcended through fusing reason and imagination. Marcuse thus proposes the *Aufhebung* of the split between science and art in a new technical base. This notion recalls the slogan of the May Events, "All Power to the Imagination," and in fact *An Essay on Liberation* (1969) is dedicated to the "young militants" of May 1968.

Although this program sounds wildly implausible, it makes a kind of intuitive sense. For example, we easily recognize the difference between the architecture of Mies van der Rohe and Frank Lloyd Wright. Mies shows us technology as a manifestation of untrammeled power, the technological sublime, while Wright's structures harmonize with nature and seek to integrate human beings with their environment. We will see that it is possible to save Marcuse's essential insight by developing this contrast.

The Neutrality of Technology

Habermas is not convinced. In "Technology and Science as 'Ideology'" he denounces the "secret hopes" of a whole generation of social thinkers —Benjamin, Adorno, Bloch, Marcuse—whose implicit ideal was the harmony of man and nature. While he too is concerned about the technocratic tendencies of advanced societies, he attacks the very notion of a new science and technology as a romantic myth; the ideal of a technology based on communion with nature applies the model of human communication to a domain of strictly instrumental relations.

In opposition to Marcuse's historical interpretation of modern technological rationality, Habermas offers a theory of the transhistorical essence of technical action in general. As Thomas McCarthy writes, "Habermas's own view is that while the specific historical forms of science and technology depend on institutional arrangements that are variable, their basic logical structures are grounded in the very nature of purposive-rational action" (McCarthy, 1981: 22). At first Habermas argued that "work" and "interaction" each have their own logic. Work is "success oriented;" it is a form of "purposive-rational action" aimed at controlling the world. On these terms, technological development is a "generic project," "a 'project' of the human species *as a whole,*" not of some particular historical epoch like class society or of a particular class like the bourgeoisie (Habermas, 1970: 87). By contrast, interaction involves communication in the pursuit of common understanding. Technocracy results not from the nature of technology, but from an imbalance between these two action-types.

Habermas not only criticizes Marcuse, but also Weber, and by implication Heidegger as well, for identifying rationalization exclusively with the extension of technical control. He identifies a process of communicative rationalization that enhances human freedom, but which has been partially blocked in the course of modern development. While this seems right in a general way, it leads to a rather slender practical result. Apparently, a new and better society can be had by tinkering with the boundaries of technical action systems. So long as technical action remains limited to merely facilitating the complex interactions required by a modern society, it poses no threat. Indeed, to criticize technization in its proper place is anti-modern and regressive.

In defense of Marcuse, it should be said that he nowhere proposes that a qualitatively different technical rationality would substitute an interpersonal relationship to nature for the objectivity characteristic of technical action. It is Habermas who uses the phrase "fraternal relation to nature" to describe Marcuse's views. This is a straw man arising from the rigid dichotomies of Habermas's worldview and not from a serious encounter with Marcuse's thought. Marcuse does advocate relating to nature as to another subject, but the concept of subjectivity implied here owes more to Aristotelian substance than to the idea of personhood. He does not recommend chatting with nature but, rather, recognizing it as possessing potentialities of its own with a certain inherent legitimacy. That recognition should be incorporated into the very structure of technical rationality. Below I will discuss the phenomenological basis of Marcuse's position.

Habermas would of course agree that technological development is influenced by social demands, but that is quite different from the notion that there are a variety of technical rationalities, as Marcuse believes. For example, Habermas is in favor of ecologically sound technology, but in his view technology as such remains *essentially* unchanged by this or any other particular realization. Technology, in short, will always be a non-social, objectivating relation to nature, oriented toward success and control. Marcuse argues, on the contrary, that the very essence of technology is at stake in ecological reform (Marcuse, 1992).

In any case, Habermas does not simply dismiss Marcuse, who had a considerable influence on his thinking. He finds in the concept of "one-dimensionality" the basis for a much better critique of technology than the one he rejects. This is Marcuse's analysis of the overextension of technical modes of thinking and acting, an approach which Habermas elaborated in his own terms. Paradoxically, although the germ of his famous "colonization thesis" appears to derive at least in part from Marcuse's critique of technology, technology itself drops out of the Habermasian equation at this point in time and never reappears. As I will show, Habermas's theory could accommodate a critique of technology in principle, but the index of *The Theory of Communicative Action* does not even contain the word. This oversight is related to his treatment of technology as neutral in its own sphere. The neutrality thesis obscures the social dimensions of technology on the basis of which a critique could be developed.

What is the outcome of this first encounter? Despite the problems in his position, Habermas prevailed. Marcuse's views were forgotten in the late '70s and '80s. Habermas had strong arguments on his side, but he also had a favorable historical context. That context was the retreat from the utopian hopes of the 1960s in the 1980s, a kind of *neue Sachlichkeit*, or "new sobriety." Habermas's views suited a time when we tamed our aspirations.

RATIONALITY IN THE CRITIQUE OF MODERNITY

Weber and Habermas
Habermas distinguishes his own critique of the "incompleteness" of modernity from what he regards as the anti-modernism of the 1960s radicals. Accordingly, *The Theory of Communicative Action* develops an implicit argument against Marcuse and the new left. I will review here one important version of Habermas's argument which I will explain in terms of Chart 3 (Habermas's figure 11), drawn from *The Theory of Communicative Action* (1984, 1987: I, 238).

Chart 3: World Relations and Basic Attitudes

Worlds Basic Attitudes	1 Objective	2 Social	3 Subjective	1 Objective
3 Expressive	Art			
1 Objectivating	Cognitive-instrumental rationality Science Social Technology Technologies		X	
2 Norm-conformative	X	Moral-practical rationality Law Morality		
3 Expressive		X	Aesthetic-practical rationality Eroticism Art	

Along the top, Habermas has listed the three "worlds" in which we participate as human beings, the objective world of things, the social world of people, the subjective world of feelings. We move constantly between the three worlds in our daily life. Along the side are listed the "basic attitudes" we can take up with respect to the three worlds: an objectivating attitude which treats everything, including people and feelings, as things; a norm-conformative attitude which views the worlds in terms of moral obligation; and an expressive attitude which approaches reality emotively.

Crossing the basic attitudes and worlds yields nine world-relations. Habermas follows Weber in claiming that only those world-relations can be rationalized that can be clearly differentiated and that build on their past achievements in a progressive developmental sequence. Modernity is based on precisely those rationalizable world-relations. They appear in the stepped double boxes: cognitive-instrumental rationality, moral-practical rationality, and aesthetic-practical rationality. However, of the three possible domains of rationalization, only the objectivating relation to the objective and social worlds, which yields science, technology, markets, and administration, has been able fully to develop in capitalist societies. Habermas argues that the pathologies of modernity are due to the obstacles capitalism places in the way of rationalization in the moral-practical sphere.

There are also three X's (at 2.1, 3.2, 1.3) on the chart which refer to non-rationalizable world relations. Two of these are of interest to us. 2.1 is the norm-conformative relation to the objective world, i.e. the fraternal relation to nature. Although he is not explicitly mentioned here, Marcuse is obviously consigned to box 2.1. Another X is placed over 3.2, the expressive relation to the social world, bohemianism, the counter-culture, exactly where Marcuse and his allies in the new left sought an alternative. In sum, the 1960s are placed under X's in zones of irrationality which can make no contribution to the reform of modern society. This figure explains more precisely than his early essay on "Technology and Science as 'Ideology'" why Habermas rejects Marcuse's most radical critique of technology.[4]

A Marcusean Reply

How might Marcuse have replied? He could have drawn on the arguments against the neutrality of science and technology developed in his work from the 1960s (Marcuse 1964; Marcuse 1968). In Habermas as in Weber, scientific-technical rationality is nonsocial, neutral, and formal. By definition it excludes the social (which would be 1.2). It is neutral because it represents a species-wide interest, a cognitive-instrumental interest which overrides all group-specific values. And it is formal as a result of the process of differentiation by which it abstracts itself from the various contents it mediates. In sum, science and technology are essentially indifferent to interests and ideology and represent the objective

---

[4] This chart is the object of an interesting debate between Habermas and Thomas McCarthy. See Bernstein (1985: pp.177ff and 203ff). Habermas seems to me to confuse the issues here by apologizing for using the chart to present his own views when in fact it was meant primarily as an explanation of Weber; but then he goes on to use it once again to present his own views. The debate is inconclusive since, as I will explain in more detail below, it poses the question of a normative relation to the objective world in terms of the possibility of a natural philosophy rather than in terms of a reconceptualized technical reason. Cf. also Thompson and Held (1982, pp. 238ff). Marcuse was none too clear on what he intended, but at least he explicitly rejected regression to a "qualitative physics" (1964: 166).

world in terms of the possibilities of understanding and control.

In his essay on Weber, Marcuse argues that the apparent neutrality of the cognitive-instrumental sphere is a special kind of ideological illusion (Marcuse 1968). He concedes that technical principles can be formulated in abstraction from any content, that is to say, in abstraction from any interest or ideology. However, as such, they are merely abstractions. As soon as they enter reality, they take on a socially specific content relative to the "historical subject" that applies them.

Although Marcuse's argument appears rather speculative—what is a historical subject?—it can be restated in simple terms. Efficiency, to take a particularly important example, is defined formally as the ratio of inputs to outputs. This definition would apply in a communist or a capitalist society, or even in an Amazonian tribe. It seems, therefore, to transcend the particularity of the social. However, concretely, when one actually gets down to applying the notion of efficiency, one must decide what kinds of things can serve as inputs and outputs, who can offer and acquire them and on what terms, what counts as discommodities, waste, and hazards, and so on. These are all socially specific, and so, therefore, is the concept of efficiency in any actual application. And insofar as the social is biased by a system of domination, so will be its efficient workings. As a general rule, formally rational systems must be practically contextualized in order to be used, and as soon as they are contextualized in a capitalist society, they incorporate capitalist values.

This approach is loosely related to Marx's original critique of the market. Unlike many contemporary socialists, Marx did not deny that markets exhibit a rational order based on equal exchange. The problem with markets is not located at this level, but in their historical concretization in a form which couples equal exchange to the relentless growth of capital at the expense of the rest of society. That concrete form shapes economic growth patterns, technological development, law, and many other aspects of social life. A rational market—rational in the narrow formal sense—produces a society that is irrational in human terms.

Economists might concede the bias of actual market societies, but they would attribute the difference between ideal models and vulgar realities to accidental "market imperfections." What they treat as a kind of external interference with the ideal-type of the market, Marx considers an essential feature of its operation under capitalism. Markets in their perfect form are simply an abstraction from one or another concrete realization in which they take on biases reflecting specific interests. The class significance of the market is relative to the way in which its basic structures are realized. Thus it is not inconsistent for Engels to recommend reliance on the market for certain purposes under socialism, as he does in the case of agriculture (Engels, 1969).

Marcuse adopts a similar line in criticizing Weber's notion of administrative rationality, a fundamental aspect of rationalization. Economic administration presupposes the separation of workers from the means of production, and that separation eventually shapes technological design. Although Weber calls capitalist management and technology "rational" without qualification, they are so only in a context where workers do not own their own tools. This social context biases Weber's concept of rationality despite his intention of elaborating a universal theory. The resulting slippage between the abstract formulation of the category and its concrete realization is ideological. Marcuse thus insists on distinguishing between rationality in general and a concrete, socially specific rationalization process: "pure" rationality is an abstraction from the life process of a historical subject. That process necessarily involves values that become integral to rationality as it is realized.

Technological Rationality

Habermas too finds Weber's rationalization theory equivocating between abstract categories and concrete instances, but his critique differs from Marcuse's. Habermas argues that a structure of rationality lies behind modern social development. The elements of this structure are realized in specific forms privileged by the dominant capitalist system (see Chart 3 above). Weber overlooked moments of potential communicative rationalization suppressed by capitalism and as a result confused the limits of capitalism with the limits of rationality as such.

Because Habermas does not challenge Weber's account of technical rationalization, he too appears to identify it with its specifically capitalist forms. Marcuse, on the contrary, attacks Weber's understanding of technical rationalization itself. Weber's error is not simply to identify all types of rationalization with technical rationalization, but more deeply to overlook the biasing of any and all technical rationality by social values. Weber's account of science and technology as nonsocial and neutral, which Habermas shares, masks the interests that preside over their genesis and application. Hence Marcuse would consider even Habermas's ideal of a balance between technical and communicative rationalization to be insufficiently critical.

Habermas might respond that these problems are mere sociological details inappropriate at the fundamental theoretical level. Raised at that level, they are a Trojan Horse for a romantic critique of rationality. The best way to keep the horse outside the city walls is to maintain a clear distinction between principle and application. Just as ethical principles must be applied, so must technical principles. That the applications never correspond exactly to principles is not a serious objection to formulating the latter in purified ideal-types. At that essential level, there is no risk of confusion between formal properties of rationality as such and social interests, although in practice the two will always be "blended" together to some extent.

Marcuse's theory is indeed a critique of rationality, but his argument is not with abstract rationality per se but with its historically concrete expression in what he calls "technological rationality." Technical principles become historically active through a culture of technology; applications are not a function of abstract principles alone but incorporate them only as they are embodied in concrete technical disciplines. As social institutions, those disciplines operate under social imperatives which influence their formulation of technical problems and solutions and show up in the applications they design. Because design is technically underdetermined, this "blending" of the technical and the social is not extrinsic and accidental as Habermas assumes, but is rather *defining* for the nature of technology.

A plausible interpretation of what Marcuse meant by his term "technological rationality" would be the most fundamental social imperatives *in the form in which they are internalized by a technical culture*. This is what, in a constructivist framework, I have called the "technical code." Such fundamental imperatives or codes tie technology not just to a particular local experience but to consistent features of basic social formations such as class society, capitalism, and socialism. They are embodied in the technical systems that emerge from that culture and reinforce its basic values. In this sense technology can be said to be "political" without mystification or risk of confusion.

Marcuse's theory makes good constructivist sense conceived on these terms. At the level of the concrete historical forms of technical culture, there is room for a variety of different "rationalities," in Marcuse's socially concrete sense of the term, and it is up to us to judge between them and chose the best. None are truly "neutral," not even modern science based technology. Each embodies a historical project, a resolution of the technically underdetermined aspects of the design of devices and systems.

The Habermasian position confuses the abstract level of pure technical principles with that of concrete social reality. It defines the technical domain as an abstraction and then attributes that definition to a supposedly "differentiated" "cultural sphere" of technical institutions, activities, and products. This confusion lends plausibility to the claim that science and technology are nonsocial, when in fact it is only the most abstract principles of those disciplines that can be so described, and not the disciplines themselves or their applications.

Constructivism, Phenomenology, and Critical Theory

Marcuse's critique of science and technology was presented in a speculative context, but its major claim—the social character of rational systems—is a commonplace of recent constructivist research on science and technology. The notion of underdetermination is central to this approach (Pinch and Bijker, 1987). Habermas himself at one time focused on this very phenomenon. In an early essay, he argued that science cannot help us decide between functionally equivalent technologies, but that values must intervene (Habermas, 1973: 270-271). He showed that the application of decision theory does not supply scientific criteria of choice, but merely introduces different valuative biases. Even in "Technology and Science as 'Ideology'" Habermas recognizes that "social interests still determine the direction, functions, and pace of technical progress" (Habermas, 1970: 105). He does not explain how this affirmation squares with his belief, expressed in the same essay, that technology is a "'project' of the human species *as a whole*" (Habermas, 1970: 87). Even this (no doubt resolvable) inconsistency seems to disappear in the later work where technology is defined as nonsocial.

But surely the earlier position was correct. If this is true, then what Habermas calls the fraternal relation to nature, 2.1., should not have an X over it. If 1.1, that is, the objective relation to the objective world, is already social, the distinction between it and 2.1 is softened. On the Marcusean view, instrumentality and normativity coexist in all real-world instances of science and technology. Does this mean that objective research cannot be distinguished from mere prejudice? Surely not. The biases that characterize the structure of entire historical eras such as the capitalist era are not mere personal idiosyncrasies. They reveal as well as conceal. Think, for example, of the obvious social background to the 17th Century's very fruitful mechanical view of nature. Hence Marcuse does not challenge the cognitive validity of the sciences on their own terrain. Habermas does not worry about this problem either because for him the important thing about rationality is not so much the purity of its source as the intersubjective redeemability of its claims. However, he does think that Marcuse's approach leads straight back to a teleological nature philosophy. What else can a normative relation to nature mean? Yet I find no evidence for this sort of thing in Marcuse. The real difference between their views lies along a different axis. The issue is not, as Habermas thinks, whether to revive a philosophy of nature; it concerns our self-understanding as subjects of technical action.

This is the argument of Steven Vogel, who points out that Habermas's chart omits an obvious domain of normative relations to the objective world: the built environment. The question of what to build and how to build it engages us in normative judgments concerning factual states of affairs. While there is no science of such judgments, they are at least as capable of rationalization as the aesthetic judgments Habermas classifies under 3.1 on his chart (Vogel, 1996: 388). Here we can give a perfectly reasonable content to the demand for an ethically informed relation to nature. Methodologically, the case is similar to medicine, which involves a normative relation to the objectified human body.

Vogel bases his position on a constructivist account of nature as a social product. Hence, it is not surprising to find him affirming our ethical responsibility for nature, particularly in relation to the environment. But this is rather different from Marcuse's phenomenological account of the lived nature with which we are immediately engaged. This account first appeared in his review-essay on Marx's *Economic and Philosophical Manuscripts,* published in 1932 (Marcuse, 1973). It resurfaces forty years later in the essay on "Nature and Revolution" (Marcuse, 1972). In these texts, Marcuse affirms our intimate connection to "sensuous" nature as participants in its life-process and source of its meaningfulness. It is *this* nature, and not the abstract constructions of natural science which has for him the status of a subject. However, the consistent development of this conception of lived nature would have taken Marcuse back to his Heideggerian roots, a return he resisted, leaving him open to Habermas's anthropomorphic misconstruction of his position.

The Heideggerian approach to nature has been developed independently of Marcuse by Augustin Berque, a Japanologist working in the tradition of humanistic geography. According to Berque, the typically modern distinctions between objectivity and subjectivity, nature and culture, occlude the realm Heidegger designated as "world," our experienced reality. In geographic terms, that reality is the landscape in which we actually live, the object of Berque's theory.

Landscape is more than a set of natural features; it is also a symbolically invested habitat, an "*écoumène,*" which Berque defines as "the earth insofar as we inhabit it" (Berque, 1996: 12). As such, landscape is not merely undifferentiated extension but a system of significant locations. The concept of location is in turn related to human constructions. As Heidegger explains in "Building Dwelling Thinking," the location that is marked by the presence of a bridge did not precede the bridge but belongs to it: "Before the bridge stands, there are of course many spots along the stream that can be occupied by something. One of them proves to be a location, and does so *because of the bridge.* Thus the bridge does not first come to a location to stand in it; rather a location comes into existence only by virtue of the bridge" (Heidegger, 1971b: 154).

Are the meanings with which nature is invested by human practices of building merely subjective associations? Not at all. They shape the landscape's physical form over the years. Thus what Berque calls the "ecosymbolicity" of lived nature precisely parallels the double aspects of technology discussed in chapter 4. Just as technology is neither purely natural nor purely social, so the nature to which it is applied also confounds such abstract distinctions. Both are simultaneously causal mechanisms and meaningful social objects. Berque concludes that "The ecosymbolicity of the *écoumène*...implies an ethic because all localities are always charged with human values....For good or ill, the human manner of inhabiting a territory can only be ethical" (Berque, 1996: 80-81). Marcuse would no doubt have expressed a similar point somewhat differently: nature belongs to history and as a historical reality it shares in all the ambiguities of the struggle between Eros and Thanatos, emancipation and domination.

Let me conclude more simply: nature would be treated as another subject where humans took responsibility for the *well-being* of the materials they transform in creating the built environment. The values in terms of which this well-being is defined, such as beauty, health, free expression and growth, may not have a scientific status and may not be the object of universal agreement, but neither are they merely personal preferences as modern value nihilism would have it. They arise in our lived experience of nature and have a history in which they have been the object of rational reflection and criticism.[5]

---

[5] Can such an approach resist the corrosive attack of value nihilism? Marcuse believed it could for reasons that we need not go into here. Marcuse's argument is developed in terms of an ontology of values based on his theory of "substantive universals" (Marcuse, 1964: 132ff). For an interesting contemporary argument against value nihilism, see Simpson (1995: chap. 7).

This is the ethical basis of democratic interventions into technology which prefigure a new style of rationalization that internalizes unaccounted costs born by "nature," i.e., some-thing or -body exploitable in the pursuit of power and profit. I call this a "rationalization" because it proceeds by technical advances made in opposition to the technocracy. There is nothing about this idea that offends against the spirit of modern science. On the contrary, to carry out this program science is needed, as Commoner has persuasively argued.

What is the result of this second phase of the debate? I think Marcuse wins this one. We are no longer in the new sobriety 1980s, but have entered the social constructivist 1990s, and his views sound much more plausible than they did twenty or thirty years ago. However there are still problems with Marcuse's position: Habermas's skepticism about its speculative foundation is difficult to dismiss. Rather than simply returning to Marcuse's original formulations, perhaps elements of his critical theory of technology can be reconstructed in a more credible framework. Does one really need a new science to get a Frank Lloyd Wright technology rather than a Mies van der Rohe technology? Couldn't one work toward such a transformation gradually, using existing technical principles but reforming them, modifying them, applying them differently? Environmentalism has shown this to be a practical approach to a long-term process of technological change.[6]

In the remainder of this chapter I propose to reformulate the Marcusean design critique inside a version of Habermas's communication theory modified to include technology.

REFORMULATING THE MEDIA THEORY

The Media Theory

Habermas's media theory explains modernity in terms of the emergence of differentiated "subsystems" based on rational forms such as exchange, law, and administration. The media concept is generalized from monetary exchange along lines proposed by Parsons. Habermas claims that power resembles money closely enough to qualify as a full-fledged medium (Habermas, 1984, 1987: II, 274). The media make it possible for individuals to coordinate their behavior while pursuing individual success in an instrumental attitude toward the world. Media-steered

---

[6] It is of course possible that this is what Marcuse intended all along, but that is far from clear.

interaction is an alternative to communicative action, to arriving at shared beliefs in the course of linguistic exchanges. Normative consensus plays no role in the market, where agents reach their ends without discussion. Administrative power too is exercised without the need for complex communication. Together, money and power "delinguistify" dimensions of social life by organizing interaction through objectifying behaviors. Roughly summarized, Habermas's aim is to right the balance between the two types of rational coordination, both of which are required by a complex modern society (Habermas, 1984, 1987: II, 330).

It is important not to exaggerate Habermas's concessions to systems theory. In his formulation media do not eliminate communication altogether, merely the need for "communicative action." This term does not refer to the general faculty of using symbols to transmit beliefs and desires, but to the special form of communication in which subjects actively pursue mutual understanding (Habermas, 1984, 1987: I, 286). Media-related communication is quite different. It consists in stereotyped utterances or symbols which aim not at mutual understanding but at successful performance. Action coordination is an effect of the structure of the mediation rather than a conscious intention of the subjects.[7]

The media theory allows Habermas to offer a much clearer explanation of technocracy than *Dialectic of Enlightenment* and *One-Dimensional Man*. Habermas distinguishes between *system*, media regulated rational institutions, such as markets and administration, and *lifeworld*, the sphere of everyday communicative interactions in which such functions as child rearing, education, and public debate go on. According to Habermas, the central pathology of modern societies is the colonization of lifeworld by system. This involves the overextension of success-oriented action beyond its legitimate range and the consequent imposition of criteria of efficiency on the communicative sphere. The lifeworld contracts as the system expands into it and delinguistifies dimensions of social life which should be mediated by language.

But, surprisingly, even though he protests what, following Luhmann, he calls the "technization of the lifeworld," Habermas scarcely mentions technology. That seems to me an obvious oversight. Surely technology, too, coordinates human action while minimizing the need for language just like the other media. This blind spot is particularly puzzling since Habermas's thought was shaped all along by his early critique of the

---

[7] For a discussion of this issue, see McCarthy (1991) and Habermas's reply in Habermas (1991).

positivist understanding of reason and its historical realization in a technocratic society. These arguments, developed especially in the essay "Technology and Science as 'Ideology'," form the basis of the theory of modern society Habermas has refined and enriched over the years. While preserving in the main the dichotomous structure of his theory, he has substituted his distinction of system rationality and lifeworld for the original contrast of work and interaction, technique and communication. Thus his project is rooted in a critique of the type of action characteristic of technology, which has provided him with a model for his later interpretation of the specific modes of "purposive-rational action" that continue to concern him focally. Why, then, isn't technology counted as a medium alongside money and power in his later work?

There is a strong objection to so enlarging the media theory, namely that technology involves causal relations to nature while the other media are essentially social. However impoverished, the codes that govern money and power are conventional and possess communicative significance, whereas those that govern technology seem to lack communicative content. Or, put in another way, technology "relieves" physical, not communicative effort.

But this argument repeats the functionalist error criticized in chapter 4. In fact technology has several different types of communicative content. Some technologies, such as automobiles and desks, communicate the status of their owners (Forty, 1986); others, such as locks, communicate legal obligations; most technologies also communicate through the interfaces by which they are manipulated. A computer program, for example, transmits the designer's conception of a field of human activity while also helping to solve problems arising in that field (Winograd and Flores, 1987: chap. 12). In any transportation system, technology can be found organizing large numbers of people without discussion; they need only follow the rules and the map. Similarly, workers in a well organized factory find their jobs almost automatically meshing through the design of the equipment and buildings—their action is coordinated—without much linguistic interaction.

Indeed, it is quite implausible to suggest as Habermas appears to that action coordination in the rationalized spheres of social life can be completely described by reference to money and power. Certainly no one in the field of management theory would subscribe to the view that a combination of monetary incentives and administrative rules suffices to organize production. The problem of motivation is far more complex than that, and unless the technical rationality of the job coordinates workers' action harmoniously, mere rules will be impotent to do so.[8]

James Beniger has shown that these observations from management theory can be extended to modern societies as a whole. The bureaucratic structure and market systems of these societies rest on elaborate technological foundations. Beniger traces the roots of the "information society" back to the 19th century when basic innovations in information processing such as the telegraph and punch cards responded to the problems posed by high-speed industrial production and rail transportation. In Beniger's terms, coordination media "preprocess" human beings in the sense that they reduce the complexity of human inputs to social subsystems. The role of technologies in such preprocessing is richly illustrated throughout his book (Beniger, 1986).

Technology as a Medium
To reduce technology to a mere causal function is to miss the results of a generation of social science research. But if one cannot reduce technology to natural causality, why exclude it from the list of media which it resembles in so many respects? Of course it is quite different from money, the paradigm medium, but if the loose analogy works for power, I would argue that it can be extended to technology as well. In Chart 4 (Habermas's figure 37), where Habermas defines money and power as media, I have listed technology (in the sense of technical control) alongside them and found a parallel for each of the terms he uses to describe them (1984, 1987: II, 274). I will not go over the whole chart, but will focus on three of the most important functions.

First, consider "generalized instrumental value." In the case of money it is utility, in the case of power it is effectiveness, and I call it productivity in the case of technical control. Those in charge of technological choices (who are not necessarily technicians) interpose devices between the members of the community, unburdening them at both the communicative and the physical levels. This generates two types of value: first, the enhanced command of resources of the equipped and coordinated individuals, and second, the enhanced command of persons gained by those who manage the technical process. This latter form of technical control resembles political power but cannot be reduced to it

---

[8] See, for an example from the management literature, Hammer and Champy (1993: chap. 5).

because it is rooted in operational autonomy rather than normative claims. Nor is it as vague as influence or prestige, media suggested by Parsons which Habermas does not retain. I believe it is *sui generis*.

Second, each of these media makes a "nominal claim": with money it is exchange value, that is, money demands an equivalent; power yields binding decisions which demand obedience; and technology generates "prescriptions," rules of action which demand compliance. Complying with instructions in operating a machine differs both from obeying political orders and from accepting an exchange of equivalents on the market. It is characterized by its own unique code. The defining communication, the one which corresponds most closely to the simplified codes of money (buy, not buy), and power (obey, disobey), is pragmatic rightness or wrongness of action.

Third, there is the sanction column, which Habermas calls the "reserve backing." In claiming that money is backed by gold Habermas skips a generous helping of economic history, but of course he is right that monetary value must refer to a credible object such as national wealth. Power requires means of enforcement; in the case of technology, the natural consequences of error have a similar function, often mediated by organizational sanctions of some sort. If you refuse the technical norms, say, by driving on the wrong side of the street, you risk your life. You burden those who would have been relieved by your compliance and who must now signal to avoid a crash. If this communicative intervention fails, nature takes its course and an accident enforces the rules encoded in law and in the technical configuration of highways and cars.

If technology is included in the media theory, the boundaries Habermas wants to draw around money and power can be extended to it as well. It makes sense to argue that technical mediation is appropriate in some spheres and inappropriate in others, just as Habermas claims for money and power. However, despite certain similarities to money and power, technical control is so thoroughly intertwined with them, and with the lifeworld, that it seems to defy a simple bounding strategy. It might therefore be objected that it is better understood as a means or mediator by which the media penetrate the lifeworld, than as a medium in its own right. Technologizing a domain of life opens it to economic and political control; technical control serves system expansion without itself being a medium.[9]

---

[9] Thomas Krogh and Torben Hviid Nielsen suggested this objection.

Chart 4: Coordination Media

Components / Medium	Standard situation	Generalized value	Nominal claim	Rational criteria	Actors' attitude	Real value	Reserve backing	Form of institutionalization
Money	exchange	utility	exchange value	profitableness	oriented to success	use value	gold	property and contract
Power	directives	effectiveness	binding decisions	success (sovereignty)	oriented to success	realization of collective goals	means of enforcement	organization of official positions
Technology	applications	productivity	prescriptions	efficiency	oriented to success	realization of goals	natural consequences	systems

But is technical control uniquely intertwined? This objection confuses two levels of the media theory. Habermas distinguishes the media as ideal-types, but in practice, of course, money and power are not so easy to separate. With money one can obtain power, with power one can obtain money; money is a means to power, power to money. Technical control is no different. It can be distinguished from money and power as an ideal-type with no difficulty, although empirically it is intertwined with them just as they are intertwined with each other. All media are mediations in this sense, all media serve as means for each other.

Historical considerations argue for this view. In each phase or type of modern development, one or another of the media plays the mediating role, facilitating general system advance. Polanyi's description of the predatory market offers a model of market-led system expansion (Polanyi, 1957). Foucault's discussion of the origins of the disciplinary society relies on the "capillary spread" of techniques (Foucault, 1977). State power is the mediator for the extension of market and technical relations into traditional lifeworlds in most theories of late modernization.

According to *The Theory of Communicative Action,* juridification plays the mediating role in the contemporary welfare state. Law, Habermas claims, is both a "complex medium" and an "institution." As a complex medium law appropriately regulates system functions. A society with contracts obviously needs laws and means of enforcement. As an institution, law also regulates lifeworld functions, for example through welfare and family legislation. But that can have pathological consequences: communication is blocked or bypassed, mistrust enters, and so on. Then law becomes an instrument of colonization of lifeworld by system.

In these respects technology offers an exact parallel to law. It, too, mediates both system and lifeworld. Following Habermas's analysis of law, one could argue that technical mediation of system functions is unobjectionable, while the application of technology to the lifeworld may give rise to pathologies. Consider, for example, the medical offensive against breast feeding in the 1930s and 1940s. In this instance, an aspect of family life was technologized in the mistaken belief that formula was healthier than breast milk. This technical mediation complicated infant care unnecessarily while opening huge markets. More recently, the widespread use of formula in countries without pure water spread infant diarrhea which in turn required medical treatment, further intruding technology on infant care. This is a clearly pathological intervention of technology into the lifeworld.

Before leaving this point, it is perhaps useful to forestall a possible misunderstanding. It would be misleading to identify technology (or any of the other media) with instrumentality as such. This is clear from the example of breast feeding which is not without its own *techne*, different from formula but "success oriented" too. If all instrumentality is designated as technological, one has no basis on which to distinguish the broad realm of technique in general from its specifically modern technological form. But there are basic differences between hand work and modern technology. The one consists in lifeworld activities carried out by individuals or small groups with small-scale means under individual control, while the other involves unusually complex activities mediated by semiautomatic devices and systems under some sort of management control. No doubt the line is fuzzy, but this general distinction is useful and allows us to judge the degree of technologization of the lifeworld.[10]

VALUE AND RATIONALITY

A Two-Level Critique

The last section sketched a communication-theoretic formulation of a critical theory of technology. Instead of ignoring the technologization of advanced societies, as Habermas and most of his followers do, this theory subjects it to analysis. The treatment of technology as a medium improves Habermas's theory of communicative action without shattering its framework. Nevertheless, it suggests some deeper problems in the theory which do place its framework under tension. I would like to address those problems now.

The synthesis sketched so far concerns only the extent and the range of instrumental mediation and not technological design. In fact Habermas's system theory offers no basis for criticizing the internal structure of any of the media. He can challenge their overextension into communicative domains but not their design in their own domain of competence. Nothing in his theory corresponds to Marcuse's critique of the neutrality of rationality. But a critical theory of technology cannot ignore design. Whether the issue concerns child labor, medical research, computer mediated communication, or environmental impacts of technology, design has normative implications and is not simply a matter of efficiency.

---

[10] Krogh (1998: 186-189) contains objections to my approach which I have tried to overcome here.

What we need is a two-level critique of instrumentality. At one level I will follow Habermas in claiming that the media have general characteristics which qualify their application. This substantivist argument justifies the demand for boundaries on their range. But a second-level critique is also needed because media design is shaped by the hegemonic interests of the society it serves. Markets, administrations, technical devices are biased and embody specific valuative choices. These designed-in biases leave a mark on the media even in those domains where they appropriately regulate affairs. Therefore, critique cannot cease at the boundary of the system but must extend deep inside it; it must become design critique.

But before we can work out such a two-level critique, a fundamental objection must be met. The two level approach appears to be self-defeating. If we blur the theoretical difference between system and lifeworld by defining both in normative terms, then how are we to maintain real boundaries between them in practical affairs? It makes no sense to protest against the extension of technological rationality into communicatively regulated domains if there is no fundamental difference between system and lifeworld in the first place.

This objection is related to the question of whether the system/lifeworld distinction is analytic or real. Axel Honneth, among others, objects to Habermas's identification of the terms of this distinction with actual institutions, e.g. state, market, family, school (Honneth, 1991: 247-248). In reality, he argues, there is no clear institutional line between system and lifeworld. Production as much as the family is constituted by a promiscuous mixture of cognitive, normative, and expressive codes, success-oriented and communicative action. The distinction is therefore purely analytic. But what then becomes of the idea of bounding the media? We can hardly place a boundary around an analytically distinguishable entity. While I agree with Honneth's main point, it seems to me that several different considerations are confused in these objections.

Habermas agrees that the distinction between system and lifeworld is analytic. No institution is a pure exemplification of one or the other category. While the types of action coordination characteristic of each—media-steered or communicative—are distinct, they are always combined in various proportions in real situations. Thus the system is not itself a social institution, but merely refers to actual institutions, such as the market or the state, in which media-steered interactions predominate. Similarly, the lifeworld is not exclusively communicative, but describes those actual institutions, such as the family, in which communication predominates (Ingram, 1987: 115-116). And surely Habermas is right to argue that there is a fundamental difference between institutions that are preponderantly shaped by markets or bureaucracies (and, I would add, technologies), and others in which personal relations or communicative interaction are primary. The fact of mixed motives and codes notwithstanding, without some such distinction one can make no sense at all of the process of modernization.

Although in principle Habermas avoids in this way a crude identification of system and lifeworld with actual institutions, in practice, the analytic distinctions tend to become indistinguishable from real ones. For instance, state and family end up exemplifying system and lifeworld despite Habermas's precautions (Habermas, 1984, 1987: II, 310). Perhaps this also explains why he does not consider technology to be a medium. It seems to be ubiquitous; how then to identify it with an institutional base in which it would support a predominance of media-steered interaction? Habermas may have thought that technology's contribution to the problems of modern society could be adequately captured by analysis of its employment in the market and administrative structures through which the colonization process advances. However, the theoretical disadvantages of thus dissolving technology into economics and politics far outweigh the advantages.

The Bias of the System

The crux of the problem is not the system/lifeworld distinction *per se*, but the identification of one of its terms with neutral formal rationality. Contemporary feminist theory, organizational sociology, and sociology of science and technology have abundantly demonstrated that no such rationality exists. For example, Nancy Fraser (1987) has shown that the high level of abstraction at which Habermas defines his categories only serves to mask their gendered realization in concrete societies. System and lifeworld, material production and symbolic reproduction, public and private, all such abstractions hide distinctions of male and female roles which invest even the apparently pure administrative and political rationality of the modern economy and state. Failing to grasp that fact leads to an overestimation of the pathologies of colonization (reification), and a corresponding underestimation of the oppression of social groups such as women.

A related problem vitiates the system concept on its own ground. Note that Habermas's system theory cuts deeper than the concept of system introduced in chapter 5. There I contrasted organizations, considered as systems, with the wider networks of actors and objects in which they are embedded and portions of which they attempt to define as their environment. My example of a system was a firm, embedded in a network including labor unions and the community. But in Habermas's Luhmannian usage, the term "system" refers in the first instance not to organizations but to the structure of interactions carried out in media such as money or power. This is the social logic that underlies the extended networks of modern societies. In the case in point, money and power mediate the forms of wage labor and urban development, and it is this which makes the organization of a firm possible in the first place.

So far so good, but what is missing from Habermas's account is any consideration of how organizations in turn structure and restructure the media, how they bias exchange and administration as they construct what de Certeau called a "Cartesian" interiority. Because Habermas does not consider this aspect of organizational activity, the media are treated as neutral realizations of a rational logic, and the social pathology associated with their overextension is reduced to the neutralization of normative considerations they bring in their wake.

This does not go far enough. The dissolution of traditional or ethical values in monetary and legal systems is only half the problem. We also need a way of talking about the implicit designed-in normative biases of rationalized institutions. And to make the theoretical challenge still more difficult, we must find a way of describing these biases without losing the distinction between system and lifeworld. This means showing how these norms enter media in media-specific forms, not as communicative understandings of the sort that characterize the lifeworld.

But this goes against the grain. If it is difficult to conceive of system rationality as normatively informed, this is because our conception of valuative bias is shaped by lifeworld contexts and experiences. We think of values as rooted in feelings or beliefs, as expressed or justified, as chosen or criticized. Values belong to the world of "ought", in contrast to the factual world of "is." We are unaccustomed to the idea that institutions based on system rationality realize objectified norms in devices and practices, and not merely in the individual beliefs or shared assumptions.

I made a start toward addressing this problem in chapter 4. I distinguished there between a functionalist understanding of technology in which technical devices stand in external relations to the social and its goals, and a hermeneutic approach for which devices possess complex meanings that include delegated norms and connotations. These valuative dimensions of technology are "embodied" in devices through design.

Habermas's difficulties stem from his fidelity to a functionalist account in which the analytic distinction between system and lifeworld ends up as a real distinction between an objective realm of technically rational means and a subjective realm of ends, values, meanings. It does not help much that he thinks valuative claims can be redeemed and given some sort of objective ground by communicative rationality. The problem is that in floating free of technical rationality, they strip the system normatively bare. The gap between value and fact Habermas transcends in the world of talk is bigger than ever in the material world. This is the ultimate result of what Latour calls the modern "purification" of nature and society (Latour, 1993). By contrast, the hermeneutic approach distinguishes system and lifeworld not as matter and spirit, means and ends, but in terms of the different ways in which fact and value are joined in different types of social objects and discourses. From this standpoint, there is no need for an unconvincing notion of pure rationality.

Critical Theory of Technology

The social theory of technology appears more plausible by contrast with Habermas's as soon as one asks what he actually means by the essence of technology, i.e. the objectivating, success-oriented relation to nature. Is there enough substance to such a definition to imagine it implemented? Is it not rather an abstract classification so empty of content as to tolerate a wide range of realizations, including Marcuse's notion of relating to nature as to another subject? Unless, that is, one smuggles in a lot of historically specific content. That is the only way one can get from the excessively general concept of a success-oriented relation to nature to the specific assertion that technology necessarily excludes respect for nature along the lines Marcuse proposes. Here Habermas repeats the very error of which he accuses Weber, identifying rationality in general with a specific historical realization of it.

The critique of norms embodied in rational systems begins with Marx's analysis of the market. Under the influence of Weber and Lukács, Critical Theory attempted to extend the Marxian approach to bureaucracy, technology, and other rational institutions. The fundamental ambition of the critique was to bring these embodied norms to consciousness where they could be identified and challenged. Habermas's notion of a nonsocial instrumental rationality puts that critique out of action. It reverses the theoretical revolution by which Marx attempted to bring philosophy down from the heaven of pure concepts to the real world, the social life process. This may explain the relentless pursuit of abstraction that is both Habermas's strength and his weakness.

Where system design embodies normative biases that are taken for granted and placed beyond discussion, only a type of critique Habermas's theory excludes can open up a truly free dialogue. In the case of technology, this critique is still undeveloped although some work has been done on the labor process, reproductive technologies, and the environment. As Marcuse had already argued, the research shows that modern technological rationality incorporates domination in its very structure. Our technical disciplines and designs, especially in relation to labor, gender, and nature, are rooted in a hegemonic order.

It is true that this pattern is often condemned in totalizing critiques of technology as such. Habermas is right to want to avoid the technophobia sometimes associated with that approach. However, Marcuse does not make this mistake. He introduces a third term between anti- and pro-technology positions: the idea of future change in the structure of technological rationality itself. As we have seen, this alternative is based on the quasi-Heideggerian distinction between technology as reduction to raw materials in the interest of control, and a differently designed technology that would free the inherent potential of its objects in harmony with human needs. We have already discussed some of the unsolved problems with this theory.

These problems do not, however, justify returning to an essentialist approach which defines technology in abstraction from any sociohistorical context. Nor will it work to claim, as Habermas does, that there is a level of technical rationality that is invariant regardless of changes in that context. Of course technical action systems and rationalities must have some common core of attributes; in chapter 9 I call these the "primary instrumentalizations." But Habermas wants to get too much—a whole social critique—out of the few abstract properties belonging to that core. No doubt it expresses, as he affirms, the objectifying, success-oriented relation to nature—but it must be embodied in technical devices and disciplines that include much else besides to provide a basis for application. It is the rationality of those concrete instantiations that is in question, since that is the form in which instrumental reason becomes historically active.

Is it possible to develop a critique of technical rationality at that concrete level while avoiding the pitfalls of Marcuse's theory? I believe this can be done through analysis of the social dimensions of technology discussed in earlier chapters. These include delegated norms, aesthetic forms, work group organization, vocational investments, and various relational properties of technical artifacts. In chapter 9, I call these "secondary instrumentalizations" by contrast with the "primary instrumentalizations" that establish the basic technical subject-object relation. Their configuration, governed by specific technical codes, characterizes distinct eras in the history of technical rationality. Consider, for example, the passage from craft to industrial production: productivity increased rapidly, a quantitative change of great significance that appears purely technical, but just as importantly, secondary instrumentalizations such as work design, management, and working life suffered a profound qualitative transformation. These transformations are not merely sociological accretions on a presocial relation to nature, or unintended consequences of technological change, but are essential to industrialization considered precisely in its technical aspect. They result from a technical code that privileges deskilling as a fundamental strategy of mechanization from Arkwright down to the present. This approach can capture something of Marcuse's contribution while also overcoming the problems in Habermas's notion of rationality.

The essence of technology can only be the sum of all the major determinations it exhibits in its various stages of development. That sum is sufficiently rich and complex to embrace numerous possibilities through shifts of emphasis among the primary and secondary instrumentalizations. This approach bears a certain resemblance to Habermas's interpretation of modernity in terms of a structural model encompassing a variety of forms of rationalization that receive differing emphases in different types of modern society (see Chart 3) (Habermas 1984, 1987: I, 238). However, I extend this approach downward into technology, which is only one component of Habermas's model, in order to introduce variety at that level. The various technical rationalities that have appeared in the course of history would each be characterized by a formal bias associated with its specific configuration. A critical account of modern technology could be developed on this basis with a view to constructive change rather than romantic retreat.[11]

Boundaries and Layers

Many of Habermas's significant advances are compatible with this enlargement of the media theory to include technology. Indeed, in

---

[11] For an all too rare attempt to defend discourse ethics by enlarging its scope to include technical relations, see Ingram 1995, Chap. 5.

recent writings he has taken a major step toward what I would call a two-level critique of law. Habermas distinguishes between the "pure" moral norms that describe "possible interactions between speaking and acting subjects in general," and legal norms that "refer to the network of interactions in a specific society" (Habermas, 1994: 124). Because they are the concrete expression of a people at a particular time and place, committed to a particular conception of the good life, these latter must incorporate substantive values. But—and this is the important point —they do so in a legally salient manner, not in a way that would erase the distinction between law and politics. Habermas concludes, "Every legal system is also the expression of a particular form of life and not merely a reflection of the universal content of basic rights" (Habermas, 1994: 124). Thus pure moral norms are insufficient to define a society; they must be concretized through choices about the good life.

The argument offered here parallels in the sphere of technology this Habermasian reflection on the relation of the right and the good. Pure technical principles do not define actual technologies. They must be concretized through a technically realized conception of the good which particularizes them and establishes them systematically in the life process of a society. Every instantiation of technical principles is socially specific, just as Habermas claims of law. For both law and technology, the abstract primary level constitutive of the action type must be realized through a secondary level that embodies context and connection. Both law and technology are thus open to criticism not only where they are inappropriately applied, but also for the defects of the form of life they embody. Like law, sometimes technology is overextended, sometimes it is politically biased, sometimes it is both. Several different critical approaches are needed, depending on the case.

Now it is clear even on Habermas's own terms why it is insufficient merely to bound technical systems; they must also be *layered* with demands corresponding to a publicly debated conception of the good life. As we saw in chapter 5, democratic rationalizations carry out this process in many domains. Each successive wave of rationalization adds new layers of significance and function as technical systems are accommodated to the demands of excluded actors. The democratic dialogue which Habermas confines to political life here enters into the technical base of the society as well. We need a method that can appreciate these occasions, even if they are few and far between, even if we cannot predict their ultimate success.

Part III.

TECHNOLOGY AND MODERNITY

8. Technology and Meaning

What Heidegger called "The Question of Technology" has a peculiar status in the academy today. After World War II, the humanities and social sciences were swept by a wave of technological determinism. If technology was not praised for modernizing us, it was blamed for the crisis of our culture. Determinism provided both optimists and pessimists with a fundamental account of modernity as a unified phenomenon. This approach has now been largely abandoned for a view that admits the possibility of significant "difference," i.e. cultural variety in the reception and appropriation of modernity. Yet the breakdown of simplistic determinism has not led to the flowering of research in philosophy of technology one might have hoped for. To a considerable extent, it is the very authority of Heidegger's answer to the "Question" that has blocked new developments. If we want to acknowledge the possibility of alternative modernities, we will have to break with Heidegger.

Heidegger is no doubt the most influential philosopher of technology in this century. Of course he is many other things besides, but it is undeniable that his history of being culminates in the technological enframing. His ambition was to explain the modern world philosophically, to renew the power of reflection for our time. This project was worked out in the midst of the vast technological revolution that transformed the old European civilization, with its rural and religious roots, into a mass urban industrial order based on science and technology. Heidegger was acutely aware of this transformation which was the theme of intense philosophical and political discussion in the Germany of the 1920s and 1930s (Sluga, 1993; Herf, 1984). At first he sought the political significance of "the encounter between global technology and modern man" (Heidegger, 1959: 166). The results were disastrous and he went on to purely philosophical reflection on the question of technology.

Heidegger claims that technology turns everything it touches into mere raw materials, which he calls "standing reserves" (*Bestand*) (Heidegger, 1977a). We ourselves are now incorporated into the mechanism, mobilized as objects of technique. Modern technology is based on methodical planning which itself presupposes the "enframing" (*Gestell*) of being, its conceptual and experiential reduction to a manipulable vestige of itself. He illustrates his theory with the contrast between a silver chalice made by a Greek craftsman and a modern dam on the Rhine (Heidegger, 1977a). The craftsman gathers the elements—form, matter, finality—and thereby brings out the "truth" of his materials. Modern technology "de-worlds" its materials and "summons" (*Herausfordern*) nature to submit to extrinsic demands. Instead of a world of authentic things capable of gathering a rich variety of contexts and meanings, we are left with an "objectless" heap of functions.

The contrast between art and craft on the one hand and technology on the other is rooted in an ontological distinction. Heidegger believes that art and craft are ontological "openings" or "clearings" (*Lichtung*) through which ordered worlds are constituted. The jug gathers together nature, man, and gods in the pouring of the libation. A Greek temple lays out a space within which the city lives and grows. The poet establishes meanings that endure and bring a world to light. All these forms of *techne* let things appear as what they most profoundly are, in some sense, prior to human willing and making. For Heidegger the fundamental mystery of existence is this self-manifesting of things in an opening provided by man.

How pathetic are technological achievements compared to this! Heidegger claims that technology does not let being appear, it makes things be according to an arbitrary will. It does not *open*, it *causes*. Or at least so the West has understood itself since antiquity. The willful making that comes to fruition in technology has been the ontological model for Western metaphysics since Plato. It was there in Christian theology, which substituted the idea of divine creation as the making of the universe for the true question of being. Today it rages over the whole planet as a human deed: modern technology. But a universe ordered simply by the will has no roots and no intrinsic meaning. In such a universe, man has no special ontological place but is merely one force among others, one object of force among others. Metaphysics swallows up the metaphysician and so contradicts itself in the terrible catastrophe that is modernity. Heidegger calls for resignation and passivity (*Gelassenheit*) rather than an active program of reform which would simply constitute a further extension of modern technology. As Heidegger explained in his last interview, "Only a god can save us" from the juggernaut of progress (Heidegger, 1977b).

In what would salvation consist? This is a difficult question for Heideggerians. Michael Zimmerman has explained at length the similarities Heidegger imagined between his own thought and National Socialism. Presumably, he believed for a time that art and technique would merge anew in the Nazi state (Zimmerman, 1990: 231). If this truly represents Heidegger's view, it would strangely resemble Marcuse's position in *An Essay on Liberation* (1969) with its eschatological concept of an aesthetic revolution in technology.[1] More plausibly, Heidegger merely hoped that art would regain the power to define worlds as we detach ourselves from technology.

In a later work, the *Discourse on Thinking (Gelassenheit)*, Heidegger proposed something he called gaining a "free relation" to technology. He admits that technology is indispensable, but "We can affirm the unavoidable use of technical devices, and also deny them the right to dominate us, and so to warp, confuse, and lay waste our nature" (Heidegger, 1966: 54). If we do so, Heidegger promises, "Our relation to technology will become wonderfully simple and relaxed. We let technical devices enter our daily life, and at the same time leave them outside, that is, let them alone, as things which are nothing absolute but remain dependent upon something higher" (Heidegger, 1966: 54).

There is a good deal more along these lines in Heidegger's text. He claims that once we achieve a free relation to technology, we will stand in the presence of technology's hidden meaning. Even though we cannot know that meaning, awareness of its existence already reveals the technological enframing as an opening, dependent on man, and disclosing being. If we can receive it in that spirit, it will no longer dominate us and will leave us open to welcome a still deeper meaning than anything technology can supply (Zimmerman, 1990: 235; Dreyfus, 1995: 102).

Translated out of Heidegger's ontological language, we could restate his main point as the claim that technology is a cultural form through which everything in the modern world becomes available for control. Technology thus violates both humanity and nature at a far deeper level than war and environmental destruction. To this culture of control corresponds an inflation of the subjectivity of the controller, a narcissistic degeneration of humanity. This techno-culture leaves nothing untouched: even the homes of Heidegger's beloved Black Forest peasants are equipped with TV antennas. The functionalization of man and society is thus a destiny from which there is no escape.

Although Heidegger means his critique to cut deeper than any social or historical fact about our times, it is by no means irrelevant to a

---

[1] Zimmerman does not cite a text and I have not been able to find one.

modern world armed with nuclear weapons and controlled by vast technically based organizations. These latter in particular illustrate the concept of the enframing with striking clarity. Alain Gras explores the inexorable growth of such macro-systems as the electric power and airline industries (Gras, 1993). As they apply ever more powerful technologies, absorb more and more of their environment, and plan ever further into the future, they effectively escape human control and indeed human purpose. Macro-systems take on what Thomas Hughes calls "momentum," a quasi-deterministic power to perpetuate themselves and to force other institutions to conform to their requirements (Hughes, 1987). Here we can give a clear empirical content to the concept of enframing.

Heidegger's critique of "autonomous technology" is thus not without merit. Increasingly, we lose sight of what is sacrificed in the mobilization of human beings and resources for goals that remain ultimately obscure. But there are significant ambiguities in Heidegger's approach. He warns us that the essence of technology is nothing technological, that is to say, technology cannot be understood through its usefulness, but only through our specifically technological engagement with the world. But is that engagement merely an attitude or is it embedded in the actual design of modern technological devices?

In the former case, we could achieve the "free relation" to technology which Heidegger demands without changing any of the devices we use. But that is an idealistic solution in the bad sense, and one which a generation of environmental action would seem decisively to refute. In the latter case, how is the break with "technological thinking" supposed to affect the design of actual devices? By osmosis, perhaps? But even such a vague indication is lacking in Heidegger, for whom technical design is totally indifferent. The lack of an answer to these questions leaves me in some doubt as to the supposed relevance of Heidegger's work to ecology.

Confronted with such arguments, Heidegger's defenders usually waffle on the attitude/device ambiguity. They point out that his critique of technology is not merely concerned with human attitudes but with the way being reveals itself. Again roughly translated out of Heidegger's language, this means that the modern world has a technological form in something like the sense in which, for example, the medieval world had a religious form. Form is no mere question of attitude but takes on a material life of its own: power plants are the gothic cathedrals of our time. But this interpretation of Heidegger's thought raises the expectation that he will offer criteria for a reform of technology. For example, his analysis of the tendency of modern technology to accumulate and store up nature's powers suggests the superiority of another technology that would not challenge nature in Promethean fashion.

Unfortunately, Heidegger's argument is developed at such a high level of abstraction he literally cannot discriminate between electricity and atom bombs, agricultural techniques and the Holocaust. In a 1949 lecture, he asserted: "Agriculture is now the mechanized food industry, in essence the same as the manufacturing of corpses in gas chambers and extermination camps, the same as the blockade and starvation of nations, the same as the production of hydrogen bombs." (Quoted in Rockmore (1992: 241)). All are merely different expressions of the identical enframing which we are called to transcend through the recovery of a deeper relation to being. And since Heidegger rejects technical regression while leaving no room for a better technological future, it is difficult to see in what that relation would consist beyond a mere change of attitude.

A CONTEMPORARY CRITIQUE

Technology and Meaning

Heidegger holds that the restructuring of social reality by technical action is inimical to a life rich in meaning. The Heideggerian relation to being is incompatible with the overextension of technological thinking. It seems, therefore, that identification of the structural features of enframing can found a critique of modernity. I intend to test this approach through an evaluation of some key arguments in the work of Albert Borgmann, the leading American representative of philosophy of technology in the essentialist vein.[2]

Borgmann identifies the "device paradigm" as the formative principle of a technological society which aims above all at efficiency. In conformity with this paradigm, modern technology separates off the good or commodity it delivers from the contexts and means of delivery. Thus the heat of the modern furnace appears miraculously from discreet sources in contrast with the old wood stove that stands in the center of

---

[2] For another contemporary approach that complements Borgmann's, see Simpson (1995). Simpson denies that he is essentializing technology, and yet he works throughout his book with a minimum set of invariant characteristics of technology independent of the sociohistorical context (Simpson, 1995: 15-16, 182). That context is then consigned to a merely contingent level of influences, conditions, or consequences rather than being integrated to the conception of technology itself.

the room and is supplied by regular trips to the woodpile. The microwaved meal emerges effortlessly and instantly from its plastic wrapping at the individual's command in contrast with the laborious operations of a traditional kitchen serving the needs of a whole family.

The device paradigm offers gains in efficiency, but at the cost of distancing us from reality. Let us consider the substitution of "fast food" for the traditional family dinner. To common sense, well prepared fast food appears to supply nourishment without needless social complications. Functionally considered, eating is a technical operation that may be carried out more or less efficiently. It is a matter of ingesting calories, a means to an end, while all the ritualistic aspects of food consumption are secondary to the satisfaction of biological need. But what Borgmann calls "focal things" that gather people in meaningful activities that have value for their own sake cannot survive this functionalizing attitude.

The unity of the family, ritually reaffirmed each evening, no longer has a comparable locus of expression today. One need not claim that the rise of fast food "causes" the decline of the traditional family to recognize a significant connection. Simplifying personal access to food scatters people who need no longer construct the rituals of quotidian interaction around the necessities of daily living. Focal things require a certain effort, it is true, but without that effort, the rewards of a meaningful life are lost in the vapid disengagement of the operator of a smoothly functioning machinery (Borgmann, 1984: 204ff).

Borgmann would willingly concede the usefulness of many devices, but the generalization of the device paradigm, its universal substitution for simpler ways, has a deadening effect. Where means and ends, contexts and commodities are strictly separated, life is drained of meaning. Individual involvement with nature and other human beings is reduced to a bare minimum, and possession and control become the highest values.

Borgmann's critique of technological society usefully concretizes themes in Heidegger. His dualism of device and meaning is also structurally similar to Habermas's distinction of work and interaction (Habermas, 1970). This dualism appears wherever the essence of technology is in question. It offers a way of theorizing the larger philosophical significance of the modernization process, and it reminds us of the existence of dimensions of human experience that are suppressed by facile scientism and the uncritical celebration of technology. Borgmann's contrast between the decontextualization of the device and the essentially contextual focal thing reprises Heidegger's distinction between modern technological enframing, and the "gathering" power of traditional craft production that draws people and nature together around a materialized site of encounter. Borgmann's solution, bounding the technical sphere to restore the centrality of meaning, is reminiscent of Habermas's strategy (although apparently not due to his influence.) It offers a more understandable response to invasive technology than anything in Heidegger.

However, Borgmann's approach suffers from both the ambiguity of Heidegger's original theory and the limitations of Habermas's. We cannot tell for sure if he is merely denouncing the modern attitude toward technology or technological design, and in the latter case, his critique is so broad it offers no criteria for constructive reform. He would probably agree with Habermas's critique of the colonization of the lifeworld, although he improves on that account by discussing the role of technology in modern social pathologies. But like Habermas, he lacks a concrete sense of the intricate connections of technology and culture beyond the few essential attributes on which his critique focuses. Since those attributes have largely negative consequences, we get no sense from the critique of the many ways in which the pursuit of meaning is intertwined with technology. And as a result, Borgmann imagines no significant restructuring of modern society around culturally distinctive technical alternatives that might preserve and enhance meaning.

But how persuasive is my objection to Borgmann's approach? After all, neither Russian nor Chinese communism, neither Islamic fundamentalism nor so-called "Asian values" have inspired a fundamentally distinctive stock of devices. Why *not* just reify the concept of technology and treat it as a singular essence? The problem with that is the existence of smaller but still significant differences which may become more important in the future rather than less so as essentialists assume. What is more, those differences often concern precisely the issues identified by Borgmann as central to a humane life. They determine our experience of education, medical care, and work, our relation to the natural environment, the functions of devices such as computers and automobiles, in ways either favorable or unfavorable to the preservation of meaning and community. Any theory of the essence of technology which forecloses the future therefore begs the question of difference in the technical sphere.

Interpreting the Computer

I would like to pursue this contention further with a specific example that illustrates concretely my reasons for objecting to this approach to technology. The example I have chosen, human communication by computer, is one on which Borgmann has commented fairly extensively and which we have already discussed in chapter 5. While not everyone who shares the essentialist view will agree with his very negative conclusions, his position adequately represents that style of technology critique, and is therefore worth evaluating here at some length.[3]

Borgmann introduces the term "hyperintelligence" to refer to such developments as electronic mail and the Internet (Borgmann, 1992: 102ff). Hyperintelligent communication offers unprecedented opportunities for people to interact across space and time, but, paradoxically, it also distances those it links. No longer are the individuals "commanding presences" for each other; they have become disposable experiences that can be turned on and off like water from a faucet. The person as a focal thing has become a commodity delivered by a device. This new way of relating has weakened connection and involvement while extending its range. What happens to the users of the new technology as they turn away from face-to-face contact?

> Plugged into the network of communications and computers, they seem to enjoy omniscience and omnipotence; severed from their network, they turn out to be insubstantial and disoriented. they no longer command the world as persons in their own right. Their conversation is without depth and wit; their attention is roving and vacuous; their sense of place is uncertain and fickle (Borgmann, 1992: 108).

This negative evaluation of the computer can be extended to earlier forms of mediated communication. In fact Borgmann does not hesitate to denounce the telephone as a hyperintelligent substitute for more deeply reflective written correspondence (Borgmann, 1992: 105).

There is an element of truth in this critique. On the networks, the pragmatics of personal encounter are radically simplified, reduced to the protocols of technical connection. It is easy to pass from one social contact to another, following the logic of the technical network that supports ever more rapid commutation. However, Borgmann's conclusions are too hastily drawn and simply ignore the role of social contextualizations in the appropriation of technology. A look, first, at the history of computer communication, and, second, at one of its innovative applica-

---

[3] For another critique of the computer similar to Borgmann's, see Slouka (1995). The case for the defense can be found in Rheingold (1993).

tions today refutes his overly negative evaluation. We will see that the real struggle is not between the computer and low tech alternatives, but within the realm of possibilities opened by the computer itself.

In the first place, the computer was not destined by some inner techno-logic to serve as a communications medium. As we saw in chapter 5, the major networks, such as the French Teletel and the Internet were originally conceived by technocrats and engineers as instruments for the distribution of data. In the course of the implantation of these networks, users appropriated them for unintended purposes and converted them into communications media. Soon they were flooded with messages that were considered trivial or offensive by their creators. Teletel quickly became the world's first and largest electronic singles bar (Feenberg, 1995: chap. 7). The Internet is overloaded with political debates dismissed as "trash" by unsympathetic critics. Less visible, at least to journalists, but more significant, other applications of computers to human communication gradually appeared, from business meetings to education, from discussions among medical patients, literary critics, and political activists to on-line journals and conferences.

How does Borgmann's critique fare in the light of this history? It seems to me there is an element of ingratitude in it. Because Borgmann takes it for granted that the computer is useful for human communication, he neither appreciates the process of making it so, nor the hermeneutic transformation it underwent in that process. He therefore also overlooks the political implications of the history sketched above. Today the networks constitute a fundamental scene of human activity. To impose a narrow regimen of data transmission to the exclusion of all human contact would surely be perceived as totalitarian in any ordinary institution. Why is it not a liberation to transcend such limitations in the virtual world that now surrounds us?

In the second place, Borgmann's critique ignores the variety of communicative interactions mediated by the networks. No doubt he is right that human experience is not enriched by much of what goes on there. But a full record of the face-to-face interactions occurring in the halls of his university would likely be no more uplifting. The problem is that we tend to judge the face-to-face at its memorable best and the computer-mediated equivalent at its transcribed worst. Borgmann simply ignores more interesting uses of computers, such as the original research applications of the Internet, and teaching applications which show great promise (Harasim, et al., 1995). It might surprise Borgmann to find the art of reflective letter writing reviving in these contexts.

Consider for example the discussion group on the Prodigy Medical Support Bulletin Board devoted to ALS (Amyotrophic Lateral Sclerosis or Lou Gehrig's Disease). In 1995, when I studied it, there were about 500 patients and caregivers reading exchanges in which some dozens of participants were actively engaged (Feenberg, et al., 1996). Much of the conversation concerned feelings about dependency, illness, and dying. There was a long-running discussion of problems of sexuality. Patients and caregivers wrote in both general and personal terms about the persistence of desire and the obstacles to satisfaction. The frankness of this discussion may owe something to the anonymity of the online environment, appropriated for very different purposes than those Borgmann criticizes. Here the very limitations of the medium open doors that might have remained closed in a face-to-face setting.

These online patient meetings have the potential for changing the accessibility, the scale, and the speed of interaction of patient groups. Face-to-face self-help groups are small and isolated. With the exception of AIDS patients they have wielded no political power. If AIDS patients have been the exception, it is not because of the originality of their demands: patients with incurable illnesses have been complaining bitterly for years about the indifference of physicians and the obstacles to experimental treatment. What made the difference was that AIDS patients were "networked" politically by the gay rights movement even before they were caught up in a network of contagion (Epstein, 1996: 229). Online networks may similarly empower other patient groups by enabling them to constitute an effective technical locale out of which to act on the global medical system. In fact, Prodigy discussion participants established a list of priorities they presented to the ALS Society of America. Computer networking feeds into the rising demand by patients for more control over their own medical care. Democratic rationalization of the computer contributes to a parallel transformation of medicine.

It is difficult to see any connection between these applications of the computer and Borgmann's critique of "hyperintelligence." Is this technologically mediated process by which dying people come together despite paralyzing illness to discuss and mitigate their plight a mere instance of "technological thinking?" Certainly not. But then how would Heidegger incorporate an understanding of it into his theory, with its reproachful attitude toward modern technology in general?

Borgmann's critique of technology pursues the larger connections and social implications masked by the device paradigm. To this extent it is genuinely dereifying. But insofar as it fails to incorporate these hidden social dimensions into the concept of technology itself, it remains still partially caught in the very way of thinking it criticizes. His theory hovers uncertainly between a description of how we encounter technology and how it is designed. Technology, i.e. the real world objects so designated, both is and is not the problem, depending on whether the emphasis is on its fetish form as pure device or our subjective acceptance of that form. In neither case can we change technology "in itself." At best, we can hope to overcome our attitude toward it through a spiritual movement of some sort.[4]

The ambiguities of the computer referred to in this section are far from unique. In fact they are typical of most technologies, especially in the early phases of their development. Recognizing this malleability of technology, we can no longer rest content with globally negative theories that offer only condemnation of the present and no guidance for the future. We need a very different conceptualization that includes what I have called the secondary instrumentalizations, i.e. the integration of technologies to larger technical systems and nature, and to the symbolic orders of ethics and aesthetics, as well as their relation to the life and learning processes of workers and users, and the social organization of work and use.

THE GATHERING

Is there anything in Heidegger that can help us in this task? I believe there is, although we will need a "free relation" to Heidegger's thought to get at it. Recall that for Heidegger modern technology is stripped of meaning by contrast with the meaningful tradition we have lost. Even the old technical devices of the past shared in this lost meaning. For example, Heidegger shows us a jug "gathering" the contexts in which it was created and functions (Heidegger, 1971a). The concept of the thing as gathering resembles Borgmann's notion of the "focal thing." These

---

[4] Andrew Light has argued that I underestimate the significance of Borgmann's distinction between device and thing for an understanding of the aesthetics of everyday life. The distinction is useful for developing a critique of mass culture and could provide criteria for democratic rationalizations of the commodified environment. The story of the ALS patients told here could be interpreted in this light as an example of the creation of a meaningful community through the creative appropriation of the hyperreal technological universe Borgmann describes (Light, 1996: chap. 9). I am in general agreement with this revision of Borgmann's position, but in some doubt as to whether Borgmann himself would be open to it.

concepts dereify the thing and activate its intrinsic value and manifold connections with the human world and nature.

Heidegger's doctrine of the thing is a puzzling combination of deep insights and idiosyncratic esotericism. In the example of the jug, Heidegger struggles to distinguish the thing as such from its representation as an object of knowledge and production. The essence of the thing is not fully understandable from either point of view. Why? Because knowing and producing presuppose the thing as their object. What it is in itself escapes: the thing, Heidegger assures us, is unknown because it has never been thought. And even the suspicion of what has been overlooked disappears in the technological enframing which absolutizes knowing and producing and annihilates the thing in its essential being.

Heidegger wants to call to our attention another mode of perception that belongs to the lost past or perhaps to a future we can only dimly imagine. In that mode we share the earth with things rather than reducing them to mere resources. This is not a matter of political or moral choice. He is demanding that we recognize fully our own unsurpassable belonging to a world in which meaning guides the rituals that crystallize around things. I thus interpret Heidegger not to be imagining some radically new relation to reality, but simply calling on us to recognize our real situation as human beings. To become aware, to "assume" our human being (*Dasein*), this would be enough. Philosophy cannot make this happen but it can rethink the thing so that we at least acknowledge what has been lost in the enframing. The concept of the gathering nature of the thing is the result of this rethinking.

Heidegger's discussion of gathering is closely conected to another still more obscure concept, the "fourfold" (*Geviert*) of earth, sky, mortals, and divinities. In the pouring of wine from the jug, humans and things— land, sun, and gods—come together, united in a ritual practice. From one poetic leap to another, Heidegger arrives at the conclusion that this gathering constitutes what he means by "world," i.e., the ordered system of connections between things, tools, locations, enacted and suffered by *Dasein* (Heidegger, 1971a). This same concept of the fourfold also appears in his discussion of the work of art which, he claims, establishes a world through its power of disclosure (*Erschlossenheit*) (Heidegger, 1971c). "To be a work means to set up a world" (Heidegger, 1971c: 44). But does the thing also disclose? The answer is not clear; in this respect the line between work and thing blurs. Heidegger does say that "The thing things world" (Heidegger, 1971a: 181). Perhaps we are meant to understand that the thing has a minor disclosive power.

Heidegger's poetic notion of the "fourfold" seems to be an attempt to capture in abstract terms the essential elements of the ritual structure of the thing, the human being, and the world they inhabit. The fourfold refers to no particular system of practices and things, but reminds us of what all such systems have in common insofar as all human lives are rooted in enacted meanings of some sort (Kolb, 1986: 191). One can judge this notion in various ways. For some readers it may be evocative and profound. I must confess that I find it rather disappointing. It seems to call me out of the meanings I encounter in my own existence toward a manufactured mystery I inevitably associate with the contingent individual, Heidegger, whom I do not feel inclined to "follow." But then Heidegger generously conceded in advance that the thought of Being is easily led astray...

Rather than dwelling on these contentious matters, I would prefer to consider a more narrowly philosophical implication of Heidegger's conception of the thing. This is the break with substance metaphysics it implies. The jug is not primarily a physical object which has gathering relations. It *is* these relations and is merely released to its existence as such by production, or known in its outward appearance by representation. Heidegger writes, for example,

> Our thinking has of course long been accustomed to *understating* the nature of the thing. The consequence, in the course of Western thought, has been that the thing is represented as an unknown X to which perceptible properties are attached. From this point of view, everything *that already belongs to the gathering nature of this thing...* appear[s] as something that is afterward read into it (Heidegger, 1971b: 153).

In sum, Heidegger grasps the thing not just as a focus of practical rituals, but as *essentially* that, as constituted *qua* thing by these involvements rather than as preexisting them somehow and acquiring them later.

At this point, a misunderstanding threatens. Could it be that Heidegger intends us to move from a substance metaphysics to a network metaphysics, a sort of field theory of things? Is the gathering thing a node in a network? In one sense the answer to these questions is yes, but it is a very special sense that needs to be worked out against the background of *Being and Time*. The notion of the thing as a gathering that discloses a world can be seen as a corrective to the overemphasis on the role of *Dasein* in disclosure in that earlier work. There "world" was defined not as "all that is," nor as an object of knowledge, but as the realm of everyday practice. To understand "world" in this sense, Heidegger required us to shift our point of view from the cognitive to the practical, to take the practical as ontologically significant on its own terms. From that point of view the world consisted in a network of ready-to-hand objects (*Zeug*) with *Dasein* at their center.

The problem is that Heidegger had little to say about those objects. *Dasein* opened up the world in which they dwelled, but they themselves never came forward in a positive role. The result was suspiciously like a theory of the subjective investment of a preexisting reality, an "X," with meaning, precisely what Heidegger wanted to avoid. Now he has found a way to right the balance. The disclosure takes place from out of the thing as much as from *Dasein*. Not just the Greek, but the Greek temple opens a world. Disclosure cannot be localized in man, an unfortunate conclusion drawn by some of Heidegger's readers, Sartre, for example.[5]

Note that the idea of the world as a network remains, but it is a network grasped from within from the practical standpoint. The world only reveals itself as such to a reflection that knows how to get behind cognition to a more primordial encounter with being. Such phenomenological reflection places us inside the flux of significance in which the world as network consists. This is not a collection of objective things, substances, but a lifeworld in which we actively participate and which only comes to light insofar as we understand participation as the most fundamental relation to reality.

If we now consider the implications of this concept of the thing for technology, we encounter a paradox right from the start. Devices, Heidegger complains, race toward our goals and lack the integrity of his favorite jug or chalice. But by what rights does he make this summary judgement on the very things that surround him? Devices are things too. Modern and technological though they may be, they too focus gathering practices that bring people together with each and with "earth and sky," joining them in a world. Recall the Prodigy support network described in the previous section. One could hardly find a better illustration of the Heideggerian notion of the thing as essentially a gathering. Indeed, this modern technology suits Heidegger's definition even better than jugs and chalices.

---

[5] For Heidegger's anti-anthropological turn, see Schürmann (1990: 209ff).

This interpretation suggests a fundamental problem with Heidegger's critique of technology. As we saw in the discussion of de Certeau in chapter 5, modern technical networks have two sides: the strategic standpoint of the system manager and the tactical standpoint of the human beings they enroll. The first understands itself in objectivistic terms as knowledge and power; the second yields its secrets to a phenomenology of lived experience. Which standpoint does Heidegger occupy in his understanding of these networks?

The answer is obvious. Heidegger's modern technology is seen from above. This is why it lacks the pathos of gathering and disclosing. The official discourse of a technological society combines narrow functionalism with awe in the face of the technological sublime. In criticizing technology, Heidegger does not so much adopt a different standpoint as reveal the meaninglessness that haunts technological thinking. But this meaninglessness is no mistake; it results from the same type of abstraction that makes system management possible in the first place. It is curious that Heidegger adopts this view of systems, while condemning them, rather than applying his phenomenological approach to the lifeworld they support.

From the standpoint of the ordinary human being—and even system managers and philosophers are ordinary human beings in their spare time—networks are lived worlds in which humans and things participate through disclosive practices. This lifeworld of technology is the place of meaning in modern societies. Our fate is worked out here as surely as on Heidegger's forest paths. Why does Heidegger insist on adopting the managerial perspective even in the course of denouncing its hollow vision? Why doesn't he view modern technology from "within," practically, in its disclosive significance for ordinary actors?

Heidegger resisted the idea that technology could share in the disclosing power of art and things, but now this implication of his theory stares us in the face. If a Greek temple can open a space for the city, why not a modern structure? At what point in its development does architecture cease to be "art" and become "technology?" Heidegger does not seem to know. Indeed, there is even a peculiar passage in which he momentarily forgives the highway bridge for its efficiency and describes it too as "gathering" right along with the old stone bridge over the village stream (Heidegger, 1971b: 152). Surely this is right.

Of course one is not always alert to the ontological significance of highway bridges. As Borgmann shows, the inauthentic relation to devices is commonplace, and, in an improvement on Heidegger, he offers a phenomenological account of that relation. But Heidegger nowhere claims that authenticity was easy before modern technology intruded. On the contrary, inauthenticity has always been the average everyday mode of *Dasein*. Heidegger maintains only the existential possibility of passing from inauthenticity to authenticity, a possibility which ought to extend to our relation to modern technological devices as well as premodern craft objects. Nothing prevents us from respecting modern technology in its "finality," to use Henry Bugbee's term for the intrinsic meaningfulness of things in the world of action. Instead of passing over technical things in our haste to reach our goals, we can dwell near them, attending to them for their own sake and ours (Bugbee, 1999).

Heidegger's undeniable insight is that every making must also include a letting be, an active connection to the meanings that emerge with the thing and which we cannot "make" but only release through our productive activity. And linked to those meanings, there is also a background, a source, that necessarily remains untransformed by our making. This is Heidegger's concept of the "earth" as a reservoir of possibilities beyond human intentions. In denying these connections technological thinking defies human finitude. Neither the meanings of our lives, nor the earth, nature, can become human deeds because all deeds presuppose them (Feenberg, 1986a: chap. 8). Yet I share David Rothenberg's interpretation, according to which Heidegger would also want us to recognize that our contact with the earth is technically mediated: what comes into focus as nature is not the pure immediate but what is lived at the limit of *techne* (Rothenberg, 1993: 195ff). Presumably, the same is true of meanings, which emerge on the horizon of our activities, not as their product but not in passive contemplation either. Despite occasional lapses into romanticism, this is after all the philosopher who placed readiness-to-hand at the center of *Dasein's* world.

The problem with Heidegger's critique is his unqualified claim that modern technology is essentially unable to recognize its limit. That is why he advocates liberation from it rather than reform of it. It is true that the dominant ideology, based on the strategic standpoint, leaves little room for respect for limits of any kind. But we must look beyond that ideology to the realities of modern technology and the society that depends on it. Heidegger's failure, like that of Habermas and many other thinkers in the humanistic tradition, to engage with actual technology is not to their credit but reveals the limits of a certain cultural tradition. Could it be that old disciplinary boundaries between the humanities and the sciences have determined the fundamental categories of social theory? If so, it is time to challenge the effects of those boundaries in our field, which is condemned to violate them by the very nature of its object.

Beyond those boundaries we discover that technology also "gathers" its many contexts through secondary instrumentalizations that integrate it to the surrounding world. Naturally, the results are quite different from the craft tradition Heidegger idealizes, but nostalgia is not a good guide to understanding the world today. When modern technical processes are brought into compliance with the requirements of the environment or human health, they incorporate their contexts into their very structure as truly as the jug, chalice, or bridge that Heidegger holds out as models of authenticity. Our models should be such things as reskilled work, medical practices that respect the person, architectural and urban designs that create humane living spaces, computer designs that mediate new social forms.

These promising innovations are the work of human beings intervening in the design of the technical objects with which they are involved. This is the only meaningful "encounter between global technology and modern man." This encounter is not simply another instance of the goal-oriented pursuit of efficiency, but constitutes an essential dimension of the contemporary struggle for a humane and livable world. In the next chapter I will explain the significance of that struggle for the essence of technology.

Part III.

TECHNOLOGY AND MODERNITY

9. Impure Reason

Habermas, Heidegger and Borgmann have described significant aspects of the technical phenomenon, but have they identified its "essence?" They seem to believe that technical action has a kind of unity that defies the complexity and diversity, the profound sociocultural embeddedness that twenty years of increasingly critical history and sociology of technology have discovered. Yet to dissolve it into the variety of its manifestations, as constructivists sometimes demand, would effectively block philosophical reflection on modernity. The problem is to find a way of incorporating these recent advances in technology studies into a conception of technology's essence rather than dismissing them, as philosophers tend to do, as merely contingent social "influences" on a reified technology "in itself" conceived apart from society. The solution to this problem is a radical redefinition of technology that crosses the usual line between artifacts and social relations assumed by common sense and philosophers alike.

The chief obstacle to this solution is the unhistorical understanding of essence to which most philosophers are committed. I propose, therefore, a historical concept of essence which combines the philosophical and the social scientific perspective. In what follows, I will define the essence of technology as the *systematic* locus for the sociocultural variables that actually diversify its historical realizations. On these terms, the essence of technology is not simply those few distinguishing features shared by all types of technical practice. Those constant determinations are merely abstractions from the socially concrete stages of a process of development. It is the logic of that process which will now play the role of the essence of technology.

I will work out this historical concept of essence in this chapter. Is the result still sufficiently "philosophical" to qualify as philosophy? In claiming that it is, I realize that I am challenging a certain prejudice against the concrete that is an occupational hazard of philosophy. Plato is usually blamed for this, but in a late dialogue he has Parmenides mock the young Socrates' reluctance to admit that there are ideal forms of "hair or mud or dirt or any other trivial and undignified objects" (Cornford, 1957: 130C-E).[1] Surely the time has come to let the social dimension of technology into the charmed circle of philosophical reflection. Let me now suggest a way of achieving this.

INSTRUMENTALIZATION THEORY

A Two-Level Theory

Substantivist philosophies of technology drew attention away from the practical question of what technology *does* to the hermeneutic question of what it *means*. The question of meaning has become defining for philosophy of technology as a distinct branch of humanistic reflection. But as Heidegger points out, from this philosophical standpoint the essence of technology has nothing to do with "the technical," i.e. the specific function of technical objects, but concerns rather the constitution of a functionalized world. More recently, constructivism has sharpened reflection on a third range of questions concerning who makes technology, why and how. This approach too seeks to understand something more fundamental than technical function, namely, the construction of the complex networks of people and things within which functions emerge. My strategy here will consist in incorporating answers to the substantivist and constructivist questions into a single framework with two levels. The first of these levels corresponds more or less to the philosophical definition of the essence of technology, the second to the concerns of social sciences. However, merging them in a two-level critical theory transforms both.

On this account, the essence of technology has not one but two aspects, an aspect which explains the *functional constitution* of technical objects and subjects, which I call the "primary instrumentalization," and another aspect, the "secondary instrumentalization," focused on the *realization* of the constituted objects and subjects in actual networks and devices. Essentialism offers insight only into the primary instrumentalization by which functions are separated from the continuum of everyday life and subjects positioned to relate to them. Primary instrumentalization characterizes technical relations in every society, although its emphasis, range of application and significance varies greatly. All forms

---

[1] Compare Latour's account of a similar episode involving Heraclitus, Latour (1993), pp. 65-66.

of technique include those constant features in historically evolving combinations with a secondary instrumentalization that includes many other aspects of the technical.

Primary Instrumentalization: Functionalization[2]

The primary instrumentalization consists in four reifying moments of technical practice. The first two correspond roughly with important aspects of Heidegger's notion of enframing, and the latter two describe the form of action implied in Habermas's media theory. Together they encompass the forms of objectification and subjectivation associated with a functional world relation.

1. *Decontextualization*

To reconstitute natural objects as technical objects, they must be "de-worlded," artificially separated from the context in which they are originally found so as to be integrated to a technical system. The isolation of the object exposes it to a utilitarian evaluation. The tree conceived as lumber, and eventually cut down, stripped of bark and chopped into boards, is encountered through its usefulness rather than in all its manifold interconnections with its environment and the other species with which it normally coexists. The isolated object reveals itself as containing technical schemas, potentials in human action systems which are made available by decontextualization. Thus inventions such as the knife or the wheel take qualities such as the sharpness or roundness of some natural thing, a rock or tree trunk for example, and release them as technical properties. The role these qualities may have played in nature is obliterated in the process. Nature is fragmented into bits and pieces that appear as technically useful after being abstracted from all specific contexts.

2. *Reductionism*

Reductionism refers to the process in which the de-worlded things are simplified, stripped of technically useless qualities, and reduced to those aspects through which they can be enrolled in a technical network. These are the qualities of primary importance to the technical subject, the qualities perceived as essential to the accomplishment of a technical program. I will therefore call them "primary qualities," it being understood that their primacy is relative to a subject's program. Primary qualities may include anything about objects that offers an affordance, such

---

[2] Many of the ideas in this section and the next were first presented in an earlier version in Feenberg (1991: chapter 8).

as weight, size, shape, sharpness or softness, color, etc. "Secondary qualities" are what remains, including those dimensions of the object that may have been most significant in the course of its pretechnical history. The secondary qualities of the object contain its potential for self-development. The tree trunk, reduced to its primary quality of roundness in becoming a wheel, loses its secondary qualities as a habitat, a source of shade, and a living, growing member of its species. The Heideggerian enframing is the reduction of all of reality to the most abstract primary qualities through formalization and quantification.

3. *Autonomization*

The subject of technical action isolates itself as much as possible from the effects of its action on its objects. Metaphorically speaking, it thus violates Newton's third law, according to which "for every action there is an equal and opposite reaction." The actor and the object in mechanics belong to the same system, hence the reciprocity of their interactions. This is not a bad description of ordinary human relations. A friendly remark is likely to elicit a friendly reply, rudeness, rudeness. By contrast, technical action "autonomizes" the subject. This is accomplished by interrupting the feedback between the object and the actor. In an apparent exception to Newton's law, the technical subject has a big impact on the world, but the world has only a very small return impact on the subject. The hunter experiences a slight pressure on his shoulder as the bullet from his gun strikes the rabbit; the driver hears a faint rustling in the wind as he hurtles a ton of steel down the highway. Administrative action too, as a technical relationship between human beings, presupposes the autonomization of the manager as subject, who must neither fear nor pity the laid-off worker. Their relation must be purely functional.

4. *Positioning*

Technical action controls its objects through their laws. There is thus a moment of passivity with respect to those laws in even the most violent technological intervention. The technical conforms with Francis Bacon's dictum "Nature to be commanded must be obeyed" (Bacon, 1939: 28). The laws of combustion rule over the automobile's engine as the laws of the market govern the investor. In each case, the subject's action consists not in modifying the law of its objects, but in using that law to advantage. Location, as they say in real estate, is everything: fortunes are made by being in the right place at the right time. By positioning itself strategically with respect to its objects, the subject turns their inherent properties to account. The management of labor and the control of the consumer through product design have a similar positional character. Of course there are no natural laws of worker and consumer behavior that would allow one to design it as one would a machine, but one can position oneself so as to induce workers and consumers to fulfill preexisting programs they would not otherwise have chosen. In these social domains, Baconian obedience is a kind of navigation in the turbulent waters of interests, expectations, and fantasies that cannot be controlled, only anticipated and used.

Secondary Instrumentalization: Realization

The primary instrumentalization lays out in skeletal fashion the basic technical relation. Far more is necessary for that relation to yield an actual system or device: technique must be *integrated* with the natural, technical, and social environments that support its functioning. In this process, technical action turns back on itself and its actors as it is realized concretely. It reappropriates some of the dimensions of contextual relatedness and self-development from which abstraction was originally made in establishing the technical relation. Realization thus compensates for some of the reifying effects of the primary instrumentalization. The underdetermination of technological development leaves room for social interests and values to participate in this process. As decontextualized elements are combined, these interests and values assign functions, orient choices and insure congruence between technology and society. The essence of technology thus includes a secondary level that works with dimensions of reality from which the primary instrumentalization abstracts.

This level includes the following four moments:

1. *Systematization*

To function as an actual device, isolated, decontextualized technical objects must be combined with each other and re-embedded in the natural environment. Systematization is the process of making these combinations and connections, in Latour's terms, of "enrolling" objects in a network (Latour, 1992). Thus individual technical objects—wheels, a handle, a container—are brought together to form a device such as a wheelbarrow. Add paint to protect the wheelbarrow from rust and the device has been embedded in its natural environment as well. The process of technical systematization is central to designing the extremely long and tightly coupled networks of modern technological societies but plays a lesser role in traditional societies. There technologies may be better adapted to the natural and social environment but more loosely related functionally. The exorbitant role of systematization in modern societies is rooted in the success of the coordination media, money, power, and (I would add) technology, and the large-scale organizations they make possible.

2. *Mediation*

Ethical and aesthetic mediations supply the simplified technical object with new secondary qualities that seamlessly embed it in its new social context. The ornamentation of artifacts and their investment with ethical meaning are integral to production in all traditional cultures. The choice of a type of stone or feather in the making of an arrow is motivated not only by sharpness and size, but also by various ritual considerations that yield an aesthetically and ethically expressive object. Heidegger's chalice exemplifies such "expressive" design. By contrast, production and aesthetics are partially differentiated in modern industrial societies. The goods are produced first, and then superficially styled and packaged for distribution. The social insertion of the industrial object appears as an afterthought. Ethical limits too are overthrown in the breakdown of religious and craft traditions. Recently, medical advances and environmental crises have inspired new interest in the ethical limitation of technical power. These limitations are eventually embodied in modified designs which condense considerations of efficiency with ethical values. A similar condensation appears in the aesthetics of good industrial design. Thus mediations remain an essential if problematic aspect of the technical process even in modern societies. I will have more to say about mediations below.

3. *Vocation*

The technical subject appears autonomous only insofar as its actions are considered in isolation from its life process. Taken as a whole, the succession of its acts adds up to a craft, a vocation, a way of life. The subject is just as deeply engaged as the object—Newton is vindicated—but in a different register. The doer is transformed by its acts: the rifleman of our earlier example will become a hunter with the corresponding attitudes and dispositions should he pursue such activities professionally. Similarly, the worker in wood becomes a carpenter, the typist at the keyboard a writer, and so on. These human attributes of the technical subject define it at the deepest levels, physically, as a person, and as a member of a community of people engaged in similar activities. "Vocation" is the best term we have for this reverse impact of tools on their users. In traditional cultures and even in some modern ones, such as the Japanese, the concept of vocation or "way" is not associated with any particular kind of work, but in most industrial societies it is reserved for medicine, law, teaching, and similar professions. This is an effect of wage labor, which substitutes temporary employment under administrative control for the lifelong craft of the independent producer, thereby reducing both the impact of any particular skill on the worker and the individual responsibility for quality implied in vocation.

4. *Initiative*

Finally, strategic control of the worker and consumer through positioning is to some extent compensated by various forms of tactical initiative on the part of the individuals submitted to technical control. Before the rise of capitalist management, cooperation was often regulated by tradition or paternal authority, and the uses of the few available devices so loosely prescribed that the line between producer programs and user appropriations was often blurred. It is capitalism that has led to the sharp split between positioning and initiative, strategy and tactics. As we saw in chapter 5, a certain margin of maneuver belongs to subordinated positions in the capitalist technical hierarchy. That margin can support conscious cooperation in the coordination of effort and user appropriation of devices and systems.

Reflexive Technology

The secondary instrumentalization constitutes a *reflexive meta-technical practice* which treats functionality itself as raw material for higher-level forms of technical action. There is of course something paradoxical about this association of reflexivity with technology; in the substantivist framework technical rationality is supposed to be blind to itself. Reflection is reserved for another type of thought competent to deal with such important matters as aesthetics and ethics. We have here the familiar split between nature and *Geist*, and their corresponding sciences.

Substantivism identifies technology as such with a particular *ideology* hostile to reflection. It is true that, abstractly conceived, technology bears an elective affinity for positivism, but that is precisely because every element of reflexivity has been left behind in extracting its essence from history. Heidegger practically admits as much when he affirms that the essence of technology is nothing technological. Ellul too warns us off early on in his major work: the "technical phenomenon" is not so much a matter of devices as of the spirit in which they are used. But in the end, these thinkers and their followers fail to develop an independent theory of technology. They seem to conclude that because at some level technology harbors the evils they have identified in positivism, instrumentalism, behaviorism, mechanism, and all the other doctrines they so effectively criticize, the critique of the one can take the place of a theory of the other.

Not so! The lack of concreteness shows up in the insoluble problems with history discussed in the Introduction. As we have seen, the problem of periodization is central to the essentialist conception. Heidegger's ontological account of the distinction between premodern and modern technology is no more plausible than Habermas's epistemological one. Philosophy ought to have more to say about the history of technology than these schematic contrasts of positivism and tradition. Above I have sketched a way of relating the characteristic distinctions between different eras in the history of technology to a variety of different structurings of the primary and secondary instrumentalizations. In contrast with Heidegger, I distinguish premodern from modern historically, rather than ontologically and I break with Habermas as well in arguing that the differentiation of modern technology from other world orientations is relatively superficial and does not reveal the truth of the technical. In what follows, I will show that the incorporation of reflexivity into the theory of technology opens up the future to multiple possibilities foreclosed by the rigid dichotomies of essentialist theory.

Chart 5: Instrumentalization Theory

	Functionalization	**Realization**
Objectification	decontextualization reduction	systematization mediation
Subjectivation	autonomization positioning	vocation initiative

THE LIMITS OF DIFFERENTIATION

The Problem of Progress

In chapter 4, I criticized the deterministic model of progress for assuming that the goals of technical advance are fixed once and for all. That model underlies the essentialism of Habermas and Heidegger, although they work it out in a sophisticated form which identifies the historicity of technology not so much with increased productivity—the usual criterion of progess—as with social differentiation. Differentiation is an apparently objective indicator that supports their critical evaluation of actually existing modernity.

Essentialism argues that a quasi-transcendental process of functionalization is differentiated from what I have called the secondary instrumentalizations in the course of technical and social development. In premodern societies there may be no clear distinction between narrowly conceived technical ends, which flow from the mastery of natural causality, and such spiritual mediations as aesthetic or ethical values. In our society, according to essentialism, these different aspects of technical work are not only clearly distinguished but often embodied in different organizations, e.g. separate engineering and styling departments.

Once technology is differentiated from other social domains, its interaction with them appears to be external. This is particularly clear in the case of mediations. Art is no longer an intrinsic part of technical practice but something added a posteriori. The Parthenon's columns are not ornamentation in our sense, but belong integrally to its design; we tack the columns on the facade after the supporting structures are completed. Ethical values regulate technology from without, through laws; they are not internal to engineering practice. This is the case, for example, with environmental regulations, which native Americans did not need to preserve their environment from harm.

Heidegger and Habermas have taken such differentiation to be the essence of modernity. In the course of it the mediations lose their concrete links to technical reality and become ineffectual ideals. Heidegger sees no way out of this situation, while Habermas's solution, communicative rationalization, is proposed without the slightest reference to the technical realities of modern societies. But what kind of social transformation is possible without changing technology? Heidegger's despair may in the end be a more realistic indication of the paltry reforms possible in this framework.

This despair is not merely an attitude, but a logical consequence of the theory of differentiation. From the standpoint of that theory, attempts at radical technical change can only lead to dedifferentiation and regression. This is an argument we have encountered before. Recall that anti-growth environmentalism, like the deterministic tradeoff model, affirms the fundamental incompatibility of ecology and economics. Whether virtuous poverty is treasured or reviled, the consequences are similar. At bottom technology remains the same whatever the modifications in its historical forms. Only the extent of its differentiation changes. Movement is either forward toward higher levels or backward toward more primitive conditions, never laterally toward a new and better type of technologically advanced society.

I have argued here, on the contrary, that technologies are not physical devices that can be extricated from contingent social values. The technical always already incorporates the social in its structure. Technology responds to social demands not through regression but through another type of change essentialism overlooks. In this process, design internalizes social constraints, condensing technical and social relations. We can still make an analytic distinction between, for example, the aesthetic form and the technical function of a streamlined vehicle, but no *real* distinction exists, any more than in the case of Heidegger's famous chalice. This is not a question of mere packaging or extrinsic influences; the design and functioning of the device is affected. But if technology is so profoundly embedded in the social, differentiation must be far less thoroughgoing than essentialist theories of modernity assume.

Technological Fetishism

The denial of history is itself a product of a certain history. Similarly, the essentialist error is not arbitrary but is a consequence of the very social dimensions of technology it denies. It is not enough therefore to dismiss it as wrong; it is also symptomatic, and requires a deeper explanation. We need to know why differentiation appears as an indicator of progress in the essentialist framework.

I will argue here that essentialism reflects the reified form of objectivity of technology in modern societies.[3] By "form of objectivity" I mean a culturally determined frame of reference rooted in a way of seeing and a corresponding way of doing, a system of practices. Forms of

---

[3] The concept of form of objectivity is derived from Lukács' early *History and Class Consciousness* (1971). See Feenberg (1986a: 70-71).

objectivity might be thought of as socially necessary "illusions" with real consequences. Such illusions are constituting for social reality insofar as we constantly act on them.

Marx offered the original analysis of this phenomenon. In his usage, the fetishism of commodities is not the love of consumption but the practical belief in the reality of the prices attached to goods on the market. As he points out, price is not in fact a "real" (physical) attribute of goods but the crystallization of a relation between manufacturers and consumers; yet the movement of goods from seller to buyer is determined by price just as though it were real. The fetishistic perception of technology similarly masks its relational character: it appears as a non-social instantiation of pure technical rationality rather than as a node in a social network. Essentialism theorizes this form and not the reality of technology.

What explains the persistent self-evidence of the reified concept of technology? In everyday practical affairs, technology presents itself to us first and foremost through its function. We encounter it as *essentially* oriented toward a use. Of course we are aware of devices as physical objects possessing many qualities that have nothing to do with function, for example, beauty or ugliness, but we tend to see these as inessential. What differentiates technology and tools in general from other types of objects is the fact that they appear always already split into "primary" and "secondary" qualities, i.e. functional qualities and all others. We do not have to make that distinction deliberately as we would in the case of a natural object since it belongs to the very form of the technical device.

Thus an initial abstraction is built into our immediate perception of technologies. That abstraction seems to set us on the path toward an understanding of the nature of technology as such. However, it is important to note that this is an assumption based on the form of objectivity of technology in *our* society. Function is not necessarily so privileged in other societies. The functional point of view may coexist peacefully with other points of view—religious, aesthetic, etc.—none of which are essentialized. To the Western observer this eclecticism appears as mere confusion but it has its rationale, as we will see. And indeed, even Westerners are capable of falling into the same "confusion" with respect to certain richly signified technical artifacts, such as houses, which we must strain to perceive as "machines for living," in Le Corbusier's phrase. In cases like this, it is obvious that a fuller picture of technology is conveyed by studying the social role of the technical object and the lifestyles it makes possible. That picture places the abstract notion of "function" in its concrete social context. Then it becomes clear that what we describe in functional language as a device is equally describable in social language as the objectification of a norm or of a symbolic content.

Of course this is not to say that the concept of function is a *useless* abstraction. On the contrary, in every society it orients users toward devices suited to their needs and in our society in particular it has an important role in management and the technical professions which must focus their efforts on narrowly defined goals. But both users and technologists act against a background of assumptions that belong to a lifeworld of technology which need not be thematized in the ordinary course of events. A hermeneutic of technology must clarify that background. From that standpoint, the secondary instrumentalizations are just as inseparable from technology's intrinsic nature as its functions.

But when we consider technologies theoretically we tend not to focus on hermeneutically complex instances like houses which we take for anomalies or ignore. Nor do we consult our rich personal involvements with technical devices that have special meaning and significance in our lives. Instead, our examples tend to be simple things like hammers. With such examples in mind, we elaborate a functionalist model in which society relates externally to technology, posing demands that are *implemented* by technical means. The notion of implementation insures a clean separation between the human subject—who has goals, values, purposes—and supposedly blind things which have no normative content but rather possess "structures" corresponding to the everyday practical evidence of function.

Technology is social only insofar as it is used "for" something, leaving the structure of technology "in itself" as a nonsocial residue. That residue consists in the systems of "parts" that enable technologies to perform their functions. Insofar as structures have an internal causal logic, they can be abstracted from their social surround as an instance of causal principles. All systematic knowledge of technology rests on this type of abstraction. Professional technical disciplines arise to explain and perfect the structures of technologies. As the prestige of these disciplines spreads, their approach to technology becomes the model for common sense and philosophy alike. Eventually, it seems obvious that technical devices *are* their structure. Function is a kind of hinge between that causal reality and the subjective intentions of users, hence also between artifact and society.

Thus the privilege we grant function over other dimensions of technology leads us to and is confirmed by the tacit identification of the functional and physical properties of the artifacts. Whereas social attributes such as the place of technologies in vocations are relational and seem therefore not to belong to technical artifacts proper, function looks like a non-relational property of technology "in itself." But in reality function is just as social as the rest. For example, the sharpness of a knife is indeed a measurable physical property, but sharpness is only a function rather than a hazard or a matter of pure indifference, through a social construction. All the properties of technologies are relational insofar as we recognize their *technological* character As Don Ihde writes, "The temptation may be strong here to leap to a contextless conclusion that the 'technology' as such is 'neutral' but takes on its significance dependent upon different 'uses.' But such a conclusion remains at most a kind of disembodied abstraction. The technology is only what it is in some use-context" (Ihde, 1990: 128). As mere physical objects abstracted from all relations, artifacts have no function and hence no properly technological character at all. But if function is social, then it should not be privileged over other equally important social dimensions of technological artifacts.

The concept of function strips technology bare of values and social contexts, focusing engineers and managers on just what they need to know to do their job. Technology emerges from this striptease as a pure instance of contrived causal interaction. To reduce technology to a device and the device to the laws of its operation is somehow obvious, but it is a typical fallacy of misplaced concreteness. Just as the parts of a clockwork mechanism lack true independence as such, even though they can be disassembled and identified as separate things, so technologies are not truly independent of the social world. That world is not merely an external environment; it traverses them with meaning.

Theory and Reality: Degrees of Differentiation

Now, there is no point in denying the existence of technical structure. It is real enough. The question is, what kind of reality does it possess? Is its rational coherence sufficient warrant for positing it as an independent object? Or is it merely an aspect, an artificial if useful cross-section, of a more complex object that includes many other dimensions? This ontological question implicit in the critique of determinist essentialism is linked to a sociological one. In the Weberian tradition, the splitting off of technical rationality from other forms of thought and dimensions of social life is a particularly important indicator of modernization. The differentiation of technical disciplines from social and religious sciences is the very condition of modern forms of rationalization. Purified objects, such as the economy of economics and the technology of engineering precipitate out of this process in their true nature. Here, in a rather different sense than Hegel intended, the rational is the real.

But how plausible is the identification of these purified objects with their real-world counterparts? Aren't these models too good to be true, mere ideal-types only loosely linked to real objects in the world? But then the essence of those real objects will not coincide with their rational "core." Rationality would be, in a phrase of Gabriel Marcel's, "eccentric with respect to the real."

I can illustrate my meaning with the example of economics. Both modern economic science and the modern economy developed through differentiation from an earlier less differentiated social magma. The science had to distinguish its object from the vaguely defined "political economy" of Adam Smith and Marx. In parallel with this theoretical development, the capitalist economy differentiated itself from institutions such as the state and religion. But economics achieves much higher levels of differentiation from social and political thought than do markets from social and political life. Long after economic science is constituted independently as a pure logic of markets, actual markets in real economies remain thoroughly intertwined with all sorts of sociological and political influences. The "real" abstraction of the actual capitalist market is nowhere near as total as the highly idealized abstractions of economic science. In a sense, then, Smith and Marx were more realistic than modern economics because they incorporated more of the relevant contexts into the object of their science.

Modern economics does take account of the broader array of factors recognized by its predecessors, but it does so in an impoverished way designed to protect the idealization which founds it. Some of these factors enter the science as background assumptions about constraints on economic behavior. For example, the study of the struggle over the length of the working day belonged to Marx's science but modern economic theory simply takes its results for granted as a condition of economic activity. Other so-called non-economic factors are recognized as "imperfections" with respect to a logical model of the "perfect" market that has never actually existed.

Of course economists are aware of the idealized character of the object of their discipline. This inclines honest members of the profession to a commendable caution when it comes to predicting the future of real economies. Unfortunately, they are not always so discreet in pronouncing on philososphical questions. If the economy of economics is so radically idealized, economic science cannot legitimately pretend to offer a philosophy that would explain social life in general; it is qualified more modestly to study economic aspects of completely stabilized, fully capitalist economies. Where this condition is met, economics provides a powerful approach to understanding economic behavior. One can hardly run a modern society without it. But where the condition is not met, the explanatory power of modern economics is small, smaller perhaps than the class and institutionally oriented methods of its predecessors.

Certainly, the case of post-communist Russia would seem to confirm this observation. Any number of historians and political commentators came closer to predicting what would happen there than Jeffrey Sacks and his colleagues at Harvard. Reformers would have done better brushing up on Smith and, yes, even Marx, than rushing headlong into the arms of Hayek and Friedmann.

The difference between the degree and type of differentiation characteristic of theories and the real-world objects they study gives rise to serious confusion. Should markets be defined simply as the object of economic science, leaving aside as does economics everything that does not fit the theory, or should they be defined in terms of their real structure, including all the aspects from which economic science abstracts? But then the essence of the market will no longer correspond exactly to the object of economics.

Similar problems arise with technology. The differentiation of technical disciplines opens cognitive access to rational structures like those economics discovers in markets. But, again like economics, those structures are abstractions from a far more complex and far less differentiated reality. That reality lies in the background of disciplines such as engineering, laying out the framework within which they define and solve problems, but it is not an object of engineering science. Engineers typically assume (as does modern common sense) that the technical device is actually identical with what they make of it and relates only externally to the society in which it is found; in fact it is a rich manifold that incorporates engineering parameters along with many others. This point might be put in another way: the selfsame device is subject to description in many discourses (engineering, artistic, ethical, etc.) none of which is "fundamental." Reconstructing the actual usage of technologies brings this complexity out clearly.[4]

Although philosophy of technology has often attacked the narrow horizons of engineering from a humanistic standpoint, paradoxically, its concept of technology is equally narrow. Its key mistake has been to assume that technical disciplines reveal the nature of their objects, not just in a certain respect for certain purposes, but generally, fundamentally. Thus limitations of those disciplines and particularly of their explicit self-understanding tend to be transferred to their objects. But once obvious social aspects of technology have been stripped away, what remains are the apparently nonsocial primary instrumentalizations: technology, in essence, decontextualizes and manipulates its objects, it is non-reflective, indifferent to values, power oriented, and so on. And that, no amount of change at the social level can alter. But an adequate definition of real technology, as opposed to the narrow, idealized cross-section studied by engineering, involves much besides the formal-rational properties of devices.

CONCRETIZATION AND TECHNICAL CHANGE

Concretization

Determinism and essentialism are attempts at articulating our actual experience of historical development as an irreversible process, a progress based on scientific and technical advance. These theories succeed in capturing the directionality of history whether it be to praise or condemn its *telos*. But their simplistic notion of a purified rationality abstracted from social life fails to capture the complexity of the technical. The problem at this point is to reconstruct a concept of progress without relying on a process of purification to explain it. Unfortunately, the philosophy of technology offers very little help in this regard. However, I have found a starting point in the work of Gilbert Simondon.[5] Although his approach

---

[4] Many reflective engineers are aware of this, particularly since their practice constantly involves them with other dimensions of technology. For theoretical accounts of the tensions between formal representations and practice in technical domains, see Star (1995) and Berg (1997).

[5] For more on this little known but very important philosopher of technology, see Dumouchel (1995) and Hottois (1993). For a further account of Simondon's concept of concretization, see Stiegler (1994).

is deterministic, it grants technology a history in a way that we can recover for a constructivist concept of progress.

Simondon explicitly distinguishes between technicity—i.e., what makes technology technical—and usefulness, which ties technologies to the needs of individuals and groups. The explanation of the technical as such must not confound it with human purposes but must be based on the laws of development of technology's independent "mode of existence." Simondon calls the fundamental law of development "concretization," by which he means something like what technologists themselves call "elegance." By contrast with a design restricted to a single function, an elegant design serves many purposes at once. Simondon's concept of concretization describes just such multifunctionality (Simondon, 1958: chap. 1).

For Simondon technologies are characterized as more or less abstract or concrete depending on their degree of structural integration. As devices develop in the course of technical progress, they are continually redesigned to multiply the functions served by their components. Concretizing innovations adapt them to a variety of demands that may at first appear disconnected or even incompatible. What started out as a collection of externally related parts ends up as a tightly integrated system. For example, the air-cooled engine does without a separate cooling system, replacing it with an engine case artfully designed not only to contain the pistons but also to dissipate the heat they generate. Two separate structures and their distinct functions are combined in a single structure with two functions. A rifle that uses its own recoil to advance a fresh cartridge merges two separate aspects of its operation into a single structure. A solar house that gets its heat from the sun rather than from burning fossil fuels internalizes environmental constraints in its design, making them in some sense part of the "machinery." The functions of shelter, warmth, and lighting are combined through the orientation of the structure toward the sun.

According to Simondon technology evolves through such elegant condensations aimed at achieving functional compatibilities. Concretization is the discovery of synergisms between the functions technologies serve and between technologies and their environments. Here the functionalization of the object is reconciled with wider contextual considerations through a special type of technical development.

The process of concretization has a progressive character: designs can be ordered in a sequence going from the most abstract to the most concrete. Concretization thus involves the type of cognitive advance usually associated with technology and to that extent it founds progress in rationality. But unlike a simple developmental criterion such as growth in productivity, concretization involves the reflexive accommodation of technologies to their social and natural environment. It describes a complex trajectory of progress, richer than simple growth. It is this higher order complexity which makes it significant for the issues under discussion here in a way mere growth is not.

Technical Pluralism

Ihde proposes the concept of technical "pluriculture" as an alternative to the notion that development leads inevitably to a unique planetary technoculture. He argues that technologies take on different meanings in different social contexts: "at the complex level of a cultural hermeneutics, technologies may be variantly embedded; the 'same' technology in another cultural context becomes quite a 'different' technology" (Ihde, 1990: 144). Technological societies can thus come to differ from each other as their traditions are reproduced in the new environment created by the ever changing panoply of devices at their disposal. The theory of democratic rationalization suggests a way of introducing Simondon's concept of concretization into the pluricultural model. This in turn will make it possible to generalize that model from the domain of national culture Ihde explores to the politics of technology.

For the most part Simondon illustrates his theory with politically neutral examples from such domains as automobile and vacuum tube design. But constructivism has now shown that social groups stand behind functions. Thus in uniting many functions in a single structure, concretizing innovations offer much more than technical improvements; they gather social groups around artifacts or systems of artifacts. What appears at first to be a necessary tradeoff, in which some groups' interests are sacrificed to others' advantage, turns out to be the site of new alliances. Concretization thus refers not merely to improvements in efficiency, but also to the positioning of technologies at the point of intersection of multiple standpoints and aspirations.

Here are examples of the sort of thing I have in mind.

1. Simondon contrasts the alienated modern worker with the craftsman, whose body is actually the "milieu" within which traditional tools function. The craftsman's tools are adapted to their human users. These latter, located at the center of the production process, are brought together socially and politically in collegial forms of work organization.

By contrast, the deskilling of industrial labor expelled the worker from a central position in production and went hand in hand with the imposition of hierarchical management. The machine emerged as a "technical individual" sufficient unto itself and requiring human input only on its margins, for example, servicing its hunger for raw materials or repairing and maintaining it. Here the "device paradigm" operates with a vengeance, alienating the worker from the work process itself.

Clearly, the situation of the craftsman is superior in important respects; the greater productive power of modern technology is bought at a price. But just how high must that price be? A general return to craft labor is impracticable, but is deskilling the last word in technical progress? It turns out that work can be redesigned to take advantage of human intelligence and skill. There is a theoretical tradition going back to Marx to which Simondon also belongs, which argues that technological advance can integrate human and machine, drawing on the full range of workers' intellectual as well as physical capacities. Concretizing innovations affecting work organization are in fact becoming more common as information technology reveals its full potential. This is a case where one might judge between several competing models of industrial development and their associated technological designs in terms of their ability to reconcile the pursuit of efficiency with the human need for interesting and fulfilling work (Hirschhorn, 1984; Zuboff, 1988).[6]

2. In both the AIDS and the Minitel cases the original design of the systems reflected the interests and concerns of technical and administrative elites. These elites imposed their technocratic conception of progress on the technologies they designed. But users resisted and succeeded in imposing another layer of function reflecting interests excluded by the original designs.[7] Concretizing innovations incorporated the new functions into the initial structures. Experiment and treatment, information and communication, were united in multifunctional systems. These examples show once again how hermeneutic diversity influences the evolution of technical artifacts and systems.

3. The stratified charge engine, developed by Honda in the early 1970s, offers a suggestive illustration from the domain of environmental

---

[6] Such advances imply more participatory forms of organization that may prove incompatible with the capitalist technical code. I have developed this argument at greater length in Feenberg (1991: chapters 5 and 7).

[7] For more on the concept of layering, see Feenberg 1995, chap. 9.

politics (Commoner, 1990: 99ff; Maruo, 1993). Since the inherent structure of this engine reduces pollution by about 90%, it requires no external add-on such as the catalytic converter to meet minimum environmental standards. What is more, properly maintaining the engine not only keeps it running at full power, but also keeps it clean. Environmentalists and drivers were reconciled in the new design, which unfortunately did not win favor at General Motors where retooling the engine assembly plants was rejected in favor of the add-on catalytic converter. As a result the automobile became significantly more complex and costly—less "concrete"—and it has an unreliable pollution control system that can and frequently does fail without the operator of the vehicle being aware of the problem, much less obliged to fix it.[8] This case may be seen as a missed opportunity, one of many for which American automobile companies bear the responsibility.

Once social constraints are internalized in this way, there is a tendency to lose sight of them. Technical devices are then seen as pure of social influences, which are conceived as essentially external, as values, ideologies, rules. The internalized social constraints concretized in design are read off the reconfigured device as its inevitable technical destiny. The concretizing process is thus a *technological unconscious*, present only in the sedimented form of technical codes that appear asocial and purely rational (Feenberg, 1991: 79ff).

Technology and Values

Strategies of concretization can adapt technology to the environment, to the vocational self-development of its human operators and to many other human needs. Here the secondary instrumentalizations overcome raw functionalization through the integration of technology with its human and natural environment. Demands for environmentally sound technology, for humane, democratic, and safe work, and for enhanced communication in society at large are thus not values against which technological efficiency must be traded off, but potential futures that can guide development.

These considerations allow us to identify a type of development that is both technically and normatively progressive. The normative standards

---

[8] Although current designs may have leapfrogged the Honda innovation, a considerable portion of urban smog today (perhaps 40%) emanates from older vehicles that would burn much cleaner had a different path been followed twenty years ago.

Chart 6: Differentiation and Concretization

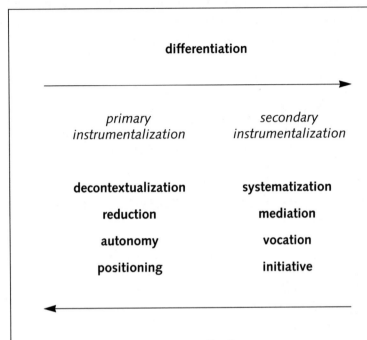

differentiation

*primary
instrumentalization*

*secondary
instrumentalization*

decontextualization

reduction

autonomy

positioning

systematization

mediation

vocation

initiative

concretization

Under modern conditions, the primary and secondary instrumentalizations are increasingly differentiated, for example, through separating technical work from styling. Yet secondary instrumentalizations with sources in ideological visions, tradition, and democratic rationalizations continue to shape technical design. The fact that these two types of instrumentalization are sometimes institutionally differentiated while at other times they are only analytically distinguishable is a source of confusion in the understanding of modern technology. The confusion is compounded by the fact that there is a constant transition from the first case to the second through concretizing advances that incorporate formerly excluded values into the technical code. Reconstructing the concept of progress requires clearly distinguishing these different relations between technology and values.

of that development are immanently derived from the resistances evoked by the technical process itself. Reified forms embodied in devices and systems which reflect a narrow spectrum of interests encounter resistance from beyond their horizon as irrationalities, inefficiencies. In reality, those resistances are reflexes of designs that suppress aspects of nature and social life the affected individuals mobilize to defend or to incorporate into improved designs through democratic rationalizations.

The theory of concretization offers a better account of the bias of technology than substantivism. This bias is not determined once and for all by the essentialized primary instrumentalization but also has a complex social dimension. To be sure, technology may enframe and colonize; but it may also liberate repressed potentialities of the lifeworld that would otherwise have remained submerged. It is thus essentially ambivalent, available for very different types of development.

CONCLUSION: THE POSSIBILITY OF ALTERNATIVES

Substantivism identifies technology in general with modern Western technology. There are undoubtedly universal achievements underlying that technology, many of them borrowed from other civilizations in the first place. However, the particular form in which these achievements have been realized in the West incorporates values that, far from being universal, belong to a definite culture and economic system. Thus the error of substantivism is not so much in the details of its description of modern technology as the failure to acknowledge its historical contingency.

That history shows that modern Western technology has been profoundly shaped by capitalist enterprise. As such it privileges the narrow goals of production and profit. The enterprise organizes the technical control of its workers and dispenses with the traditional responsibilities for persons and places that accompanied technical power in the past. It is this peculiar indifference of modern capitalism to its social and natural environment that frees the entrepreneur to extend technical control to the labor force, the organization of work, and aspects of the natural environment that were formerly protected from interference by custom and tradition. To define technology as such on these terms is ethnocentric.

Why, if capitalism is the problem was communism not the solution? It is too easy to clear capitalism of responsibility on the grounds that the Soviets did no different and no better. The regime never constituted a serious alternative; it followed the capitalist example in essential respects, importing technology and management methods, in some cases, such as protection of the environment, carrying capitalist irresponsibility even further. While early illusions about the Soviet Union are understandable, it is hard to see how anyone can argue in good faith today that the principles of socialism were tested in the one-party bureaucratic state it eventually became. This rearguard defense of the essentialist position will not wash (Feenberg, 1991: chap. 6).

What does a broader historical picture show? Contrary to Heideggerian substantivism, there is nothing unprecedented about our technology. Its chief features, such as the reduction of objects to raw materials, the use of precise measurement and plans, the management of some human beings by others, large scales of operation, are commonplace throughout history. The same could be said of Borgmann's device paradigm. It is the exorbitant role of these features that is new, and this does have unprecedented consequences.

Those consequences include the suppression of many traditional features of technology that stand in the way of the maximum exploitation of human and natural resources. Getting rid of these barriers was not merely a matter of ideology and law but involved radical reconstruction of existing work processes and technological designs. Our world is the inheritor of that sharp break with the past. Only a critique of the resulting designs is adequate to the problems, and only such a critique can recover the lost dimensions of technique.

If we define technology exclusively in modern capitalist terms, we ignore many currently marginalized practices that belonged to it in the past and may prove central to its future development. For example, before Taylorism, technical experience was essentially vocational experience. Using technology was associated with a way of life; it was a matter not just of productivity but also of character development. This is the realm of meaning in which Heidegger's craftsman flourished. This link with things was broken when capitalist deskilling transformed workers into mere objects of technique, no different from raw materials or machines. Here, not in some mysterious dispensation of being, lies the source of the "total mobilization" of modern times.

A different type of social system that restored the role of the secondary instrumentalizations would determine a different type of technical development in which these traditional technical values might be expressed in new ways. Thus social reform involves not merely limiting the reach of the media, as Habermas advocates, but building a different technology based on a wider range of human and technical potentials.

Marxian socialism first proposed such an alternative modernity. To Marx, overcoming capitalism meant not just ending economic injustices and crises, but also democratizing technical systems, bringing them under the control of the workers they enroll. This change would release technology from the grip of capitalist imperatives to a different development (Feenberg, 1991: chap. 2). Whatever our view of Marxism, a conception of technology open to a wider range of values remains essential to any real break with "technological thinking."

For the most part the socialist movement has failed in this task. It has focused on the crude opposition of market and plan, rich and poor, and overlooked the question of technology. Occasionally anti-capitalist movements have demanded not just nationalizations and redistribution but fundamental technical change. As we saw in chapter 2, as recently as the French May Events of 1968, self-management was proposed to overcome the split between conception and execution, substituting control from below for bureaucratic control from above. The themes of substantivist critique were in the air right alongside the socialist critique of capitalism. This is the heady air we must breath if we want to make a fundamental difference in the shape of technical advance.

Because its hegemony rests on extending technical control beyond traditional boundaries to embrace the labor force, capitalism tends to identify technique as a whole with the means through which that control is secured. Meanwhile, other aspects of technique are forgotten or treated as non-technical. It is this capitalist technical rationality that is reflected unwittingly in the essentialism of Heidegger and Habermas. Precisely because they characterize technology as such on the terms of capitalist modernity, they are unable to develop a socially and historically concrete conception of its essence and an alternative to it. They take their own labor of abstraction, by which they eliminate the sociohistorical dimensions of technical action, for evidence of the nonsocial nature of technology.

But unexpected struggles over issues such as nuclear power, access to experimental treatment, and user participation in computer design remind us that the technological future is by no means predetermined. The very existence of these struggles suggests the possibility of a change in the form of technical rationality. They prefigure a general reconstruction of modernity in which technology gathers a world to itself rather than reducing its natural, human and social environment to mere resources. The goal would be to define a better way of life, a viable ideal of abundance, and a free and independent human type, not just to obtain more goods in the prevailing socioeconomic system. To the extent that technology is thus swept into the democratic movement of history, we can hope to inhabit a very different future from the one projected by essentialist critique. In that future technology is not a fate one must chose for or against, but a challenge to political and social creativity.

References

Achterhuis, et al. (1997). *Van Stoommachine tot Cyborg: Denken over Techniek in de Nieuwe Wereld.* Amsterdam: Ambo.

Adorno, Theodor and Horkheimer, Max (1972). *Dialectic of Enlightenment.* trans. J. Cummings. New York: Herder & Herder.

Aldridge, Alexandra (1984). *The Scientific World View in Dystopia.* Ann Arbor: UMI Research Press.

Aronowitz, Stanley (1973). *False Promises.* New York: McGraw Hill.

Bacon, Francis (1939). "Aphorisms Concerning the Interpretation of Nature and the Kingdom of Man," in E. A. Burtt, ed., *The English Philosophers from Bacon to Mill.* New York: Modern Library.

Barber, Benjamin (1984). *Strong Democracy.* Berkeley: University of California Press.

Baudrillard, Jean (1968). *Le Système des Objets.* Paris: Gallimard.

—(1970). *La Société de Consommation.* Paris: Gallimard.

Beck, Ulrich, Giddens, Anthony, and Lash, Scott (1994). *Reflexive Modernization: Politics, Tradition and Aesthetics in the Modern Social Order.* Stanford: Stanford University Press.

van den Belt, Henk and Rip, Arie (1990). "The Nelson-Winter-Dosi Model and Synthetic Dye Chemistry," in W. Bijker, T. Hughes, and T. Pinch, eds., *The Social Construction of Technological Systems.* Cambridge, Mass.: MIT Press.

Beniger, James (1986). *The Control Revolution: Technological and Economic Origins of the Information Society.* Cambridge, Mass.: Harvard University Press.

Benjamin, Walter (1968). *Illuminations,* ed. H. Arendt, trans. H. Zohn. New York: Schocken.

Berg, Marc (1997). "Of Forms, Containers and the Electronic Medical Record: Some Tools for a Sociology of the Formal," in *Science, Technology and Human Values,* no. 22.

Bernstein, Richard, ed. (1985). *Habermas and Modernity.* Cambridge: Polity Press.

Berque, Augustin (1996). *Être Humains sur la Terre.* Paris: Gallimard.

Besançon, Julien (1968). *Les Murs Ont la Parole.* Paris: Tchou, 1968.

Bidou, Catherine, Guillaume, Marc, and Prévost, Véronique (1988). *L'Ordinaire de la Télématique: Offre et usages des services utilitaires grand-public.* Paris: Editions de l'Iris.

Bijker, Wiebe (1987). "The Social Construction of Bakelite: Toward a Theory of Invention," in W. Bijker, T. Hughes, and T. Pinch, eds., *The Social Construction of Technological Systems.* Cambridge, Mass.: MIT Press.

— (1998). "Democratization of Technology. Who are the Experts?" http://www.desk.nl/%7Eacsi/WS/speakers/bijker2.htm.

Bijker, Wiebe, Hughes, Thomas, and Pinch, Trevor (1987). *The Social Construction of Technological Systems.* Cambridge, Mass.: MIT Press.

Bijker, Wiebe and Law, John., eds. (1992). *Shaping Technology/Building Society: Studies in Sociotechnical Change.* Cambridge, Mass.: MIT Press.

Bloor, David (1991). *Knowledge and Social Imagery.* Chicago: University of Chicago Press.

Blueprint for Survival (1974). New York: Signet Books.

Borgmann, Albert (1984). *Technology and the Character of Contemporary Life.* Chicago: University of Chicago Press.

—(1992). *Crossing the Postmodern Divide.* Chicago: University of Chicago Press.

Braverman, Harry (1974). *Labor and Monopoly Capital.* New York: Monthly Review.

de la Bruhèze, Adri (1992). "Closing the Ranks: Definition and Stabilization of Radioactive Wastes in the US Atomic Energy Commission, 1945-1960," in W. Bijker and J. Law, eds., *Shaping Technology/Building Society: Studies in Sociotechnical Change.* Cambridge, Mass.: MIT Press.

Bugbee, Henry (1999). *The Inward Morning.* Athens, Georgia: University of Georgia Press.

Burke, John (1972). "Bursting Boilers and the Federal Power," in M. Kranzberg and W. Davenport, eds., *Technology and Culture.* New York: New American Library.

Callon, Michel (1987). "Society in the Making: The Study of Technology as a Tool for Sociological Analysis," in T. Pinch, T. Hughes, and W. Bijker, eds., *The Social Construction of Technological Systems.* Cambridge, Mass.: MIT Press.

Cambrosio, Alberto and Limoges, Camille (1991). "Controversies as Governing Processes in Technology Assessment," *Technology Analysis and Strategic Management,* vol. 3, no. 4.

Le Capitalisme Monopoliste d'Etat (1971). Two volumes. Paris: Editions Sociales.

Centre Universitaire d'Etude et de Formation Marxiste-Leniniste (1968). *Les Etudiants, les Cadres et la Révolution.*

de Certeau, Michel (1980). *L'Invention du Quotidien.* Paris: UGE.

Charon, Jean-Marie (1987). "Teletel, de l'interactivité homme/machine à la communication médiatisée," in *Les Paradis Informationnels,* M. Marchand, ed. Paris: Masson.

Commoner, Barry (1971). *The Closing Circle.* New York: Bantam.

—Testimony of B. Commoner (1972a). Hearings before the Committee on Interior and Insular Affairs, House of Representatives, on "Fuel and Energy Resources," April 14-19, *Congressional Record,* Serial no. 92-94

—(1972b). "Labor's Stake in the Environment/The Environment's Stake in Labor," speech given to the Conference on "Jobs and the Environment," San Francisco, Nov. 28.

—(1973a). "Motherhood in Stockholm," *Harpers Magazine.* Dec.

—(1973b). "Workplace Burden," *Environment,* July/Aug.

—(1990). *Making Peace with the Planet.* New York: Pantheon Press.

Commoner, B., Ehrlich, P., and Holdren, J., (1972). "Dispute: The Closing Circle," *Environment,* Vol. 14, no. 3.

Cornford, Francis (1957). *Plato and Parmenides.* New York: Liberal Arts Press.

Cunningham, Frank (1987). *Democratic Theory and Socialism.* Cambridge: Cambridge University Press.

Daedalus, Winter, 1968.

Darnovsky, Marcy (1991). "Overhauling the Meaning Machines: An Interview with Donna Haraway," *Socialist Review,* vol. 21, no. 2.

Dewey, John (1980). *The Public and Its Problems.* Athens, Ohio: Swallow Press.

Dodier, Nicolas (1995). *Les Hommes et les Machines: La Conscience Collective dans les Sociétés Technicisées.* Paris: Métailié.

Dosi, G. (1982). "Technological Paradigms and Technological Trajectories: A Suggested Interpretation of the Determinants of Technical Change," *Research Policy,* no. 11.

Dreyfus, Hubert (1992). "On the Ordering of Things: Being and Power in Heidegger and Foucault," in T. Armstrong, ed., *Michel Foucault Philosopher.* New York: Routledge.

—(1995). "Heidegger on Gaining a Free Relation to Technology," in A. Feenberg and A. Hannay, eds, *Technology and the Politics of Knowledge.* Bloomington and Indianapolis: Indiana University Press.

Dubois, P. et al. (1971). *Grèves Revendicatives ou Grèves Politiques?* Paris: Anthropos.

Dumouchel, Paul (1995). "Gilbert Simondon's Plea for a Philosophy of Technology," in A. Feenberg and A. Hannay, eds., *Technology and the Politics of Knowledge.* Bloomington and Indianapolis: Indiana University Press.

Ehn, Pelle (1989). *Work-Oriented Design of Computer Artifacts.* Stockholm: Arbetslivscentrum.

Ehrlich, Paul (1968). *The Population Bomb.* New York: Ballantine

—(1970). "Letter," *The New York Times,* June 9, p. 32.

—(1972). "Letter," *The New York Times,.* Feb. 6, part VII, p. 42.

Ehrlich, P. and Holdren, J. (1972). "One-dimensional Ecology Revisited," *The Bulletin of the Atomic Scientists,* June.

Ehrlich, P., and Harriman, R. (1971). *How To Be a Survivor.* New York: Ballantine.

Ehrlich, Paul and Ehrlich, Anne (1990). *The Population Explosion,* New York: Simon and Schuster.

Elster, Jon (1983). *Explaining Technical Change.* Cambridge: Cambridge University Press.

Ellul, Jacques (1964). *The Technological Society,* trans. J. Wilkinson, New York: Vintage.

Engels, Frederick (1969). "The Peasant Question in France and Germany," in *Karl Marx and Frederick Engels: Selected Works.* New York: International Publishers.

Epstein, Steven (1996). *Impure Science: AIDS, Activism, and the Politics of Knowledge.* Berkeley: University of California Press.

Feenberg, Andrew (1986a). *Lukács, Marx, and the Sources of Critical Theory.* New York: Oxford University Press.

—(1986b). "Network Design: An Operating Manual for Computer Conferencing," *IEEE Transactions on Professional Communications,* Vol. PC-29, no. 1.

—(1991). *Critical Theory of Technology.* New York: Oxford University Press.

—(1993). "Building a Global Network: The WBSI Experience," in L. Harasim, ed., *Global Networks: Computerizing the International Community.* Cambridge, Mass.: MIT Press.

—(1995). *Alternative Modernity: The Technical Turn in Philosophy and Social Theory.* Los Angeles: University of California Press.

Feenberg, Andrew, Licht, J., Kane, K., Moran, K., and Smith, R. (1996). "The Online Patient Meeting," *Journal of the Neurological Sciences,* no. 139.

Fiorino, Daniel (1989). "Environmental Risk and Democratic Process: A Critical Review," *Columbia Journal of Environmental Law,* vol. 14, no. 2.

Florman, Samuel (1981). *Blaming Technology: The Irrational Search for Scapegoats.* New York: St. Martin's.

Ford II, Henry (1970). *The Human Environment and Business*. New York: Weybright & Talley.

Forty, Adrian (1986). *Objects of Desire*. New York: Pantheon.

Foucault, Michel (1976). *Histoire de la Sexualité 1: La Volonté de Savoir*. Paris: Editions Gallimard.

—(1977). *Discipline and Punish*, trans. A. Sheridan. New York: Pantheon.

—(1980). *Power/Knowledge*, trans. C. Gordon. New York: Pantheon.

Frankenfeld, Philip J. (1992). "Technological Citizenship: A Normative Framework for Risk Studies," *Science, Technology, and Human Values*, vol. 17, no. 4.

Fraser, Nancy (1987). "What's Critical about Critical Theory?" in S. Benhabib and D. Cornell, eds., *Feminism As Critique*. Cambridge: Polity Press.

Garaudy, Roger (1968). "La Révolte et la Révolution," *La Démocratie Nouvelle*, April-May.

Glucksmann, André (1968). *Stratégie et Révolution en France 1968*. Paris: Christian Bourgois.

Gouldner, Alvin (1970). *The Coming Crisis of Western Sociology*. New York: Basic Books.

Gras, Alain (1993). *Grandeurs et Dépendence: Sociologie des Macro-Systèmes Techniques*. Paris: Presses Universitaires de France.

"Group Seeks to Shift Protests on Pollution" (1971). *The Los Angeles Times*, Wed., May 5, Part I, p. 25.

Guin, Yannick (1969). *La Commune de Nantes*. Paris: Maspero.

Habermas, Jürgen (1970). "Technology and Science as 'Ideology,'" in *Toward a Rational Society*, trans. J. Shapiro. Boston: Beacon Press.

—(1973). "Dogmatism, Reason, and Decision: On Theory and Praxis in our Scientific Civilization," in *Theory and Practice*, trans. J. Viertel. Boston: Beacon Press.

—(1984, 1987). *The Theory of Communicative Action: Lifeworld and System: A Critique of Functionalist Reason*, trans. T. McCarthy. Boston: Beacon.

—(1991). "A Reply," in A. Honneth and H. Joas eds., *Communicative Action*, trans. J. Gaines and D. Jones. Cambridge, Mass.: MIT Press.

—(1994). "Struggles for Recognition in the Democratic Constitutional State," in A. Gutman, ed. *Multiculturalism*, Princeton: Princeton University Press.

—(1996). *Between Facts and Norms: Contributions to a Discourse Theory of Law and Democracy*, trans. W. Rehg. Cambridge, Mass.: MIT Press.

Hammer, Michael and Champy, James (1993). *Reengineering the Corporation: A Manifesto for Business Revolution*. New York: HarperBusiness.

Hamon, Hervé and Rotman, Patrick (1987). *Génération*. Paris: Seuil.

Hansard's Debates, Third Series: Parliamentary Debates 1830-1891, vol. LXXIII.

Harasim, Linda, Hiltz, S. R., Teles, L., and Turoff, M. (1995). *Learning Networks: A Field Guide to Teaching and Learning Online*. Cambridge, Mass.: MIT Press.

Haraway, Donna (1991). "Situated Knowledges: The Science Question in Feminism and the Privilege of Partial Perspective," in *Simians, Cyborgs, and Women: The Reinvention of Nature*. New York: Routledge.

Hardin, Garret (1970). "The Tragedy of the Commons," in G. de Bell, ed., *The Environmental Handbook*. New York: Ballantine.

—(1971). "The Survival of Nations and Civilization," *Science*, vol. 172, p. 1792.

Harrison, Paul (1987). *The Greening of Africa: Breaking Through in the Battle for Land and Food*. London: Paladin Grafton Books.

Heidegger, Martin (1959). *An Introduction to Metaphysics,* trans. R. Manheim. New York: Doubleday Anchor.

—(1966). *Discourse on Thinking,* trans. J. Anderson. New York: Harper & Row.

—(1971a). "The Thing," in A. Hofstadter, ed. and trans., *Poetry, Language, and Thought.* New York: Harper & Row.

—(1971b). "Building Dwelling Thinking," in A. Hofstadter, ed. and trans., *Poetry, Language, and Thought.* New York: Harper & Row.

—(1971c). "On the Origin of the Work of Art," in A. Hofstadter, ed. and trans., *Poetry, Language, and Thought.* New York: Harper & Row.

—(1977a). *The Question Concerning Technology,* trans. W. Lovitt. New York: Harper & Row.

—(1977b). "Only a God Can Save Us Now," trans. D. Schendler. *Graduate Faculty Philosophy Journal,* 6(1).

Heilbroner, Robert (1974). *An Inquiry into the Human Prospect.* New York: Norton.

Herf, Jeffrey (1984). *Reactionary Modernism: Technology, Culture, and Politics in Weimar and the Third Reich.* Cambridge: Cambrige University Press.

Hickman, Larry (1990). *John Dewey's Pragmatic Technology.* Bloomington: Indiana University Press.

Hill, Gladwin (1970). "Scientific and Welfare Groups Open a 4-Day Study of Population Growth," *The New York Times,* June 9, p. 32.

Hirschhorn, Larry (1984). *Beyond Mechanization: Work and Technology in a Postindustrial Age.* Cambridge, Mass.: MIT Press.

Hoffman, Lily (1989). *The Politics of Knowledge: Activist Movements in Medicine and Planning.* Albany: SUNY Press.

Honneth, Axel (1991). *The Critique of Power: Reflective Stages in a Critical Social Theory,* trans. K. Baynes. Cambridge, Mass.: MIT Press.

Hottois, Giles (1993). *Simondon et la Philosophie de la 'Culture Technique.'* Brussels: de Boeck.

Hughes, Thomas (1987). "The Evolution of Large Technological Systems," in W. Bijker, T. Hughes, and, T. Pinch, eds., *The Social Construction of Technological Systems.* Cambridge, MA: MIT Press.

Hunnicutt, Benjamin (1988). *Work Without End: Abandoning Shorter Hours for the Right to Work.* Philadelphia: Temple University Press.

Ihde, Don (1990). *Technology and the Lifeworld.* Bloomington and Indianapolis, Indiana University Press.

Ingram, David (1987). *Habermas and the Dialectic of Reason.* New Haven: Yale University Press.

—(1995). *Reason, History, and Politics: the Communitarian Grounds of Legitimation in the Modern Age.* Albany: State University of New York Press.

Kellner, Douglas (1977). *Karl Korsch: Revolutionary Theory.* Austin: University of Texas Press.

—(1984). *Herbert Marcuse and the Crisis of Marxism.* Berkeley: University of California Press.

—(1995). *Media Culture: Cultural Studies, Identity and Politics Between the Modern and the Postmodern.* New York: Routledge.

Kerr, Clark (1963). *The Uses of the University.* Boston: Harvard.

Kolb, David (1986). *The Critique of Pure Modernity: Hegel, Heidegger, and After.* Chicago: University of Chicago Press.

Krogh, Thomas (1998). *Technology and Rationality*. Aldershot: Ashgate Publishing.

Kuhn, Thomas (1962). *The Structure of Scientific Revolutions*. Chicago: University of Chicago Press.

Laclau, Ernesto, and Mouffe, Chantal (1985). *Hegemony and Socialist Strategy: Towards a Radical Democratic Politics*. London and New York: Verso.

Latour, Bruno (1992). "Where Are the Missing Masses? The Sociology of a Few Mundane Artifacts," in W. Bijker, and J. Law, eds., *Shaping Technology/Building Society: Studies in Sociotechnical Change*. Cambridge, Mass: MIT Press.

—(1993). *We Have Never Been Modern*, trans. C. Porter. Cambridge, Mass.: Harvard University Press.

Law, John (1987). "Technology and Heterogeneous Engineering: The Case of Portuguese Expansion," in W. Bijker, T. Hughes, and T. Pinch, eds., *The Social Construction of Technological Systems*. Cambridge, Mass.: MIT Press.

Leiss, William (1976). *The Limits to Satisfaction*. Toronto: University of Toronto.

Levathes, Louise (1994). *When China Ruled the Seas: The Treasure Fleet of the Dragon Throne, 1405-33*. New York: Simon & Schuster.

Lie, Merete and Sorensen, Knut (1996). *Making Technology Our Own? Domesticating Technology into Everyday Life*. Oslo: Scandinavian University Press.

Light, Andrew (1996). *Nature, Class, and the Built World: Philosophical Essays between Political Ecology and Critical Technology*. Dissertation, University of California, Riverside.

Lukács, George (1971). *History and Class Consciousness,* trans. R. Livingstone. Cambridge, Mass.: MIT Press.

Luxemburg, Rosa (1970). "The Mass Strike, the Political Party and the Trade Unions," in Mary-Alice Waters, ed., *Rosa Luxemburg Speaks*. New York: Pathfinder.

Lyotard, Jean François (1979). *La Condition Postmoderne*. Paris: Editions de Minuit.

Mallet, Serge (1963). *La Nouvelle Classe Ouvrière*. Paris: Seuil.

—(1971). *Le Pouvoir Ouvrier*. Paris: Anthropos.

Mansholt, Sico (1972.) *La Lettre Mansholt*. Paris: Pauvert.

Marcuse, Herbert (1964). *One-Dimensional Man*. Boston: Beacon Press.

—(1968). "Industrialization and Capitalism in the Work of Max Weber," in *Negations*, trans. J. Shapiro. Boston: Beacon Press.

—(1969). *An Essay on Liberation*. Boston: Beacon Press.

—(1972). "Nature and Revolution," in *Counter-Revolution and Revolt*. Boston: Beacon Press.

—(1973). "The Foundation of Historical Materialism," in *Studies in Critical Philosophy,* trans. J. de Bres. Boston: Beacon Press.

—(1992). "Ecology and the Critique of Modern Society," in *Capitalism, Nature, Socialism*, vol. 3, no. 11.

Marglin, Steven (1996). "Farmers, Seedsmen, and Scientists: Systems of Agriculture and Systems of Knowledge," in F. Appfel-Marglin and S. Margin, eds., *Decolonizing Knowledge: From Development to Dialogue*. Oxford: Clarendon Press.

Maruo, Kanehira (1993). "The Uncompleted Catalysis: A History of Competitions and a Rhetorical Closure around Automobile Emission Control Technology," in L. Hickman and E. Porter, eds., *Technology and Ecology*. Carbondale, Illinois: Society for Philosophy and Technology.

Marvin, Carolyn (1988). *When Old Technologies Were New: Thinking about Electric Communication in the Late Nineteenth Century*. New York: Oxford University Press.

Marx, Karl (1906 reprint). *Capital,* trans. E. Aveling. New York: Modern Library.

McCarthy, Thomas (1981). *The Critical Theory of Jürgen Habermas.* Cambridge, Mass.: MIT Press.

—(1991). "Complexity and Democracy: or the Seducements of Systems Theory," in A. Honneth and H. Joas eds., *Communicative Action,* trans. J. Gaines and D. Jones. Cambridge, Mass.: MIT Press.

McLuhan, Marshall (1964). *Understanding Media.* New York: McGraw Hill.

Meadows, D., Randers, D.J., and Behrens III, W.W., (1972). *The Limits to Growth.* New York: Universe Books.

Merchant, Carolyn (1980). *The Death of Nature: Women, Ecology, and the Scientific Revolution.* New York: Harper and Row.

Miss Ann Thropy, (1987). "Population and AIDS," *The Earth First! Journal,* Jan. 5.

Mitcham, Carl (1994). *Thinking Through Technology: The Path Between Engineering and Philosophy.* Chicago: University of Chicago Press.

Morone, Joseph and Woodhouse, Edward (1989). *The Demise of Nuclear Energy?* New Haven: Yale University Press.

Nelson, Richard and Winter, Sidney (1982). *An Evolutionary Theory of Economic Change.* Cambridge, Mass.: Harvard University Press.

Newhall, Beaumont (1964). *The History of Photography.* New York: Museum of Modern Art.

Noble, David (1984). *Forces of Production.* New York: Oxford University Press.

Oppenheimer, J. Robert (1955). *The Open Mind.* New York: Simon & Schuster.

Pacey, Arnold (1983). *The Culture of Technology.* Cambridge, Mass.: MIT Press.

Paddock, William and Paddock, Paul (1967). *Famine—1975!* Boston: Brown.

Penley, Constance and Ross, Andrew, eds. (1991). *Technoculture.* Minneapolis: University of Minnesota Press.

Pinch, Trevor, and Bijker, Wiebe (1987). "The Social Construction of Facts and Artefacts," in W. Bijker, T. Hughes, and T. Pinch, eds., *The Social Construction of Technological Systems.* Cambridge, Mass.: MIT Press.

Pippin, Robert (1995). "On the Notion of Technology as Ideology: Prospects," in A. Feenberg and A. Hannay, eds., *Technology and the Politics of Knowledge,* Bloomington and Indianapolis: Indiana University Press.

Polanyi, Karl (1957). *The Great Transformation.* Boston: Beacon Press.

Prévost, Claude (1968). "Les Foundations de l'Idéologie Gauchiste," *La Nouvelle Critique,* June.

Radder, Hans (1996). *In and About the World: Philosophical Studies of Science and Technology.* Albany: SUNY Press.

Rheingold, Howard (1993). *The Virtual Community: Homesteading on the Electronic Frontier.* Reading, Mass.: Addison-Wesley.

Richards, Paul (1985). *Indigenous Agricultural Revolution.* London and Boulder: Hutchinson Press and Westview Press.

Ricoeur, Paul (1979). "The Model of the Text: Meaningful Action Considered as a Text," in P. Rabinow and W. Sullivan, eds., *Interpretive Social Science: A Reader.* Berkeley: University of California Press.

Rip, Arie and Kemp, R. (1998). "Towards a Theory of Socio-Technical Change," in S. Rayner and E.L. Malone, eds., *Human Choice and Climate Change,* vol. II, Columbus, Ohio: Battelle Press.

Rockmore, Tom (1992). *On Heidegger's Nazism and Philosophy.* Berkeley: University of California Press.

Rogers, Everett (1995). *Diffusion of Innovations.* New York: The Free Press.

Rothenberg, David (1993). *Hand's End: Technology and the Limits of Nature.* Los Angeles: University of California Press.

Rybczynski, Witold (1991). *Paper Heroes: Appropriate Technology: Panacea or Pipe Dream?* New York: Penguin.

Saint-Just, Louis Antoine de (1963). *L'Esprit de la Révolution.* Paris: UGE.

Schivelbusch, Wolfgang (1988). *Disenchanted Light,* trans. A. Davies, Berkeley: University of California Press.

Schnapp, P. and Vidal-Naquet, P. (1968). *La Commune Etudiante.* Paris: Seuil.

—(1971). *The French Student Uprising.* Boston: Beacon Press.

Schrader-Frechette, Kristin (1991). "Reductionist Approaches to Risk," in D. Mayo and R. Hollander, eds. *Acceptable Evidence: Science and Values in Risk Management.* New York: Oxford University Press.

Schürmann, Reiner (1990). *Heidegger on Being and Acting: From Principles to Anarchy.* Bloomington: Indiana University Press.

Schweickart, David (1993). *Against Capitalism.* Cambridge: Cambridge University Press.

Sclove, Richard (1995). *Democracy and Technology.* New York: Guilford Press.

Seeman, Melvin (1972). "The Signals of '68: Alienation in Pre-Crisis France," *American Sociological Review,* Volume 37, no. 4.

Sejersted, Francis (1995). *After Technological Determinism,* Unpublished manuscript.

Silk, Leonard (1972). "Questions Must be Raised About the Immanence of Disaster," *The New York Times,* March 13, p. 35.

Silverstone, R. and Haddon, L. (1996). "Design and the Domestication of Information and Communication Technologies: Technical Change and Everyday Life," in R. Mansel and R. Silversone, eds., *Communication by Design: The Politics of Information and Communication Technologies.* New York: Oxford University Press.

Silverstone, R., Hirsch, E., and Morley, D. (1992). "Information and communication technologies and the moral economy of the household," in R. Silverstone, and E. Hirsch, eds., *Consuming Technologies: Media and Information in Domestic Spaces,* London: Routledge.

Simondon, Gilbert (1958). *Du Mode d'Existence des Objets Techniques.* Paris: Aubier.

Simpson, Lorenzo (1995). *Technology, Time, and the Conversations of Modernity.* New York: Routledge.

Singer, Daniel (1970). *Prelude to Revolution.* New York: Hill & Wang.

Slouka, Mark (1995). *War of the Worlds: Cyberspace and the High-Tech Assault on Reality.* New York: Basic Books.

Sluga, Hans (1993). *Heidegger's Crisis: Philosophy and Politics in Nazi Germany.* Cambridge, Mass.: Harvard University Press.

Smith, Alice K. (1965). *A Peril and a Hope.* Cambridge: MIT Press.

Smith, Merritt Roe and Marx, Leo (1994). *Does Technology Drive History? The Dilemma of Technological Determinism.* Cambridge, Mass.: MIT Press.

Star, Susan Leigh (1995). "The Politics of Formal Representations: Wizards, Gurus, and Organizational Complexity," in S. Star, ed., *Ecologies of Knowledge: Work and Politics in Science and Technology.* Albany: SUNY Press.

Stiegler, Bernard (1994). "La Maieutique de l'Objet Comme Organisation de l'Inorganique," in *Gilbert Simondon: Une Pensée de l'Individuation et de la Technique.* Paris: Albin Michel.

Stiglitz, Joseph (1994). *Whither Socialism?* Cambridge, Mass.: MIT Press.

Suchman, Lucy (1987). *Plans and Situated Actions: The Problem of Human-Machine Communication.* Cambridge: Cambridge University Press.

—(1994). "Do Categories Have Politics? The Language/Action Perspective Reconsidered," *Computer Supported Cooperative Work,* no. 2.

Swantz, Marja-Liisa and Tripp, Aili Mari (1996). "'Big fish' or 'Small Fish'? A Study of Contrasts in Tanzania's Fishing Sector," in F. Appfel-Marglin and S. Margin, eds., *Decolonizing Knowledge: From Development to Dialogue.* Oxford: Clarendon Press.

Thomas, Paul (1994). *Alien Politics: Marxist State Theory Revisited.* New York: Routledge.

Thompson, John B. and Held, David, eds. (1982). *Habermas: Critical Debates.* Cambridge, Mass.: MIT Press.

Touraine, Alain (1968). *Le Mouvement de Mai ou le Communisme Utopique.* Paris: Seuil.

Ullrich, Otto (1979). *Weltniveau: In der Sackgasse des Industriesystems.* Berlin: Rotbuch Verlag.

Visvanathan, Shiv (1996). "Footnotes to Vavilov: An Essay on Gene Diversity," in F. Appfel-Marglin, and S. Margin, eds., *Decolonizing Knowledge: From Development to Dialogue.* Oxford: Clarendon Press.

Vogel, Steven (1996). *Against Nature: The Concept of Nature in Critical Theory.* Albany: SUNY Press.

Weber, Henri (1988). *Vingt Ans Après: Que Reste-t-il de 68?* Paris: Seuil.

Weber, Max (1958). *The Protestant Ethic and the Spirit of Capitalism,* trans. T. Parsons. New York: Scribners.

Wells, H.G. (1967). *The Food of the Gods.* New York: Berkley Highlands Publishing Co.

White, Lynn (1972). "The Historical Roots of Our Ecological Crisis," in C. Mitcham and R. Mackey, eds., *Philosophy and Technology: Readings in the Philosophical Problems of Technology.* New York: The Free Press.

de Wilde, Rein (1997). "Sublime Futures: Reflections on the Modern Faith in the Compatibility of Community, Democracy, and Technology," in S. Myklebust, ed., *Technology and Democracy: Obstacles to Democratization—Productivism and Technocracy.* Oslo: Center for Technology and Culture.

Winner, Langdon (1986). "Do Artifacts Have Politics," in *The Whale and the Reactor.* Chicago: University of Chicago.

—(1995). "Citizen Virtues in a Technological Order," in A. Feenberg and A. Hannay, eds., *Technology and the Politics of Knowledge.* Bloomington and Indianapolis: Indiana University Press.

Winograd, Terry (1995). "Heidegger and the Design of Computer Systems," in A. Feenberg, and A. Hannay, eds., *Technology and the Politics of Knowledge.* Bloomington and Indianapolis: Indiana University Press.

Winograd, Terry and Flores, Fernando (1987). *Understanding Computers and Cognition.* Reading, Mass.: Addison-Wesley.

Zimmerman, Michael (1990). *Heidegger's Confrontation with Modernity: Technology, Politics, Art.* Bloomington: Indiana University Press.

Zuboff, Shoshana (1988). *In the Age of the Smart Machine: The Future of Work and Power.* New York: Basic Books.

Index